SSCP®

Systems Security Certified Practitioner Practice Exams

ABOUT THE AUTHOR

Nick Mitropoulos is the CEO of Scarlet Dragonfly and has more than 11 years of experience in security training, cybersecurity, incident handling, vulnerability management, security operations, threat intelligence, and data loss prevention. He has worked for a variety of companies (including the Greek Ministry of Education, AT&T, F5 Networks, JP Morgan Chase, KPMG, and Deloitte) and has provided critical advice to many clients regarding various aspects of their security. He's a certified (ISC)² and EC-Council instructor, as well as a GIAC advisory board member and has an MSc in Advanced Security and Digital Forensics (with distinction) from Edinburgh Napier University. He holds over 25 security certifications, including SSCP, GCIH, GISF, Security+, CCNA Cyber Ops, CCNA Security, CCNA Routing & Switching, CCDA, CEH, CEI, Palo Alto (ACE), Qualys (Certified Specialist in AssetView and ThreatPROTECT, Cloud Agent, PCI Compliance, Policy Compliance, Vulnerability Management, Web Application Scanning), and Splunk Certified User.

About the Technical Editor

Pantelis Stoufis, CISSP, GNFA, GCFA, GREM, CCNP Security, is a cybersecurity professional with over ten years of experience in the field of incident response, threat intelligence, network security, and malware analysis, with the majority of his experience originating from working in several financial institutions. He has been a Cisco Champion since 2015, holding more than 15 network and cybersecurity certifications. He has a MEng in Electrical and Electronic Engineering from the University of Bristol and a MSc in Information Technology, Management, and Organisational Change from the University of Lancaster.

He is currently working for a Fortune 100 company leading a team of cybersecurity analysts focusing on incident response and threat analysis for macOS and Linux platforms.

SSCP®

Systems Security Certified Practitioner Practice Exams

Nick Mitropoulos

New York   Chicago   San Francisco
Athens   London   Madrid   Mexico City
Milan   New Delhi   Singapore   Sydney   Toronto

Sponsoring Editor Wendy Rinaldi	**Technical Editor** Pantelis Stoufis	**Composition** Cenveo Publisher Services
Editorial Supervisor Janet Walden	**Copy Editor** Lisa McCoy	**Illustration** Cenveo Publisher Services
Project Manager Snehil Sharma, Cenveo® Publisher Services	**Proofreader** Claire Splan	**Art Director, Cover** Jeff Weeks
Acquisitions Coordinator Claire Yee	**Production Supervisor** Lynn M. Messina	

This book is dedicated to my mother,
Johanna, who was taken from us so abruptly,
and to my father, Charalambos, whom I love so much.

CONTENTS

ACKNOWLEDGMENTS

This book wouldn't have been possible without the contribution of various people participating at each phase, from initial discussions about the idea and how it can help readers, all the way to finding its way to the bookshelves and online retailers.

I would like to specially thank Wendy Rinaldi from McGraw-Hill for entrusting me to write this book, as well as Claire Yee for always providing prompt support and input.

Special thanks goes to my good friend and technical reviewer, Pantelis Stoufis. He's an amazing individual with in-depth knowledge on all aspects of security. He has always been very helpful, and his feedback has been far more than constructive. I feel truly lucky to have worked on this book with him, as I believe it wouldn't have been the same without his input.

INTRODUCTION

Studying for IT certifications is quite hard. Studying for security certifications is often thought to be even harder, but it's definitely worth every minute. The SSCP (Systems Security Certified Practitioner) certification is considered an introductory security certification but shouldn't be taken lightly. Even if you have some basic security experience, it is highly recommended to plan for additional study so you can maximize the chances of passing the exam. SSCP includes the following domains (the percentage indicates each domain's weight in relation to the exam total questions):

1.0	Access Controls	16%
2.0	Security Operations and Administration	15%
3.0	Risk Identification, Monitoring, and Analysis	15%
4.0	Incident Response and Recovery	13%
5.0	Cryptography	10%
6.0	Network and Communications Security	16%
7.0	Systems and Application Security	15%

The SSCP exam consists of 125 multiple-choice questions that you have three hours to answer. The passing score is 700 out of 1,000 points. In order to become certified, you will need to pass the exam and apply for (ISC)² membership. If you don't have at least one full year of experience in one or more of the noted domains (or don't hold a degree relating to an approved cybersecurity program, which can act as a waiver), then you can still become an (ISC)² associate until the required experience is gained. After becoming an (ISC)² associate, you are given a two-year period in which you need to gain the required one-year experience. For more information about the exam and overall process, visit https://www.isc2.org/Certifications/SSCP, which is the official (ISC)² web page about SSCP.

This book aims to help you be as prepared for the exam as possible. However, you shouldn't expect to pass the exam just by reading this book, nor to get the same questions in the exam as the ones contained in this book, as that would be against the (ISC)² Code of Ethics. The goal is to make you be as prepared as possible by familiarizing you with the style of the questions and related material and to allow you to identify the areas where you lack preparation and need to study more. That is actually very important. Don't attempt the exam if you are not fully prepared. Often enough, getting an accreditation is crucial to someone's current role or even key to getting a new one. Try to be realistic about the expectations you set and the commitment that is required to study for the exam.

Some of the book questions might be more challenging to answer, while others might seem fairly straightforward. This is by design. The exam itself doesn't only contain hard questions that you need to spend several minutes thinking about, as that wouldn't allow you enough time to complete it. Technically speaking, it is still an introductory certification, so it wouldn't be fair for everything to be difficult. However, do note that even easy questions can be answered wrong just by not carefully reading them.

Different readers have different backgrounds. As such, some of the in-depth explanations might seem too deep to some readers, while to others (who are possibly more knowledgeable or have gained significant security experience through their work) these might seem more superficial. I have tried to strike a reasonable balance, keeping in mind that the certification is predominantly aimed at people who don't have an in-depth security background. As such, enough information is provided so that novice readers can understand why an answer is correct and also why the rest of the answers are not suitable ones.

I have compiled the following list of hints that you need to consider as you're answering the questions in this book, as well as when taking the actual exam:

- **Be aware of absolute statements.** If a question states "which of the following encryption types is *never* used," then you have to be absolutely sure that this encryption type is *never* used. However, the easiest way to tackle this is to identify a scenario that would make this statement false. So if you manage to identify a situation where the encryption type is actually used, then you automatically invalidate that statement and you know it's not a correct answer.

- **When answering book questions, consider what you don't know.** It's not enough to identify a question's correct answer. Identifying why the other options are wrong is equally important because an exam question might relate to those. In addition, always know the background of the answers. Don't just identify the correct option and think you kind of know why the others are wrong. Read the in-depth explanations before you proceed to the next question. When studying, time is on your side. When taking an exam, it isn't. If you invest more time preparing, you will need less time to answer questions when taking the exam.

- **Think of examples as much as you can**, especially from practical experience. For example, if a question mentions access controls, think about what types of access control mechanisms you have in your company in order to make associations about what you are being asked. There's really no substitute for experience.

- **Try to identify distractors.** Sometimes, a few answers seem really wrong or flat-out unsuitable for the context of the question. Those are usually distractors placed there to confuse you. Read all theory about the seven domains carefully before attempting to answer any questions. That will instill the concepts in your mind, and you will have less chance of getting confused by such distractors.

- **Review all possible answers as carefully as the questions.** Especially when the questions use phrases like "least possible," "most probable," "best answer," "least effective," "less likely," and similar ones. That means you need to evaluate all possible options carefully so the appropriate answer can be identified.

- **Some questions will seem vague or may contain things you have never heard of before.** An effort has been made to include such questions in the book in order to simulate the conditions of the exam. Don't be afraid of these questions. Try to read the question and all answers as carefully as possible and rule out what you think is not suitable.

- **Read scenario- or command output–related questions closely.** Any questions relating to a short scenario or command output would require you to review that closely. Usually, the answer or some really good hints about it are within the scenario or command output. Review those carefully before answering.

- **Sometimes more than one answer may seem fitting.** Read the question and all possible answers again in order to distinguish the one that is actually correct.

- **Don't dwell on what you don't know or can't remember.** There's no point in stressing about something you don't remember or might not even know when taking the exam. Again, preparation is key. Try to review any theory in advance so you are familiar with all related concepts.

- **Use the book's objectives map.** The book contains an objectives map, which describes what questions relate to a specific domain. That makes it easier for you to test your knowledge on a specific domain. However, it is highly recommended that you review all related SSCP theory before starting to answer questions, as that will make you aware of any possible options that are placed as distractors or that relate to something totally different than what the question may be asking.

If you have any questions or want to provide any feedback, please feel free to send those to feedback@scarlet-dragonfly.com

In This Book

This book contains a total of 500 different exam questions, which will help the reader prepare for the SSCP exam. 250 of these questions are contained in the printed copy, while an additional 250 questions are accessible through the online test engine.

Pre-assessment Test

This book contains a pre-assessment test with a collection of questions across all seven domains. It can help you identify the areas you need to improve your knowledge in, so you can focus your study accordingly.

Practice Exams

In addition to the practice questions included in this book, 250 practice questions are provided in an electronic test engine. You can create custom exams by chapter, or you can take multiple timed, full-length practice exams. For more information, please see Appendix B.

Exam Objectives Map

The following SSCP exam objectives map contains a reference of the domain and objective each question relates to and can help you focus on a specific domain during your study. Note that it is highly beneficial to have a sound understanding of all related SSCP theory before attempting to answer any of the book questions or start focusing on a set of questions relating to a particular domain.

SSCP Exam

Official Exam Domain and Objective	Ch #	Question #
1.0 Access Controls		
1.1 Implement and maintain authentication methods	1	1–2, 5–13, 16–20, 25–27, 31, 33–35, 37, 39
1.2 Support internetwork trust architectures	1	28, 38
1.3 Participate in the identity management lifecycle	1	4, 36
1.4 Implement access controls	1	3, 14–15, 21–24, 29–30, 32, 40
2.0 Security Operations and Administration		
2.1 Comply with codes of ethics	2	13, 23, 36
2.2 Understand security concepts	2	10, 17, 25, 28
2.3 Document, implement, and maintain functional security controls	2	11, 18, 37
2.4 Participate in asset management	2	14, 20
2.5 Implement security controls and assess compliance	2	7, 9, 16, 26
2.6 Participate in change management	2	21, 24, 27, 34
2.7 Participate in security awareness and training	2	1–6, 8, 12, 19, 30–33
2.8 Participate in physical security operations (e.g., data center assessment, badging)	2	15, 22, 29, 35, 38
3.0 Risk Identification, Monitoring, and Analysis		
3.1 Understand the risk management process	3	1, 4, 8–9, 15, 17–18, 29–30, 38
3.2 Perform security assessment activities	3	2–3, 6–7, 19–20, 23, 25–28, 31–35
3.3 Operate and maintain monitoring systems (e.g., continuous monitoring)	3	5, 11, 13–14, 16, 21, 24, 36–37
3.4 Analyze monitoring results	3	10, 12, 22

Official Exam Domain and Objective	Ch #	Question #
4.0 Incident Response and Recovery		
4.1 Support incident lifecycle	4	1, 16–18, 22, 24, 28–30
4.2 Understand and support forensic investigations	4	5–7, 12–13, 20, 33
4.3 Understand and support Business Continuity Plan (BCP) and Disaster Recovery Plan (DRP) activities	4	2–4, 8–11, 14–15, 19, 21, 23, 25–27, 31–32
5.0 Cryptography		
5.1 Understand fundamental concepts of cryptography	5	1, 7, 9–10, 16, 20, 24–25
5.2 Understand reasons and requirements for cryptography	5	2–3, 13
5.3 Understand and support secure protocols	5	4–6, 11–12, 15, 17–19, 21
5.4 Understand Public Key Infrastructure (PKI) systems	5	8, 14, 22–23
6.0 Network and Communications Security		
6.1 Understand and apply fundamental concepts of networking	6	1–6, 25–28, 30
6.2 Understand network attacks and countermeasures (e.g., DDoS, man-in-the-middle, DNS poisoning)	6	7–10, 31–33
6.3 Manage network access controls	6	18, 29
6.4 Manage network security	6	11–15, 34–36
6.5 Operate and configure network-based security devices	6	16–17, 24, 37–38
6.6 Operate and configure wireless technologies (e.g., Bluetooth, NFC, Wi-Fi)	6	19–23, 39–40
7.0 Systems and Application Security		
7.1 Identify and analyze malicious code and activity	7	1–8, 11, 18–22, 29, 37
7.2 Implement and operate endpoint device security	7	14–17, 23–25, 31–32
7.3 Operate and configure cloud security	7	26–28, 33–35
7.4 Operate and secure virtual environments	7	9–10, 12–13, 30, 36, 38

Access Controls

This chapter includes questions from the following objectives:
- 1.1   Implement and maintain authentication methods
- 1.2   Support internetwork trust architectures
- 1.3   Participate in the identity management lifecycle
- 1.4   Implement access controls

This chapter contains a complete set of questions and answers regarding various methods and best practices that can be used to implement user and device authentication (single/dual/multifactor authentication, SSO, federated access, centralized/decentralized authentication); different trust models (one-way, two-way, transitive trust); and network types (internet, intranet, and extranet) that can be utilized. Additionally, it contains questions regarding the identity management lifecycle (identity proofing, provisioning and authentication, maintenance and entitlement, de-provisioning), as well as the various access control models (DAC, MAC, RBAC, ABAC, subject/object based) that can be enforced.

1. An army officer needs to access a secure area. For that purpose, she enters her unique six-digit username, personal password, and answer to a security question. Which of the following describes the type of authentication being used?

    A. Multifactor authentication

    B. Strong authentication

    C. Single-factor authentication

    D. Two-factor authentication

2. Which of the following is indicative of a better biometric authentication system?

    A. Higher FAR

    B. Higher FRR

    C. Lower DER

    D. Lower CER

3. John is a security manager and is creating an Excel file containing his team's shift plan. He wants his team to be able to read the file in order to know what shift they are working in but doesn't want them to be able to edit the file and change shifts at will. Which of these access control models would be most suitable to accomplish this?

    A. Mandatory

    B. Discretionary

    C. Rule-based

    D. Role-based

4. The process of creating user accounts and granting them access to appropriate resources is called:

    A. Provisioning

    B. Authorization

    C. Entitlement

    D. Proofing

5. Bob wants to log on to a company system and is presented with a screen asking him to enter a username and password, followed by a second screen asking for an OTP. Which of these elements falls under identification?

    A. Password

    B. OTP

    C. Username

    D. Username and password combination

6. How many primary types of authentication factors are there?

   A. 2

   B. 3

   C. 7

   D. 4

7. Which of the following passwords is the strongest as per NIST's SP 800-63B?

   A. YouCan'tTouchThi$12

   B. *iQ23!T

   C. abcdefgh

   D. Copenhagen

8. Sarah, a customer of Glober Bank, has successfully logged on to the bank's website and wants to complete a transaction. In order for that to be finalized, after inserting the destination account details she is required to use a device that generates an eight-digit number that she needs to provide to the website within 40 seconds of its creation time in order for the transaction to be verified and allowed. This is an example of:

   A. Static password

   B. Authentication

   C. Synchronous dynamic password

   D. Asynchronous dynamic password

9. Captain Cramer is reviewing a biometric authentication system that will be used at a nuclear missile silo. Which of the following is the most likely reason that would prevent him from approving the usage of this device?

   A. Low CER

   B. Increased amount of type 1 errors

   C. Increased amount of type 2 errors

   D. High FRR

10. What mechanism does Kerberos use to protect transmission confidentiality?

   A. Symmetric encryption

   B. Asymmetric encryption

   C. TGT

   D. KDC

11. What is the primary purpose of SSO?

 A. Authorization

 B. Confidentiality

 C. Availability

 D. Authentication

12. Which of the following is the best method of performing device authentication?

 A. MAC address filtering

 B. Dynamic IP addressing

 C. Cookies

 D. Certificate-based authentication

13. Josh is going away on a two-week holiday, but his Windows domain password expires in three days. He wants to still be able to use his laptop to access company network resources while he's away. What does he need to do?

 A. Change his domain password before it expires

 B. Call his company's IT team while away so they can have his password changed

 C. Do nothing, as he can always use his cached credentials after the first three days

 D. Log in to his laptop as a local administrator and reset his password

14. Which of these statements is true regarding DAC and non-DAC access control?

 A. In non-DAC models, users have ownership of their resources.

 B. In non-DAC models, security administrators control the access granted to users.

 C. DAC models are best for avoiding catastrophic system modifications.

 D. DAC models don't use any type of ACL.

15. Felly Corp. wants to improve the level of current security policies. As such, employees won't be allowed to connect to critical infrastructure using corporate machines from the guest network. This is an example of:

 A. Role-based Access Control (RBAC)

 B. MAC

 C. ABAC

 D. DAC

16. Nadia is on holiday and needs to access her banking website to make a transaction. She uses her friend's computer to log on to the bank's website, and after entering her credentials she is requested to enter her mother's maiden name. This is an example of:

A. Passphrase

B. OTP

C. Cognitive password

D. Static password

17. An attacker is using a brute-force tool in order to crack a user's password and gain access to online medical information. Which is the best option in order to protect against this type of attack?

A. Account lockout policy

B. Minimum password length

C. Password history

D. Maximum password age

18. Which is the best option for managing passwords?

A. Write them down and save them in a safe to which only you have the key.

B. Save them on a local text file.

C. Store them on an external USB.

D. Use KeePassXC.

19. Which is not a protocol for asynchronous dynamic password creation?

A. HOTP

B. OPIE

C. TOTP

D. S/KEY

20. Elizabeth books a SSCP exam, and when she reaches the exam center she realizes that a palm vein scan is required. This is an example of which authentication factor?

A. Something you know

B. Something you are

C. Something you have

D. Biometrics

21. Which data classification scheme does the U.S. government use (listed from lowest to highest classification level)?

   A. Top Secret, Secret, Confidential, Unclassified

   B. Unclassified, Confidential, Secret, Top Secret

   C. Unclassified, Classified, Secret, Top Secret

   D. Unclassified, Classified, Confidential, Top Secret

22. Which of these statements is not correct regarding the Bell-LaPadula model?

   A. It uses the "no read up" rule.

   B. It uses the "no write down" rule.

   C. It is used to enforce confidentiality.

   D. It is used to enforce integrity.

23. Which of these models uses the "simple integrity axiom"?

   A. Biba

   B. Clark-Wilson

   C. Brewer-Nash

   D. Bell-LaPadula

24. A large law firm has a team (designated Alpha) representing a manufacturing client, while another team (designated Bravo) is working on a case relating to one of the manufacturing client's biggest competitors. Bravo team would greatly benefit from information that Alpha team has access to. Which of these models would be the most appropriate to ensure that a conflict of interest is avoided?

   A. Bell-LaPadula

   B. Biba

   C. Clark-Wilson

   D. Brewer-Nash

25. Dian signs in to her Gmail account and checks her e-mail. She then wants to access her YouTube channel to upload a new video, which she accesses without entering any further login details. This is an example of:

   A. Federated access

   B. SSO

   C. Decentralized authentication

   D. Two-step verification

26. Which of these combinations provides the strongest and most accurate authentication?

    A. Username, cognitive password, PIN

    B. Dynamic password, fingerprint

    C. Retina scan, OTP

    D. Symantec's VIP Access, Google Authenticator

27. Which of these statements regarding passwords is not true?

    A. Use one strong password across various systems.

    B. Change passwords often.

    C. Never give out your password.

    D. Use passphrases whenever possible.

28. Fine Investments Bank has a partnership with Gradie Security to share resources in order for the latter to manage their firewalls. They aim to exchange a lot of network documentation via a web-based portal, which will only be accessible by Gradie Security. This is an example of a(n):

    A. DMZ

    B. PAN

    C. Intranet

    D. Extranet

29. Mesquite Investment Group wants to allow their employees to browse Facebook only after their workday finishes. Which of these attributes is best to use?

    A. Location

    B. Group membership

    C. Remote access

    D. Temporal

30. A user accesses a document. Which of these statements is correct?

    A. The user is the object.

    B. The document is the object.

    C. The document is the subject.

    D. The user is both the subject and object.

31. Anemone Investment Group is using a two-step verification process (user's password combined with an OTP sent via SMS) to allow remote access to its secure file server. It is 2:00 A.M. on a Saturday, and one of their employees realizes his personal e-mail account has been compromised. He is using the same compromised credentials to access Anemone Investment Group's network remotely. The IT team only works Monday through Friday. How should he proceed?

    A. Call the company CEO and report the issue.

    B. Immediately drive to the office and change their password.

    C. Send an e-mail to the IT team and follow up with them on Monday morning.

    D. Delete their personal e-mail account.

32. Captain Jones has been granted top secret access. According to the Bell-LaPadula model, which rule ensures that she doesn't write information to a lower security level?

    A. Simple integrity axiom

    B. Star property

    C. Simple security property

    D. Star integrity axiom

33. Danny attempts to enter his credentials in order to log in to his corporate laptop. After entering a wrong password three times, he is unable to enter any credentials again. What is the most likely reason?

    A. Maximum password age.

    B. Password history.

    C. Account has been deleted.

    D. Account has been locked out.

34. An attacker managed to obtain the password file from Lara's laptop and is using a brute-force tool to guess her password. Which of the following is the best option in order to protect her account from this type of attack?

    A. Account lockout policy

    B. Password complexity

    C. Password history

    D. Password length

35. What is the greatest disadvantage of using a retina scanner?

    A. The scan can potentially identify and reveal the subject's medical conditions.

    B. They are often unreliable.

    C. The scan takes too long.

    D. There is a large amount of false positives.

36. Which of the following isn't included in the identity and access management lifecycle?

    A. Entitlement

    B. Proofing

    C. De-provisioning

    D. Deletion

37. Which of the following is an example of a passphrase?

    A. ILoveS@l@miAndCh33s3

    B. P@ssw0rd

    C. IUOIUQJHJH1987287!!dslkUYQ62

    D. passphrase

38. A home network serving the needs of a small family can be classified as a:

    A. WAN

    B. PAN

    C. LAN

    D. MAN

39. Which of the following is not an SSO technology?

    A. SAML

    B. SecureAuth IdP

    C. Kerberos

    D. OpenIDConnect

40. Which model is known as the "Chinese Wall" model?

    A. Biba

    B. Brewer-Nash

    C. Bell-LaPadula

    D. Clark-Wilson

1. C	11. D	21. B	31. C
2. D	12. D	22. C	32. B
3. B	13. A	23. A	33. D
4. A	14. B	24. D	34. B
5. C	15. C	25. B	35. A
6. B	16. C	26. C	36. D
7. A	17. A	27. A	37. A
8. C	18. D	28. D	38. C
9. C	19. C	29. D	39. B
10. A	20. B	30. B	40. B

1. An army officer needs to access a secure area. For that purpose, she enters her unique six-digit username, personal password, and answer to a security question. Which of the following describes the type of authentication being used?

   A. Multifactor authentication

   B. Strong authentication

   C. Single-factor authentication

   D. Two-factor authentication

   ☑ **C.** Both the previously mentioned authentication attributes (password, answer to a security question) belong to the same authentication category, which is "something you know." As you may remember, the first step to answering any authentication factor–related question is to identify the different factors used to authenticate the user. In the example, there's only one factor in use, therefore resulting in the system using single-factor authentication. Also note that the six-digit username is used for identification (not authentication).

   ☒ **A, B,** and **D** are incorrect. **A** is incorrect because in order to have a multifactor authentication system in place, attributes would need to be present from at least two different types of factors. **B** is incorrect because there is no authentication factor known as "strong authentication." **D** is incorrect because in order to have a two-factor authentication system in place, attributes would need to be present from exactly two different types of factors.

2. Which of the following is indicative of a better biometric authentication system?

   A. Higher FAR

   B. Higher FRR

   C. Lower DER

   D. Lower CER

   ☑ **D.** CER (Crossover Error Rate) is where the FRR (False Rejection Rate) and FAR (False Acceptance Rate) cross over. A good biometric authentication system should have a low CER.

   ☒ **A, B,** and **C** are incorrect. **A** is incorrect because FAR relates to the percentage of times a system falsely identifies an unknown user as a genuine system user who should be granted access to the system; thus, a larger FAR isn't indicative of a good biometric system. **B** is incorrect because FRR relates to the percentage of time a system denies access to a perfectly valid system user. As in the previous case, a larger FRR is not indicative of a good biometric system being in use. **C** is incorrect because DER is not a term used in biometric authentication systems.

3. John is a security manager and is creating an Excel file containing his team's shift plan. He wants his team to be able to read the file in order to know what shift they are working in but doesn't want them to be able to edit the file and change shifts at will. Which of these access control models would be most suitable to accomplish this?

A. Mandatory

B. Discretionary

C. Rule-based

D. Role-based

☑ **B.** Discretionary access control (DAC) grants access to objects based on the identity of each subject. It also provides data owners the ability to grant permissions to subjects.

☒ **A, C,** and **D** are incorrect. **A** is incorrect because mandatory access control (MAC) uses labels to identify subjects and objects. It is often used in military environments, as it provides the maximum level of security between all access models. **C** is incorrect because Rule-based Access Control uses rules that establish access to resources. **D** is incorrect because Role-based Access Control defines access by using roles or groups and is often incorporated by organizations with large groups of users (i.e., a group of employees that belong to the security team could utilize a role named "security members," and each time new employees are hired they can be assigned to that particular group).

4. The process of creating user accounts and granting them access to appropriate resources is called:

A. Provisioning

B. Authorization

C. Entitlement

D. Proofing

☑ **A.** The definition of provisioning is "The process of creating user accounts and assigning them access to suitable resources."

☒ **B, C,** and **D** are incorrect. **B** is incorrect because authorization refers to providing proper account privileges (for the accounts created via the provisioning process). **C** is incorrect because entitlement refers to what privileges are provided to users and ensuring those align with their role (i.e., an employee who left the HR department and moved to accounting shouldn't have access to other employees' bonuses, since they are now performing a different function, meaning they are not entitled to that data anymore). **D** is incorrect because proofing refers to establishing an individual's identity prior to account creation.

5. Bob wants to log on to a company system and is presented with a screen asking him to enter a username and password, followed by a second screen asking for an OTP. Which of these elements falls under identification?

   A. Password

   B. OTP

   C. Username

   D. Username and password combination

   ☑ **C.** Bob first enters a username to claim his identity. Please note that at this point he just claims to be Bob, without providing any further evidence to support that (like his password).

   ☒ **A, B,** and **D** are incorrect. **A** is incorrect because the password is used to authenticate the user and not identify him. **B** is incorrect because OTP (one-time password) is used as a second step of a two-step verification process. The user would typically encounter this screen only after entering a valid username and corresponding password (meaning he has claimed he is Bob and has provided Bob's correct password). **D** is a distractor, as a username and password pair can't be used in order to provide identification of a user. Passwords are used for authentication.

6. How many primary types of authentication factors are there?

   A. 2

   B. 3

   C. 7

   D. 4

   ☑ **B.** There are three primary types of authentication factors. Those are "something you know," "something you have," and "something you are."

   ☒ **A, C,** and **D** are incorrect because there are three primary types of authentication (as mentioned earlier). However, please do note that in some sources, you might find five authentication factors mentioned, which in essence includes two additional types: "somewhere you are" and "something you do." These are less reliable than the three primary types already noted. For example, "somewhere you are" usually requires some type of geolocation mechanism to be active and allows the user to connect to a system only if he is originating from a specific location. However, depending on the source machine configuration, that can easily be defeated by using third-party proxy software in order to "trick" the system into accepting an incoming connection from a source location that it shouldn't.

7. Which of the following passwords is the strongest as per NIST's SP 800-63B?

   A. YouCan'tTouchThi$12

   B. *iQ23!T

   C. abcdefgh

   D. Copenhagen

   ☑ **A.** "YouCan'tTouchThi$12" is a passphrase that is in accordance with NIST's SP 800-63B password recommendations. Actually, it also includes a combination of lowercase and uppercase letters, a special character ($), and two numbers to make it stronger.

   ☒ **B, C,** and **D** are incorrect. **B** is incorrect because although "*iQ23!T" might seem strong at first glance (having a combination of lowercase and uppercase letters, as well as numbers and special characters), but has a length of seven characters, while NIST's recommendation is a minimum of eight. **C** is incorrect because "abcdefgh" is considered a weak password. **D** is incorrect because "Copenhagen" would most likely be present in a dictionary of common words that could be used to brute-force the user's password.

8. Sarah, a customer of Glober Bank, has successfully logged on to the bank's website and wants to complete a transaction. In order for that to be finalized, after inserting the destination account details she is required to use a device that generates an eight-digit number that she needs to provide to the website within 40 seconds of its creation time in order for the transaction to be verified and allowed. This is an example of:

   A. Static password

   B. Authentication

   C. Synchronous dynamic password

   D. Asynchronous dynamic password

   ☑ **C.** A synchronous dynamic password is generated by a token, which changes the password at given intervals (in this example, every 40 seconds).

   ☒ **A, B,** and **D** are incorrect. **A** is incorrect because the question suggests that the password changes every 40 seconds; thus, it can't be a static one, as that wouldn't change. **B** is incorrect, as the question states Sarah has already logged on successfully to the bank's website, meaning authentication has already taken place. **D** is incorrect because an asynchronous password wouldn't need to be provided within a specific time frame (i.e., 40 seconds).

9. Captain Cramer is reviewing a biometric authentication system that will be used at a nuclear missile silo. Which of the following is the most likely reason that would prevent him from approving the usage of this device?

   A. Low CER

   B. Increased amount of type 1 errors

C. Increased amount of type 2 errors

D. High FRR

☑ **C.** A type 2 error (also known as FAR, False Acceptance Rate) can affect a system in a more negative way, as it means that it improperly allows access to illegitimate users, which would be detrimental in the case of a nuclear silo.

☒ **A, B,** and **D** are incorrect. **A** is incorrect because ideally a good biometric system needs to have a low CER (Crossover Error Rate), as that means it is performing better. **B** is incorrect because type 1 errors refer to FRR (False Rejection Rate), meaning the system doesn't allow access to a legitimate user. Although this is a nuisance, it doesn't even come close to how worse things can become by allowing illegitimate users to enter the secure premises (which is what answer C depicts). **D** is incorrect, as it has exactly the same meaning as B but instead of the term "type 1 error," FRR is used.

10. What mechanism does Kerberos use to protect transmission confidentiality?

A. Symmetric encryption

B. Asymmetric encryption

C. TGT

D. KDC

☑ **A.** Kerberos uses symmetric encryption in order to protect the transmission confidentiality.

☒ **B, C,** and **D** are incorrect. **B** is incorrect because not all Kerberos versions use asymmetric encryption (for example, version 5 is able to use asymmetric encryption). **C** is incorrect because TGT is a term used to indicate the time-stamped ticket (known as ticket-granting ticket) that the Kerberos server will provide to the client. **D** is incorrect because the term KDC (also known as Key Distribution Center) is used to refer to the Kerberos server via another term.

11. What is the primary purpose of SSO?

A. Authorization

B. Confidentiality

C. Availability

D. Authentication

☑ **D.** SSO (single sign-on) is mainly used to identify and authenticate users. Hence, from the available answers, authentication is the correct one.

☒ **A, B,** and **C** are incorrect. **A** is incorrect because SSO doesn't provide authorization, as it is not responsible for the services the user can access after being authenticated to a system. **B** is incorrect because SSO doesn't provide confidentiality (which is usually achieved by using encryption). **C** is incorrect because SSO doesn't provide availability, which has to do with the system being available for usage.

12. Which of the following is the best method of performing device authentication?

    A. MAC address filtering

    B. Dynamic IP addressing

    C. Cookies

    D. Certificate-based authentication

    ☑ **D.** Out of the proposed answers, certificate-based authentication is the best method, as it entails a digital certificate to be installed on the device in order to authenticate when used to connect to a network.

    ☒ **A, B,** and **C** are incorrect. **A** is incorrect because MAC addresses can be easily spoofed. **B** is incorrect because dynamic IP addressing won't help uniquely identify a device, as the IP address would be different each time. **C** is incorrect because cookies can be deleted or manipulated and don't offer a fully reliable authentication mechanism.

13. Josh is going away on a two-week holiday, but his Windows domain password expires in three days. He wants to still be able to use his laptop to access company network resources while he's away. What does he need to do?

    A. Change his domain password before it expires

    B. Call his company's IT team while away so they can have his password changed

    C. Do nothing, as he can always use his cached credentials after the first three days

    D. Log in to his laptop as a local administrator and reset his password

    ☑ **A.** The only way for Josh to maintain access to company resources while he's away on holiday is to ensure he changes his password before leaving. The question doesn't mention that a VPN client is configured, thus implying that Josh's laptop has no way of connecting to the corporate network once he's away.

    ☒ **B, C,** and **D** are incorrect. **B** is incorrect because even if an IT administrator changes Josh's password at the Windows server level, his laptop will have no way of connecting to the corporate network (since there's no VPN present) to get the updated password. **C** is incorrect because although Josh can use locally cached credentials after the first three days, that won't allow him access to the corporate network resources but only to the local system ones. **D** is incorrect because a local administrator would only be able to administer local accounts, not Windows domain accounts.

14. Which of these statements is true regarding DAC and non-DAC access control?

    A. In non-DAC models, users have ownership of their resources.

    B. In non-DAC models, security administrators control the access granted to users.

    C. DAC models are best for avoiding catastrophic system modifications.

    D. DAC models don't use any type of ACL.

☑ **B.** In non-DAC models (i.e., MAC), security administrators control the access provided to users, allowing for very robust but less granular control.

☒ **A, C,** and **D** are incorrect. **A** is incorrect because users have ownership of their resources in DAC systems, thus allowing for access granularity. **C** is incorrect because non-DAC models are best for avoiding catastrophic system modifications, as they provide the system owner less control, which provides greater system protection. **D** is incorrect because DAC models do use discretionary ACLs (also known as DACLs).

15. Felly Corp. wants to improve the level of current security policies. As such, employees won't be allowed to connect to critical infrastructure using corporate machines from the guest network. This is an example of:

A. RBAC (Role-based Access Control)

B. MAC

C. ABAC

D. DAC

☑ **C.** ABAC works by evaluating subject and object attributes (i.e., a user attempting to log in to a finance server from the guest network) and allows/rejects accordingly.

☒ **A, B,** and **D** are incorrect. **A** is incorrect because Role-based Access Control defines access by using roles or groups and isn't suitable for this scenario. **B** is incorrect because MAC uses labels for subject and object identification. **D** is incorrect because DAC models grant access to objects based on the identity of each subject (i.e., Alice has read and write permissions to a file).

16. Nadia is on holiday and needs to access her banking website to make a transaction. She uses her friend's computer to log on to the bank's website, and after entering her credentials she is requested to enter her mother's maiden name. This is an example of:

A. Passphrase

B. OTP

C. Cognitive password

D. Static password

☑ **C.** Entering the mother's maiden name is a typical example of a cognitive password, which is something that only a valid system user would know (similar to a dog's name, first school that was attended, favorite color, or city of birth). It is worth noting that in real life, the answer to such a question doesn't need to be truthful, and actually this is a good way of not allowing an unauthorized user to discover accurate information and gain access to someone's account. For example, if a user's cognitive password is his favorite color (i.e., yellow), then an attacker can identify that in little time (often enough an attacker will use open source intelligence techniques, like browsing to someone's Facebook profile where a favorite color is being depicted). However, if an answer of "fever31" is set, the chance of someone identifying that as a favorite color is very slim.

☒ **A, B,** and **D** are incorrect. **A** is incorrect because the mother's maiden name doesn't constitute a passphrase (although arguably, based on the earlier comment about not providing true answers to the system's questions, someone might indeed use a passphrase as an answer). **B** is incorrect because an OTP is generated by some type of hardware or software token. **D** is incorrect because although the maiden name doesn't change, it is not being used as a password here. Remember that Nadia already provided her credentials to the banking system but was requested to provide a cognitive password due to the fact that she is using her friend's machine, which is a new device that the banking system hasn't encountered before, so it needs to verify the legitimacy of the connection.

17. An attacker is using a brute-force tool in order to crack a user's password and gain access to online medical information. Which is the best option in order to protect against this type of attack?

    A. Account lockout policy

    B. Minimum password length

    C. Password history

    D. Maximum password age

    ☑ **A.** Configuring a lockout policy with a low number of attempts to enter a password (commonly three to five) will mitigate the risk of an attacker brute forcing a user's password. That means that if a wrong password is entered five consecutive times, the user's account is locked, which will require an administrator to unlock it.

    ☒ **B, C,** and **D** are incorrect. **B** is incorrect because a minimum password length policy doesn't guarantee a password won't be brute forced. For example, setting a password at a minimum of seven characters doesn't guarantee that the attacker won't guess it if they have enough time and processing power. Furthermore, it doesn't guarantee that the password is strong enough, as someone might use "abcdefg," which is considered very common. **C** is incorrect because password history (i.e., the system having a record of the most recently used passwords) doesn't guarantee a strong password is being used. Someone might switch "abcdefg" with "qwertyu," again not using a strong password. **D** is incorrect because maximum password age refers to how often users are compelled to alter their account passwords, which also doesn't guarantee a strong password is in use or an attacker can't brute force it.

18. Which is the best option for managing passwords?

    A. Write them down and save them in a safe to which only you have the key.

    B. Save them on a local text file.

    C. Store them on an external USB.

    D. Use KeePassXC.

☑ **D.** Using a password manager (like KeePassXC or Windows Credential Manager) ensures that you store your passwords in an encrypted database, which can only be accessed via a main password (also known as a master password). As long as you ensure your master password is strong enough, then the data is fairly secure.

☒ **A, B,** and **C** are incorrect. **A** is incorrect because passwords should never be written down. If they are, there's a possibility they are read, regardless of where they are stored. **B** is incorrect because saving them on a local file presents the risk of that file being read, especially if the machine is compromised or stolen. **C** is incorrect because an external USB can be read, lost, or stolen, thus compromising your passwords.

19. Which is not a protocol for asynchronous dynamic password creation?

    A. HOTP

    B. OPIE

    C. TOTP

    D. S/KEY

    ☑ **C.** TOTP (Time-based One Time Password) is a protocol that is used for creating time-based synchronous dynamic passwords.

    ☒ **A, B,** and **D** are incorrect, as all three protocols relate to asynchronous dynamic password creation.

20. Elizabeth books a SSCP exam, and when she reaches the exam center she realizes that a palm vein scan is required. This is an example of which authentication factor?

    A. Something you know

    B. Something you are

    C. Something you have

    D. Biometrics

    ☑ **B.** A palm vein scan falls under "something you are," as it uses a person's unique characteristics (palm vein feature) in order to provide authentication.

    ☒ **A, C,** and **D** are incorrect. **A** is incorrect because "something you know" refers to a password or something else that the user has knowledge of. **C** is incorrect because "something you have" refers to an item that the user is in possession of, like a token or card. **D** is incorrect because although a palm vein scan is considered a biometric authentication method, the authentication factor that this falls under is "something you are." There's no authentication factor known as biometrics.

21. Which data classification scheme does the U.S. government use (listed from lowest to highest classification level)?

    A. Top Secret, Secret, Confidential, Unclassified

    B. Unclassified, Confidential, Secret, Top Secret

    C. Unclassified, Classified, Secret, Top Secret

    D. Unclassified, Classified, Confidential, Top Secret

☑ **B.** The U.S. government classification order (from lowest to highest) is Unclassified, Confidential, Secret, and Top Secret.

☒ **A, C,** and **D** are incorrect. **A** is incorrect because it presents the classification in an order of highest to lowest. **C** and **D** are incorrect, and note that they also contain a data classification level named "Classified" that doesn't exist as part of the actual data classification scheme used. For the U.S. government, any information that is not categorized as unclassified is considered classified, and it is assigned a level of Confidential, Secret, or Top Secret.

22. Which of these statements is not correct regarding the Bell-LaPadula model?

    A. It uses the "no read up" rule.

    B. It uses the "no write down" rule.

    C. It is used to enforce confidentiality.

    D. It is used to enforce integrity.

☑ **C.** The primary goal of the Bell-LaPadula model is to enforce confidentiality.

☒ **A, B,** and **D** are incorrect. **A** is incorrect because Bell-LaPadula does use the "no read up" rule in order to ensure that a subject that has access to a security level can't read an object found at a higher security level (as they are not authorized to access that information). **B** is incorrect because Bell-LaPadula also uses the "no write down" rule to ensure that subjects with access to a security level don't write to objects at a lower security level. **D** is incorrect because the primary goal of this model is not to enforce integrity, but to enforce confidentiality, which is exactly why it uses the mentioned "no read up" and "no write down" rules.

23. Which of these models uses the "simple integrity axiom"?

    A. Biba

    B. Clark-Wilson

    C. Brewer-Nash

    D. Bell-LaPadula

☑ **A.** The Biba model uses the "simple integrity axiom," which states that subjects with access to a security level can't read a lower security level object.

☒ **B, C,** and **D** are incorrect. **B** is incorrect because Clark-Wilson uses certification and enforcement rules for separation of duties enforcement. **C** is incorrect because Brewer-Nash works by creating a logical barrier that prevents conflicts of interest but doesn't have anything to do with the "simple integrity axiom." **D** is incorrect because Bell-LaPadula uses the "no read up" and "no write down" rules but not the "simple integrity axiom."

24. A large law firm has a team (designated Alpha) representing a manufacturing client, while another team (designated Bravo) is working on a case relating to one of the manufacturing client's biggest competitors. Bravo team would greatly benefit from information that Alpha team has access to. Which of these models would be the most appropriate to ensure that a conflict of interest is avoided?

A. Bell-LaPadula

B. Biba

C. Clark-Wilson

D. Brewer-Nash

☑ **D.** The Brewer-Nash model (also known as the Chinese Wall model) is primarily used to avoid conflicts of interest. According to that, an ethical screen model is used to classify data to distinct conflict-of-interest classes. In this case, a simple way of classifying data would be to ensure that the manufacturing client is placed in one class while their competitor is in another one. Hence, if Bravo team has access to the competitor class, it can't access data from the conflicting class of the manufacturing client.

☒ **A, B,** and **C** are incorrect. **A** is incorrect because Bell-LaPadula is used for enforcing confidentiality. **B** is incorrect because Biba is used for enforcing integrity. **C** is incorrect because Clark-Wilson is also used to enforce integrity. Hence, the most appropriate choice is the Brewer-Nash model.

25. Dian signs in to her Gmail account and checks her e-mail. She then wants to access her YouTube channel to upload a new video, which she accesses without entering any further login details. This is an example of:

A. Federated access

B. SSO

C. Decentralized authentication

D. Two-step verification

☑ **B.** SSO refers to a single user authentication instance while the system allows for the same credentials to be used for the remainder of the session (typically until the user closes his browser or logs out of the application). Dian used her credentials to log in to her Gmail account, and when she browsed to YouTube, SSO was used, which is why she didn't have to re-enter her username and password.

☒ **A, C,** and **D** are incorrect. **A** is incorrect because federated access refers to the ability of a single login to users in different networks, but Dian is only using Google's network so no federated access is being used. **C** is incorrect because in decentralized authentication, credentials to access different systems are stored in separate databases.

That means that if two systems were accessed, two different login sessions would be required. **D** is incorrect because two-step verification relates to using a second factor to authenticate to a system (i.e., user enters his username and password and then a one-time code is sent to his mobile phone, which needs to be entered into the system to complete the authentication process).

26. Which of these combinations provides the strongest and most accurate authentication?

   A. Username, cognitive password, PIN

   B. Dynamic password, fingerprint

   C. Retina scan, OTP

   D. Symantec's VIP Access, Google Authenticator

   ☑ **C.** Using a retina scan and OTP (one-time password) entails that a two-factor authentication system is in place (combining "something you are" and "something you have"). If you take a look at the other answers, A and D only use one factor (as explained later on). However, B also mentions two factors of authentication being in place: a dynamic password (which is another way of describing OTP) and a fingerprint. Note that a retina scan is considered one of the most accurate biometric authentication types and is certainly more accurate than a fingerprint, thus making it the best option.

   ☒ **A, B,** and **D** are incorrect. **A** is incorrect because a cognitive password and PIN both belong to the same authentication factor, which is "something you know," making this a weak option (note that the username provides identification and not authentication). **B** is incorrect because it does entail two factors of authentication (dynamic password and fingerprint), which would be equivalent to what C mentions (OTP and retina scan). However, as a retina scan is more accurate, this is not the best answer. **D** is incorrect because Symantec's VIP Access and Google Authenticator both belong to the same authentication factor, that being "something you have," not making this the best answer.

27. Which of these statements regarding passwords is not true?

   A. Use one strong password across various systems.

   B. Change passwords often.

   C. Never give out your password.

   D. Use passphrases whenever possible.

   ☑ **A.** Although the answer mentions a strong password is in use, that doesn't make it impossible to be intercepted, stolen, or provided unintentionally to an attacker. If that password is used across various systems, the malicious party will have access to everything, which could prove quite damaging for an organization.

   ☒ **B, C,** and **D** are incorrect. **B** is incorrect because it is a good practice to change passwords often. **C** is incorrect, as it is highly recommended not to give your password out to anyone. **D** is incorrect because using passphrases is a great way of creating secure passwords.

28. Fine Investments Bank has a partnership with Gradie Security to share resources in order for the latter to manage their firewalls. They aim to exchange a lot of network documentation via a web-based portal, which will only be accessible by Gradie Security. This is an example of a(n):

A. DMZ

B. PAN

C. Intranet

D. Extranet

☑ **D.** An extranet is a network that uses the Internet to host resources and would be the best way for Fine Investments Bank to provide documentation and other internal information to Gradie Security.

☒ **A, B,** and **C** are incorrect. **A** is incorrect because a DMZ hosts resources that are available to everyone on the Internet, while an extranet is used to exchange information only with a trusted third party. **B** is incorrect because a PAN is a very small network, commonly used by an individual (i.e., creating a PAN between a laptop, tablet, and a phone). **C** is incorrect because an intranet is the internal network of an organization and would never be accessible by a third party (like Gradie Security).

29. Mesquite Investment Group wants to allow their employees to browse Facebook only after their workday finishes. Which of these attributes is best to use?

A. Location

B. Group membership

C. Remote access

D. Temporal

☑ **D.** Assuming that the working day runs from 9:00 A.M. to 5:00 P.M., then Mesquite Investment Group wants to only allow Facebook usage out of those hours, which is something that can easily be done using the temporal attribute.

☒ **A, B,** and **C** are incorrect. **A** is incorrect because the location is irrelevant, as the question doesn't limit this to one company branch (i.e., the Chicago branch). **B** is incorrect, as this refers to groups of subjects that are granted access to objects (i.e., admins, local admins, users). **C** is incorrect because the remote access attribute refers to allowing users to remotely connect to the company network.

30. A user accesses a document. Which of these statements is correct?

A. The user is the object.

B. The document is the object.

C. The document is the subject.

D. The user is both the subject and object.

☑ **B.** An object is the resource being accessed; hence, the document is the object.

☒ **A, C,** and **D** are incorrect. **A** is incorrect because the user is the one that accesses a resource, thus making him the subject. **C** is incorrect because a subject accesses a resource, but here the document is the resource being accessed. **D** is incorrect because the user is the one accessing the document, meaning he is strictly the subject, not both subject and object.

31. Anemone Investment Group is using a two-step verification process (user's password combined with an OTP sent via SMS) to allow remote access to its secure file server. It is 2:00 A.M. on a Saturday, and one of their employees realizes his personal e-mail account has been compromised. He is using the same compromised credentials to access Anemone Investment Group's network remotely. The IT team only works Monday through Friday. How should he proceed?

    A. Call the company CEO and report the issue.

    B. Immediately drive to the office and change their password.

    C. Send an e-mail to the IT team and follow up with them on Monday morning.

    D. Delete their personal e-mail account.

    ☑ **C.** One of the greatest advantages of using a two-factor authentication scheme is that even if the user's password is compromised, the attacker would still need an OTP (which in this case he can only get if he obtains the user's mobile phone) to access the account. Based on that, the user can safely notify the IT team via e-mail at the time he was made aware of the issue and be diligent and follow up with them as soon as they are available.

    ☒ **A, B,** and **D** are incorrect. **A** is incorrect because calling the company CEO to report an issue like this is out of his remit and a bit of an overkill. Reporting this to the IT team is the best way to move forward, as they are responsible for resetting or monitoring the user's account, checking access logs, and performing other similar activities. **B** is incorrect because (as mentioned earlier) a two-factor authentication system is in place; hence, there's no need to drive to the office in the middle of the night to change the account password. **D** is incorrect because even if the user deletes his personal e-mail account, this will have no effect on enhancing the corporate account's security.

32. Captain Jones has been granted top secret access. According to the Bell-LaPadula model, which rule ensures that she doesn't write information to a lower security level?

    A. Simple integrity axiom

    B. Star property

    C. Simple security property

    D. Star integrity axiom

    ☑ **B.** The star property (also known as "no write down") ensures that subjects with access to a security level don't write to objects at a lower security level.

☒ **A, C,** and **D** are incorrect. **A** is incorrect because it's a rule encountered in the Biba model, which doesn't allow the reading of objects at a lower security level. **C** is incorrect because the simple security property (also known as "no read up") ensures that a subject that has access to a security level can't read an object found at a higher security level. **D** is incorrect because the star integrity axiom is used in the Biba model and relates to not allowing subjects who are granted access at a security level to write to an object of a higher security level.

33. Danny attempts to enter his credentials in order to log in to his corporate laptop. After entering a wrong password three times, he is unable to enter any credentials again. What is the most likely reason?

    A. Maximum password age.

    B. Password history.

    C. Account has been deleted.

    D. Account has been locked out.

    ☑ **D.** After entering a wrong password three times, Danny's account most likely was locked out in order to prevent a brute-force attack from taking place.

    ☒ **A, B,** and **C** are incorrect. **A** is incorrect because the maximum password age defines how often users are obligated to change their account passwords (i.e., every ten days). **B** is incorrect because password history relates to changing a user's password. The system remembers previous passwords that a user has used (i.e., last eight) in order to prevent him from using the same password again. **C** is incorrect because an account wouldn't normally be deleted just because a user entered a wrong password.

34. An attacker managed to obtain the password file from Lara's laptop and is using a brute-force tool to guess her password. Which of the following is the best option in order to protect her account from this type of attack?

    A. Account lockout policy

    B. Password complexity

    C. Password history

    D. Password length

    ☑ **B.** Password complexity is the best weapon against offline brute-force attacks. The more complex the password is, the less chance a brute-force attack has of identifying it.

    ☒ **A, C,** and **D** are incorrect. **A** is incorrect because an account lockout policy would be very beneficial if this was an online brute-force attack. However, the attacker is using an offline tool while having the password file at his disposal, hence there's no account that can be locked out. **C** is incorrect because password history (as already mentioned in the previous question) relates to changing a user's password. **D** is incorrect because the password length doesn't ensure a strong password was used. For example, even if the password length is seven characters, if the password of choice is "hackers," then there's a higher chance of the password being identified by an attacker using any standard brute-force dictionary.

35. What is the greatest disadvantage of using a retina scanner?

    A. The scan can potentially identify and reveal the subject's medical conditions.

    B. They are often unreliable.

    C. The scan takes too long.

    D. There is a large amount of false positives.

    ☑ **A.** The biggest disadvantage of a retina scanner is the fact that a scan can identify and reveal a subject's medical conditions, which makes it less popular to the majority of the population.

    ☒ **B, C,** and **D** are incorrect. **B** is incorrect because retina scans are very reliable and are actually considered one of the best biometric authentication methods. **C** is incorrect because the subject's identity is verified very quickly. **D** is incorrect because retina scans have a very low rate of false positives (as well as false negatives).

36. Which of the following isn't included in the identity and access management lifecycle?

    A. Entitlement

    B. Proofing

    C. De-provisioning

    D. Deletion

    ☑ **D.** There's no term known as deletion in the identity and access management lifecycle. Account deletion will normally take place at the de-provisioning phase.

    ☒ **A, B,** and **C** are incorrect. **A** is incorrect because entitlement refers to what privileges are provided to users and ensuring those align with their role. **B** is incorrect because proofing refers to establishing an individual's identity prior to account creation. **C** is incorrect because de-provisioning relates to ensuring that inactive accounts are disabled and deleted.

37. Which of the following is an example of a passphrase?

    A. ILoveS@l@miAndCh33s3

    B. P@ssw0rd

    C. IUOIUQJHJH1987287!!dslkUYQ62

    D. passphrase

    ☑ **A.** A passphrase is defined as a lengthy character sequence that is meaningful to the user. ILoveS@l@miAndCh33s3 is a passphrase derived from "ILoveSalamiAndCheese" where the letter "a" has been replaced with the character "@" and the letter "e" with "3" in order to provide enhanced security.

    ☒ **B, C,** and **D** are incorrect. **B** is incorrect because P@ssw0rd is just a password containing a combination of lowercase and uppercase letters, numeric digits, and special characters. That doesn't constitute a passphrase. **C** is incorrect because

IUOIUQJHJH1987287!!dslkUYQ62 might again be a lengthy password (even longer than the passphrase used in option A); however, this doesn't have any meaning at all to the user. It is just random characters, and it would be impossible to remember. **D** is incorrect because, similarly to B, "passphrase" is just a word (which would be a poor password) and doesn't constitute a passphrase.

38. A home network serving the needs of a small family can be classified as a:

   A. WAN

   B. PAN

   C. LAN

   D. MAN

   ☑ **C.** Home networks can be classified as LANs, as they are a group of connected devices within a small geographical area, which in this case is the user's residence.

   ☒ **A, B,** and **D** are incorrect. **A** is incorrect because a WAN would be used for connecting devices across vast areas. **B** is incorrect because a PAN is a very small network, commonly used by an individual, and it wouldn't be suitable for a home network. **D** is incorrect because a MAN is a collection of various networks spanning over large geographical areas, like a large corporate complex spread across several miles.

39. Which of the following is not an SSO technology?

   A. SAML

   B. SecureAuth IdP

   C. Kerberos

   D. OpenIDConnect

   ☑ **B.** SecureAuth IdP provides mobile device management and doesn't have anything to do with SSO.

   ☒ **A, C,** and **D** are incorrect. **A** is incorrect because SAML is used to provide SSO. **C** is incorrect because Windows domains and Linux/UNIX realms do use Kerberos for SSO. **D** is incorrect because OpenIDConnect is an SSO technology.

40. Which model is known as the "Chinese Wall" model?

   A. Biba

   B. Brewer-Nash

   C. Bell-LaPadula

   D. Clark-Wilson

   ☑ **B.** The Brewer-Nash model is also known as the Chinese Wall model.

   ☒ **A, C,** and **D** are incorrect. All other models (Biba, Bell-LaPadula, Clark-Wilson) are unrelated to the Chinese Wall model.

CHAPTER 2

Security Operations and Administration

This chapter includes questions from the following objectives:

- 2.1 Comply with codes of ethics
- 2.2 Understand security concepts
- 2.3 Document, implement, and maintain functional security controls
- 2.4 Participate in asset management
- 2.5 Implement security controls and assess compliance
- 2.6 Participate in change management
- 2.7 Participate in security awareness and training
- 2.8 Participate in physical security operations (e.g., data center assessment, badging)

This chapter contains a complete set of questions and answers regarding the (ISC)^2 code of ethics; basic security concepts (confidentiality, integrity, availability); security control types (preventive, detective, corrective); asset management; security controls implementation and compliance assessment; change management; and participation in physical security operations. In addition, there's variety of questions focusing on security awareness and training (attack types, malicious code, performing security audits, and understanding security policies).

1. Ben is a system administrator, and he was told that users are experiencing slow response times when trying to access the corporate website. Upon investigation, he notices that the web server shows a high number of established connections and thinks an attack might be taking place. Based on this, which of the following statements is correct?

   A. The website is experiencing a DoS attack.

   B. A DDoS attack is underway.

   C. The server is experiencing increased traffic.

   D. A port scan is taking place.

2. Jason is the CFO of sales, and he just received an e-mail inviting him to access a Dropbox URL sharing financial projections for the next quarter. The URL is http://xteyjsurls.com. This is an example of:

   A. A valid method of sharing company financial data

   B. Spear phishing

   C. Vishing

   D. Whaling

3. Which of the following is classified as PHI?

   A. Company name

   B. Business address

   C. Fingerprint

   D. Healthcare provider

4. Next Gemini Bank is developing a new proprietary algorithm. What is the most suitable data classification label for that information?

   A. Proprietary

   B. Confidential

   C. Public

   D. Sensitive

5. Don is on his way to work and wants to review the material for the morning meeting. For that purpose, he powers on his laptop and opens the spreadsheet application to access the related file. What is this an example of?

   A. Data in use

   B. Data in motion

   C. Data in transit

   D. Data at rest

6. In which corporate policy are these statements most likely to be present?

Employees are not allowed to access social media sites.
Company information is not allowed to be stored in USB drives.
Client data must never be provided to any individual who is not a corporate employee.
It is not allowed to connect any personal devices to the company network.

   A. Backup policy

   B. Network access policy

   C. Guest access policy

   D. Acceptable use policy

7. A network administrator is considering placing a new firewall at the network perimeter. Which type of control is this?

   A. Detective

   B. Corrective

   C. Preventive

   D. Recovery

8. Which of these security practices is not a part of system hardening?

   A. Update operating system

   B. Enable appropriate services

   C. Enable firewall

   D. Remove unused protocols

9. James is searching for a way to apply critical patches across his company's network. Which of the following would be inappropriate for that purpose?

   A. TPM

   B. WSUS

   C. SCCM

   D. ConfigMgr

10. Dianne is working on a critical system implementation and needs to ensure that proper audit logging is in place to be able to account for any administrator action. This is an example of:

   A. Authentication

   B. Integrity

   C. Nonrepudiation

   D. Confidentiality

11. Which of these is considered a detective control?

    A. IPS

    B. IDS

    C. Security camera

    D. Disaster recovery plan

12. Jane is a system administrator and has chosen to allow company users to connect USB flash drives in read-only mode (i.e., users can only copy data from flash drives to company devices) so data loss can be avoided. What is the biggest disadvantage of that?

    A. Company employees don't have any way of sharing information.

    B. Malware will still be copied from any infected corporate machine to the USB flash drives.

    C. Standard users (non-administrator) can easily bypass the read-only setting.

    D. Company antivirus software won't be able to remove any infected files that exist on the flash drives.

13. Janet is a network administrator. Upon reviewing records of a recent network change, she realizes that one of her colleagues made a mistake and, in an attempt to cover his tracks, he deleted the related audit logs. How should Janet proceed?

    A. Do nothing in order not to create tension in the workplace.

    B. Confront her colleague by telling him she knows what happened so he should report it to the team's manager himself.

    C. Report the incident to her manager.

    D. Help her colleague recover the audit logs from the related backups and ask him to never let this happen again.

14. A security analyst is investigating a possible network misconfiguration issue, resulting in increased internal network traffic. The offending machine's IP and MAC addresses have been identified, but the analyst needs to trace those to the machine owner in order to verify the legitimacy of the traffic. What is the best way of achieving this?

    A. Search the company's incident management software to identify cases that involve the same IP/MAC combination.

    B. Check the asset register.

    C. Connect to the host in question via RDP to get the necessary information.

    D. Block the host from the network to stop a further increase in traffic.

15. Which of these controls is the most appropriate to stop tailgating?

    A. Security camera

    B. Access badge

    C. Mantrap

    D. Physical security policy

16. How often do PCI merchants need to perform network scans according to PCI-DSS requirements?

    A. Monthly

    B. Quarterly

    C. Biannually

    D. Annually

17. Which of the following should a large bank's mergers and acquisitions team ensure has taken place before a major acquisition of an investment firm happens?

    A. Due diligence

    B. Due care

    C. Separation of duties

    D. Confidentiality

18. A company backup policy primarily uses magnetic tapes for backups. They also regularly back up data to the company cloud. Which type of control does the company cloud represent?

    A. Detective

    B. Deterrent

    C. Recovery

    D. Compensating

19. Which of the following is not a security policy characteristic?

    A. Mission statement

    B. Enforcement section

    C. Sanctions statement

    D. Accountability statement

20. Which of these is not included in asset management?

    A. Hardware

    B. People

    C. Data

    D. Software

21. What is the primary goal of change management?

    A. Review changes

    B. Minimize disruption

    C. Document changes

    D. Provide resource allocation

22. You are tasked with enhancing your company's physical security controls in order to ensure a proper audit trail exists. Which action would accomplish that goal?

    A. Place access card readers at the interior of secure operation rooms.

    B. Replace external 16-foot fences with taller ones.

    C. Increase security guard presence to achieve patrolling in pairs.

    D. Suggest hiring an external party to perform a physical security assessment.

23. What process would take place if an (ISC)² member doesn't comply with the (ISC)² code of ethics?

    A. Any violators will be reported to the company the member is working for.

    B. (ISC)² will revoke their certifications.

    C. A review from a peer panel will take place.

    D. They will get a one-off warning.

24. Which of the following is not a step of the change management process?

    A. Change approved or rejected

    B. Change resolved

    C. Change reviewed

    D. Change submitted

25. A system administrator is installing an IPS, a firewall, and a vulnerability scanner while at the same time drafting new security policies and training materials for his company. Which best describes his goal?

    A. Confidentiality

    B. Due diligence

    C. Accountability

    D. Defense in depth

26. In order for a merchant to comply with PCI-DSS, a network scan is required to be completed by which of the following?

    A. SAQ

    B. ASV

    C. QSA

    D. ISA

27. Which of the following changes wouldn't require CAB approval?

A. Standard

B. Emergency

C. Normal

D. Expedited

28. An attacker manages to compromise a critical server, with no central logging capability enabled. After obtaining the information of interest, the audit logs are accessed and the related entries showing what actions the attacker performed are removed. Which of the following is being compromised?

A. Least privilege

B. Availability

C. Accountability

D. Authentication

29. Employee badges are primarily used for:

A. Identification

B. Authentication

C. Provisioning

D. Entitlement

30. John powers on his computer and successfully installs a new application. After a few minutes he realizes that he's unable to launch the newly installed application, as that is being blocked by the antivirus program. What would the antivirus most probably be using to block the application at that point?

A. Antivirus blacklisting

B. Scheduled scan

C. On-demand scan

D. Heuristic-based detection

31. Which of the following is most suitable to protect against phishing attacks?

A. Spam filtering provider

B. User education

C. E-mail gateway

D. Antivirus

32. Which of the following wouldn't be used during an SQL injection attack?

    A. SELECT

    B. --

    C. <>

    D. ;

33. An attacker compromises a fashion retailer's website and places malware on its web page. The goal is for the malware to be downloaded by clients that visit the website to place future orders. This is an example of:

    A. Malvertising

    B. Trapdoor

    C. Drive-by download

    D. Rootkit

34. Which of these statements about configuration management is not accurate?

    A. Puppet uses Python.

    B. Microsoft offers "Group Policy" for system configuration.

    C. Imaging is a commonly used method.

    D. Ansible can be used in a Linux environment.

35. In which of these control goal and class combinations does a motion sensor fall into?

    A. Preventive, technical

    B. Detective, technical

    C. Preventive, physical

    D. Detective, physical

36. Which of the following is not included in the (ISC)² code of ethics?

    A. Act honorably.

    B. Provide adequate service.

    C. Advance and protect the profession.

    D. Provide diligent service to principals.

37. Which of the following can be part of more than one control type (i.e., combine being detective and preventive)?

    A. Security policy

    B. IDS

    C. IPS

    D. Audit logs

38. A secure facility requires individuals to sign in at the reception desk and swipe their cards at the card readers. However, the security personnel do an end-of-shift check and realize that there's a mismatch between the two records, showing 150 people signing in at the reception desk but only 140 swiping in. What is the most likely reason for that?

A. People signing in at reception more than once.

B. Tailgating has occurred.

C. Some employees signed in at reception but entered the building via nonstandard entrances.

D. Card reader system experienced an error.

1. C	**11.** B	**21.** B	**31.** B
2. D	**12.** D	**22.** A	**32.** C
3. D	**13.** C	**23.** C	**33.** C
4. B	**14.** B	**24.** B	**34.** A
5. A	**15.** C	**25.** D	**35.** D
6. D	**16.** B	**26.** B	**36.** B
7. C	**17.** A	**27.** A	**37.** C
8. B	**18.** D	**28.** C	**38.** B
9. A	**19.** C	**29.** A	
10. C	**20.** B	**30.** D	

1. Ben is a system administrator, and he was told that users are experiencing slow response times when trying to access the corporate website. Upon investigation, he notices that the web server shows a high number of established connections and thinks an attack might be taking place. Based on this, which of the following statements is correct?

   A. The website is experiencing a DoS attack.

   B. A DDoS attack is underway.

   C. The server is experiencing increased traffic.

   D. A port scan is taking place.

   ☑ **C.** The question states that there is a high number of established connections. However, that is not necessarily an indicator that an attack is taking place. Without performing additional investigation, this would most likely be considered a time when the server is experiencing a peak traffic flow, which would account for the increased traffic.

   ☒ **A, B,** and **D** are incorrect. **A** is incorrect because if a DoS (denial of service) attack was underway, users wouldn't be able to browse the website or their experience would be severely degraded, whereas at this time there's just a report of website slowness (also note that at this time, the slowness is just a user's subjective opinion, as no investigation has been performed to corroborate that claim). **B** is incorrect because for a DDoS (distributed denial of service) attack to take place, traffic would need to originate from different sources, which are all sending multiple packets to the web server. **D** is incorrect because a port scan would try to identify open ports on a target machine (while there's no indication of that here), and in addition, an attacker performing a port scan would typically try to remain undetected.

2. Jason is the CFO of sales, and he just received an e-mail inviting him to access a Dropbox URL sharing financial projections for the next quarter. The URL is http://xteyjsurls.com. This is an example of:

   A. A valid method of sharing company financial data

   B. Spear phishing

   C. Vishing

   D. Whaling

   ☑ **D.** Whaling is a specific category of spear phishing where an attacker targets a C-level company executive (like CEO, CFO, or COO). In this example, the CFO (chief financial officer) was enticed to click a URL posing to be a Dropbox link. Upon a simple URL review, it can be noticed that http://xteyjsurls.com has nothing to do with Dropbox.

   ☒ **A, B,** and **C** are incorrect. **A** is incorrect because even if the Dropbox link was genuine, it wouldn't be the preferred method of sharing sensitive company data. **B** is incorrect because "spear phishing" usually targets a team of people or a whole organization. Even if one specific individual is targeted via a spear-phishing e-mail, when that person is a high-level executive, the appropriate term used to describe this attack is "whaling." **C** is incorrect because "vishing" is a social engineering technique that uses the phone (not e-mail) as an attack vector.

3. Which of the following is classified as PHI?

    A. Company name

    B. Business address

    C. Fingerprint

    D. Healthcare provider

    ☑ **D.** An individual's healthcare provider is considered PHI (protected health information), as it's classified as personal information about someone's health.

    ☒ **A, B,** and **C** are incorrect. **A** is incorrect because a company name is publicly available. **B** is incorrect because a business address should be publicly available so potential clients can reach the business in question. **C** is incorrect because biometric information (like a fingerprint) is classified as PII (personally identifiable information).

4. Next Gemini Bank is developing a new proprietary algorithm. What is the most suitable data classification label for that information?

    A. Proprietary

    B. Confidential

    C. Public

    D. Sensitive

    ☑ **B.** A newly designed proprietary algorithm would be classified as highly important information and would need to have the highest classification assigned. Given the possible answers, that would be "confidential."

    ☒ **A, C,** and **D** are incorrect. **A** is incorrect because although the algorithm is proprietary in nature, an organization wouldn't typically have a label named "proprietary." Labels should be generic and depict the protection level the data requires. **C** is incorrect because highly sensitive information would never be classified as "public." **D** is incorrect because "sensitive" is not strong enough to depict the importance of proprietary data as well the information leakage impact at that level.

5. Don is on his way to work and wants to review the material for the morning meeting. For that purpose, he powers on his laptop and opens the spreadsheet application to access the related file. What is this an example of?

    A. Data in use

    B. Data in motion

    C. Data in transit

    D. Data at rest

☑ **A.** When Don opened his spreadsheet application and accessed the related file, it was transferred into his computer's memory. That data (residing in memory or being processed) is "data in use."

☒ **B, C,** and **D** are incorrect. **B** is incorrect because "data in motion" refers to a network being used for data transmission. **C** is incorrect because "data in transit" is just another term used to describe "data in motion." **D** is incorrect because the term "data at rest" in this example would be used to describe the data file stored on the hard drive before being opened and accessed by Don.

6. In which corporate policy are these statements most likely to be present?

Employees are not allowed to access social media sites.
Company information is not allowed to be stored in USB drives.
Client data must never be provided to any individual who is not a corporate employee.
It is not allowed to connect any personal devices to the company network.

A. Backup policy

B. Network access policy

C. Guest access policy

D. Acceptable use policy

☑ **D.** An acceptable use policy defines what is and is not considered proper use of organizational hardware and information assets. All new employees must usually confirm they are aware of the policy and agree to adhere to it before commencing their work.

☒ **A, B,** and **C** are incorrect. **A** is incorrect because a backup policy defines organizational backup procedures and would include items such as how often company assets need to be backed up, what type of backup method is to be used (e.g., incremental or full backup), and where the data should be backed up to (e.g., cloud or off-site location). **B** is incorrect because a network access policy refers to the rights and privileges of specific subjects when they gain access to the corporate network. This policy would most likely include information about company VPN connectivity, type of information that can be accessed through a workstation, authentication techniques, and access control mechanisms. **C** is incorrect because a guest access policy states the company's policy for allowing guests to connect to the corporate network. Additionally, the question mentions connecting devices to the company network and accessing client data, both of which wouldn't be related to a guest access policy.

7. A network administrator is considering placing a new firewall at the network perimeter. Which type of control is this?

A. Detective

B. Corrective

C. Preventive

D. Recovery

☑ **C.** A firewall is classified as a preventive control, as it has the ability to prevent an attack by stopping offending traffic.

☒ **A, B,** and **D** are incorrect. **A** is incorrect because a detective control would only be able to identify an attack when it's taking place or after it has happened. **B** is incorrect because a corrective control would perform an activity to counter the attack. **D** is incorrect because a recovery control aims to restore a system after an incident has happened.

8. Which of these security practices is not a part of system hardening?

   A. Update operating system

   B. Enable appropriate services

   C. Enable firewall

   D. Remove unused protocols

   ☑ **B.** Enabling appropriate services wouldn't take place during a system hardening. On the contrary, during such an activity, services that are not absolutely needed would be disabled.

   ☒ **A, C,** and **D** are incorrect. **A** is incorrect because updating the operating system is something highly recommended during a hardening process. **C** is incorrect because if a system does have an available firewall, this would definitely be enabled during this activity. **D** is incorrect because any unused protocols would be removed in order not to be exploited by an attacker.

9. James is searching for a way to apply critical patches across his company's network. Which of the following would be inappropriate for that purpose?

   A. TPM

   B. WSUS

   C. SCCM

   D. ConfigMgr

   ☑ **A.** TPM (Trusted Platform Module) is a hardware chip used by various computer models (like Microsoft Surface Pro devices) for full disk encryption and has nothing to do with patching.

   ☒ **B, C,** and **D** are incorrect. **B** is incorrect because WSUS (Windows Server Update Services) is often used for patch management. **C** is incorrect because SCCM (System Center Configuration Management) is also used for patching. **D** is incorrect because ConfigMgr (also known as Configuration Manager) provides patch management.

10. Dianne is working on a critical system implementation and needs to ensure that proper audit logging is in place to be able to account for any administrator action. This is an example of:

    A. Authentication

    B. Integrity

    C. Nonrepudiation

    D. Confidentiality

☑ **C.** Nonrepudiation is the most suitable term in this case, as it refers to an individual not being able to refuse an action that was taken. Enabling audit logs will allow tracking of related administrator actions.

☒ **A, B,** and **D** are incorrect. **A** is incorrect because authentication refers to verifying an individual's identity. **B** is incorrect because integrity refers to being able to detect any unauthorized data alteration. **D** is incorrect because confidentiality refers to information being accessible only by authorized individuals.

11. Which of these is considered a detective control?

   A. IPS

   B. IDS

   C. Security camera

   D. Disaster recovery plan

   ☑ **B.** An IDS (intrusion detection system) is considered a detective control, as it only has the ability to provide event detection.

   ☒ **A, C,** and **D** are incorrect. **A** is incorrect because an IPS (intrusion prevention system) is able to prevent an attack, as it can drop offending traffic before reaching the target network. **C** is incorrect because a security camera aims to prevent offenders from attempting to enter the secure premises. **D** is incorrect because a disaster recovery plan is considered a corrective control, as it's unable to detect an incident but can help restore the system in the state that it was prior to the incident taking place.

12. Jane is a system administrator and has chosen to allow company users to connect USB flash drives in read-only mode (i.e., users can only copy data from flash drives to company devices) so data loss can be avoided. What is the biggest disadvantage of that?

   A. Company employees don't have any way of sharing information.

   B. Malware will still be copied from any infected corporate machine to the USB flash drives.

   C. Standard users (non-administrator) can easily bypass the read-only setting.

   D. Company antivirus software won't be able to remove any infected files that exist on the flash drives.

   ☑ **D.** Company antivirus software that identifies malicious files on any flash drives won't be able to delete those, as it would need "write permissions" on the flash drives to do so.

   ☒ **A, B,** and **C** are incorrect. **A** is incorrect because although using flash drives is a very common way of file sharing, it is not the only one, or the most secure for that matter. Employees should be prompted to use alternative methods, such as secure company network shares or company cloud solutions supporting adequate data encryption. **B** is incorrect because no data from a corporate machine can be copied to the flash drives (since write permission has been disabled). **C** is incorrect because only administrators have adequate permissions to edit the related policy.

13. Janet is a network administrator. Upon reviewing records of a recent network change, she realizes that one of her colleagues made a mistake and, in an attempt to cover his tracks, he deleted the related audit logs. How should Janet proceed?

   A. Do nothing in order not to create tension in the workplace.

   B. Confront her colleague by telling him she knows what happened so he should report it to the team's manager himself.

   C. Report the incident to her manager.

   D. Help her colleague recover the audit logs from the related backups and ask him to never let this happen again.

   ☑ C. According to the second cannon of the (ISC)² code of ethics, a member should "act honorably, honestly, justly, responsibly and legally." In accordance with that, Janet should report the incident to her manager as soon as possible in order for appropriate actions to be taken.

   ☒ A, B, and D are incorrect. A is incorrect because doing nothing is not an option when employee misconduct has taken place. B is incorrect because taking matters into one's own hands and confronting others may have severe consequences even though the intention may be correct. D is incorrect because being complicit and helping to cover up what has happened is not acting "honorably and justly," not to mention it's illegal.

14. A security analyst is investigating a possible network misconfiguration issue, resulting in increased internal network traffic. The offending machine's IP and MAC addresses have been identified, but the analyst needs to trace those to the machine owner in order to verify the legitimacy of the traffic. What is the best way of achieving this?

   A. Search the company's incident management software to identify cases that involve the same IP/MAC combination.

   B. Check the asset register.

   C. Connect to the host in question via RDP to get the necessary information.

   D. Block the host from the network to stop a further increase in traffic.

   ☑ B. Checking the company's asset register (or asset management software) is the best way to obtain information about any type of equipment an organization has, as well as to identify the owner of a device. Devices such as mobile phones, computers, routers, etc., should all be present in the asset register.

   ☒ A, C, and D are incorrect. A is incorrect because searching past cases might not provide up-to-date information. For example, just because three months ago an incident was raised about the machine in question, which indicated it was owned by Jane, doesn't make that accurate, as Jane might not be working for the company anymore. C is incorrect because it means taking a form of offensive action, as the analyst would be trying to connect to another individual's machine, having access to all of the information residing in that machine. **D** is incorrect because an increase in traffic doesn't provide enough evidence to warrant blocking the host machine. That could very well be a critical company server, and blocking its operation might have severe consequences for the business.

15. Which of these controls is the most appropriate to stop tailgating?

    A. Security camera

    B. Access badge

    C. Mantrap

    D. Physical security policy

    ☑ **C.** A mantrap is one of the best mechanisms that can be used to avoid tailgating, as it can control the flow of people entering a building or secure area.

    ☒ **A, B,** and **D** are incorrect. **A** is incorrect because although a security camera might record tailgating, the odds of someone monitoring that in real time at peak hours and acting each time a tailgater is present are very low. **B** is incorrect because access badges allow access to the building or area, but that doesn't stop a valid employee (in possession of an access badge) to tailgate one of his colleagues. **D** is incorrect because even if there's an appropriate organizational policy in effect, that is not enough to stop people from violating it. Only physical restrictions (i.e., a mantrap, turnstile) will be able to do that.

16. How often do PCI merchants need to perform network scans according to PCI-DSS requirements?

    A. Monthly

    B. Quarterly

    C. Biannually

    D. Annually

    ☑ **B.** PCI defines four merchant levels: 4 (lowest) to 1 (highest). In all levels, quarterly scans are required.

    ☒ **A, C,** and **D** are incorrect as they all present wrong answers. As mentioned, quarterly scans are mandatory for all four merchant levels.

17. Which of the following should a large bank's mergers and acquisitions team ensure has taken place before a major acquisition of an investment firm happens?

    A. Due diligence

    B. Due care

    C. Separation of duties

    D. Confidentiality

☑ **A.** "Due diligence" refers to all the necessary actions the bank will need to take to verify that the investment firm and its profits are legal in order to ensure the legality of the acquisition. This is often a task outsourced to business intelligence firms, which perform an investigation and provide a full report to the requestor (i.e., the bank) raising anything that might need to be clarified or further investigated before the transaction happens.

☒ **B, C,** and **D** are incorrect. **B** is incorrect because "due care" refers to ensuring appropriate actions are taken to protect company assets. **C** is incorrect because "separation of duties" refers to not allowing one individual to possess full control of a critical process. **D** is incorrect because confidentiality refers to information being accessible only by authorized individuals.

18. A company backup policy primarily uses magnetic tapes for backups. They also regularly back up data to the company cloud. Which type of control does the company cloud represent?

    A. Detective

    B. Deterrent

    C. Recovery

    D. Compensating

    ☑ **D.** The cloud provider is being used in case the backup tape (which is primarily used as a backup media) fails, thus making it a compensating control.

    ☒ **A, B,** and **C** are incorrect. **A** is incorrect because a detective control has the ability to provide event detection, which is not true in the case of a backup to the cloud. **B** is incorrect because a deterrent control aims to deter an attacker from performing a hostile action. **C** is incorrect because a recovery control aims to restore a system after an incident has happened. Please note that the question focuses on what type of control the company cloud is, making the correct answer a "compensating" one. However, if the question focused on what type of control a backup policy is, then the correct answer would be a recovery control.

19. Which of the following is not a security policy characteristic?

    A. Mission statement

    B. Enforcement section

    C. Sanctions statement

    D. Accountability statement

    ☑ **C.** A security policy doesn't have a "sanctions statement." Any related actions that can be pursued if the policy is not followed will be included in the "enforcement section."

☒ **A, B,** and **D** are incorrect. **A** is incorrect because a "mission statement" should be present and describe the overarching organizational vision. **B** is incorrect because an "enforcement section" would describe how a policy is going to be enforced and what steps might be taken in case personnel don't adhere to it. **D** is incorrect because an "accountability statement" would describe the specific role types (i.e., security staff) that have a responsibility to follow the policy.

20. Which of these is not included in asset management?

    A. Hardware

    B. People

    C. Data

    D. Software

    ☑ **B.** Although people might be referred to as organizational assets, they don't fall under asset management, which deals with how valuable company assets are managed.

    ☒ **A, C,** and **D** are incorrect. **A** is incorrect because hardware should be managed from the moment that it first appears in a company up until the time that it is discarded. **C** is incorrect because "data" refers to how data is handled (i.e., categorized or labelled), as well as what media are used for storage (i.e., keeping a record of the serial numbers of all devices that store company data). **D** is incorrect because all software (including version and patch) should be properly listed for licensing and organizational security/awareness (i.e., if a new vulnerability is published about a software version the company is using, it should be able to search the asset register and identify what devices are using that software and require patching to be protected against that vulnerability).

21. What is the primary goal of change management?

    A. Review changes

    B. Minimize disruption

    C. Document changes

    D. Provide resource allocation

    ☑ **B.** The primary goal of change management is to ensure any organizational disruption is kept to a minimum by carefully reviewing the proposed changes and their associated impact and approve or reject them accordingly.

    ☒ **A, C,** and **D** are incorrect. **A** is incorrect because although change management will review a change thoroughly prior to approving/rejecting it, this is not the primary goal. The change is being reviewed with the goal of minimizing business impact. **C** is incorrect because documenting changes is part of change management process, but is not its primary goal. **D** is incorrect because resource allocation is not a part of change management. Change management is concerned about the change's impact, not about who will be performing it.

22. You are tasked with enhancing your company's physical security controls in order to ensure a proper audit trail exists. Which action would accomplish that goal?

   A. Place access card readers at the interior of secure operation rooms.

   B. Replace external 16-foot fences with taller ones.

   C. Increase security guard presence to achieve patrolling in pairs.

   D. Suggest hiring an external party to perform a physical security assessment.

   ☑ A. Placing access card readers at the interior of secure areas would be a good starting point, as it will ensure that individuals who have swiped their cards to get access into the room will also do the same when exiting, creating a proper physical audit trail.

   ☒ B, C, and D are incorrect. B is incorrect because replacing 16-foot fences with taller ones will not be an audit trail improvement. C is incorrect because although having more security guards is great, increasing presence to have them patrol in pairs doesn't improve the auditing capability. D is incorrect because hiring an external company to perform a physical assessment may lead to suggestions improving the organization's physical security stance but won't have any immediate impact on the existing audit trail process.

23. What process would take place if an (ISC)² member doesn't comply with the (ISC)² code of ethics?

   A. Any violators will be reported to the company the member is working for.

   B. (ISC)² will revoke their certifications.

   C. A review from a peer panel will take place.

   D. They will get a one-off warning.

   ☑ C. In the event that a member violates the (ISC)² code of ethics, a peer review panel is formed so the case can be examined and a recommendation on how to proceed be made.

   ☒ A, B, and D are incorrect. A is incorrect because (ISC)² doesn't have the remit to reach out to the company a member might be working for. B is incorrect because certifications aren't revoked straight away. That might be a recommendation from an appropriate panel, but a ruling will come out after it convenes. D is incorrect because a code of ethics violation is a very serious matter, which doesn't warrant any warnings.

24. Which of the following is not a step of the change management process?

   A. Change approved or rejected

   B. Change resolved

   C. Change reviewed

   D. Change submitted

☑ **B.** The change management process doesn't include any step named "resolved," which is a term used to describe a ticket or incident status (in related ticketing/incident management tools). However, the term "change implemented" is used to describe a change request's implementation and associated documentation.

☒ **A, C,** and **D** are incorrect. **A** is incorrect because at the "change approved or rejected" step, a decision will be made about whether this change will proceed to implementation or not. **C** is incorrect because at the "change reviewed" step, the change request can be thoroughly reviewed and discussed. **D** is incorrect because the "change submitted" phase is actually the first step of the change management process where an individual submits a specific change request regarding a change to be made on a device or system.

25. A system administrator is installing an IPS, a firewall, and a vulnerability scanner while at the same time drafting new security policies and training materials for his company. Which best describes his goal?

A. Confidentiality

B. Due diligence

C. Accountability

D. Defense in depth

☑ **D.** "Defense in depth" is achieved by combining a variety of security devices and protocols to achieve a multilayered security approach. As such, installing an IPS, a firewall, and a vulnerability scanner and drafting new policies and training materials will aid in creating a multilayered security approach.

☒ **A, B,** and **C** are incorrect. **A** is incorrect because confidentiality refers to information being accessible only by authorized individuals. **B** is incorrect because due diligence refers to a series of steps being undertaken by an organization or individual in order to minimize organizational risk. **C** is incorrect because accountability means being able to attribute an action to a specific individual.

26. In order for a merchant to comply with PCI-DSS, a network scan is required to be completed by which of the following?

A. SAQ

B. ASV

C. QSA

D. ISA

☑ **B.** An ASV (Approved Scanning Vendor) is an external security entity that uses authorized scanners to perform a scan. Merchants of all levels are required to use such a provider for any scans that are performed.

☒ **A, C,** and **D** are incorrect. **A** is incorrect because an SAQ (Self-Assessment Questionnaire) can be used by an entity with a low number of credit card transactions to perform a compliance audit. **C** is incorrect because a QSA (Quality Security Assessor) is an external party that can perform an audit at a client site. **D** is incorrect because an ISA (Internal Security Assessor) is an internal company employee (who is ISA certified) able to perform specific client-site audits.

27. Which of the following changes wouldn't require CAB approval?

    A. Standard

    B. Emergency

    C. Normal

    D. Expedited

    ☑ **A.** Not all changes require CAB (Change Authorization Board) approval. If a change is well documented and has taken place in the past (as in the case of a standard change), then no CAB approval is typically required.

    ☒ **B, C,** and **D** are incorrect. **B** is incorrect because an emergency change will need CAB approval to ensure it has minimal business impact. **C** is incorrect because normal changes are not repetitive changes (like standard ones), so they also need to be reviewed by CAB. **D** is incorrect because expedited changes are normal changes that need to be implemented quickly (usually within four to six hours) and as such also require CAB review.

28. An attacker manages to compromise a critical server, with no central logging capability enabled. After obtaining the information of interest, the audit logs are accessed and the related entries showing what actions the attacker performed are removed. Which of the following is being compromised?

    A. Least privilege

    B. Availability

    C. Accountability

    D. Authentication

    ☑ **C.** In the event that an attacker manages to access and manipulate the audit logs, the log integrity would be compromised, making accountability very difficult to achieve.

    ☒ **A, B,** and **D** are incorrect. **A** is incorrect because "least privilege" refers to users having enough access to perform their role but not more than that. **B** is incorrect because availability refers to appropriate individuals being able to access necessary resources whenever they need them. **D** is incorrect because authentication refers to verifying an individual's identity, which doesn't relate to log manipulation.

29. Employee badges are primarily used for:

A. Identification

B. Authentication

C. Provisioning

D. Entitlement

☑ **A.** Employee badges are primarily used for identification, as they typically contain an individual's full name along with a picture. Badges are also used to provide authentication, but the primary purpose is still identification.

☒ **B, C,** and **D** are incorrect. **B** is incorrect because (as mentioned earlier) authentication may be provided in addition to a badge's primary purpose, which is identification. **C** is incorrect because "provisioning" refers to user account creation and proper permissions being assigned to it. **D** is incorrect because "entitlement" refers to ensuring a user has appropriate privileges for the role that is being performed at any given moment in time (i.e., if a user changes role, privileges from the previous role should be revoked accordingly).

30. John powers on his computer and successfully installs a new application. After a few minutes he realizes that he's unable to launch the newly installed application, as that is being blocked by the antivirus program. What would the antivirus most probably be using to block the application at that point?

A. Antivirus blacklisting

B. Scheduled scan

C. On-demand scan

D. Heuristic-based detection

☑ **D.** When heuristic detection is used, some activities might be suspended if the antivirus application considers certain behaviors suspicious. In this example, the antivirus agent considered that the newly installed application was performing actions that were deviating from what is expected, and in order to protect the operating system, it blocked further usage of the application in question.

☒ **A, B,** and **C** are incorrect. **A** is incorrect because since the application was successfully installed, it couldn't have been blacklisted by the antivirus agent. **B** is incorrect because a scheduled scan would be performed at regular intervals that the user specified (which is not something that the question mentions). **C** is incorrect because on-demand scanning (similarly to a scheduled scan) would be performed at the user's request (but the question didn't mention the user requested such a scan).

31. Which of the following is most suitable to protect against phishing attacks?

   A. Spam filtering provider

   B. User education

   C. E-mail gateway

   D. Antivirus

   ☑ **B.** User education is the most effective way to protect a company from phishing attacks. No matter how many technical controls are put in place, human nature is always going to be a primary target for any attacker.

   ☒ **A, C,** and **D** are incorrect. **A** is incorrect because a spam filtering provider will deal with some (or even the majority) of the phishing e-mails an organization may receive, but the ones that do get past it will end up in user mailboxes. **C** is incorrect because an e-mail gateway will filter out some of the phishing e-mails (it will mainly identify various e-mails as spam) but not necessarily all of them. **D** is incorrect because an antivirus agent might detect some types of content as malicious (i.e., attachment contained in a phishing e-mail), but that would mean the attack has already penetrated the company's security mechanisms and managed to reach the end user (since an antivirus program would typically be running at a user's machine or a company server).

32. Which of the following wouldn't be used during an SQL injection attack?

   A. SELECT

   B. --

   C. <>

   D. ;

   ☑ **C.** The "<>" character sequence would typically be used during a cross-site scripting (XSS) attack in order to insert HTML or JavaScript code.

   ☒ **A, B,** and **D** are incorrect. **A** is incorrect because "SELECT" is an SQL statement that could be used during an SQL injection attack. **B** is incorrect because two hyphens "--" indicate a comment in SQL, which could be used in an SQL attack. **D** is incorrect because a semicolon ";" is used to indicate an SQL command termination, which could be used in an SQL attack

33. An attacker compromises a fashion retailer's website and places malware on its web page. The goal is for the malware to be downloaded by clients that visit the website to place future orders. This is an example of:

   A. Malvertising

   B. Trapdoor

   C. Drive-by download

   D. Rootkit

☑ **C.** During a "drive-by download" attack, a web server will typically be compromised and malware will be inserted so victims that later visit the target website download that malware.

☒ **A, B,** and **D** are incorrect. **A** is incorrect because "malvertising" uses seemingly legitimate ads (which are in fact malicious) to spread malware. **B** is incorrect because a "trapdoor" is usually created by software developers in order to gain later access to systems (usually to troubleshoot some issue or as an emergency access method). **D** is incorrect because a "rootkit" obtains full target system access and is very difficult to detect and remove. Although an attacker might have actually planted a rootkit on the website, there's no evidence to support that claim based on the question's information. However, the information provided does show typical signs of a drive-by attack being staged.

34. Which of these statements about configuration management is not accurate?

    A. Puppet uses Python.

    B. Microsoft offers "Group Policy" for system configuration.

    C. Imaging is a commonly used method.

    D. Ansible can be used in a Linux environment.

    ☑ **A.** Puppet doesn't use Python but actually uses a proprietary language or Ruby DSL (domain-specific language).

    ☒ **B, C,** and **D** are incorrect. **B** is incorrect because "Group Policy" is a common feature used for configuration management in large Microsoft environments. **C** is incorrect because "imaging" is a typical method of configuration management whereby the IT team creates a system image best fitting the needs of the organization and that is then used for deployment across the estate. **D** is incorrect because Ansible can indeed be used for configuration management in a Linux environment (similar to Puppet and Chef).

35. In which of these control goal and class combinations does a motion sensor fall into?

    A. Preventive, technical

    B. Detective, technical

    C. Preventive, physical

    D. Detective, physical

    ☑ **D.** A motion sensor is a detective control, as its primary goal is to trigger an alarm if it detects any environmental movement. As it is something that can be touched, it is classified as a physical control (similar to a smoke detector or a door alarm).

    ☒ **A, B,** and **C** are incorrect. **A** is incorrect because a motion sensor can't prevent someone from entering the area it monitors and is not a technical control. **B** is incorrect because although a motion sensor is a detective control, it doesn't fall into the technical control class. **C** is incorrect because although a motion sensor is classified as a physical control, it can't prevent someone from entering the area of supervision.

36. Which of the following is not included in the (ISC)² code of ethics?

    A. Act honorably.

    B. Provide adequate service.

    C. Advance and protect the profession.

    D. Provide diligent service to principals.

    ☑ **B.** The (ISC)² code of ethics doesn't have a canon about providing "adequate service." The third canon, however, does clearly state that a member has to "provide diligent and competent service to principals."

    ☒ **A, C,** and **D** are incorrect. **A** is incorrect, as the second canon states "act honorably, honestly, justly, responsibly and legally." **C** is incorrect, as the fourth canon states "advance and protect the profession." **D** is incorrect, as the third canon states "provide diligent and competent service to principals."

37. Which of the following can be part of more than one control type (i.e., combine being detective and preventive)?

    A. Security policy

    B. IDS

    C. IPS

    D. Audit logs

    ☑ **C.** An IPS (intrusion prevention system) is predominantly used as a preventive control. However, in principle, it combines both detective and preventive control categories, as it can detect and act on malicious traffic. In addition, an IPS can be configured to act as an IDS (like when the IPS is in learning mode, prior to allowing anomaly detection to take place).

    ☒ **A, B,** and **D** are incorrect. **A** is incorrect because a security policy is classified as a preventive control. **B** is incorrect as an IDS is a detective control and can't take preventive or corrective actions. **D** is incorrect because audit logs are a detective control (logging an action that has taken place on a particular system).

38. A secure facility requires individuals to sign in at the reception desk and swipe their cards at the card readers. However, the security personnel do an end-of-shift check and realize that there's a mismatch between the two records, showing 150 people signing in at the reception desk but only 140 swiping in. What is the most likely reason for that?

    A. People signing in at reception more than once.

    B. Tailgating has occurred.

    C. Some employees signed in at reception but entered the building via nonstandard entrances.

    D. Card reader system experienced an error.

☑ **B.** Tailgating is the most likely reason for the mismatch. People will typically sign in at the reception desk, as they need to go past the security guards. However, when they need to swipe in, they will often tailgate others, especially during morning peak hours.

☒ **A, C,** and **D** are incorrect. **A** is incorrect because having multiple people signing in more than once is highly unlikely, especially when they are supervised by a security guard. **C** is incorrect because most buildings have all entrances monitored or protected via an access card or some other form of access control. Since the question mentions employees have to sign in and swipe in to gain access, the odds of such a company leaving other entrances unmonitored are very low. **D** is incorrect because if the card reader experienced errors, the security team would most likely be notified of that fact by some type of alert.

Risk Identification, Monitoring, and Analysis

This chapter includes questions from the following objectives:

- 3.1 Understand the risk management process
- 3.2 Perform security assessment activities
- 3.3 Operate and maintain monitoring systems (e.g., continuous monitoring)
- 3.4 Analyze monitoring results

This chapter contains a complete set of questions and answers regarding risk definition (threat sources, threat events, vulnerabilities, and threat intelligence); risk management (risk register, CVSS, RMF, and risk treatment); and risk assessment (threat modelling, vulnerability analysis, and risk assessment steps). In addition, it refers to operation and maintenance of monitoring systems (IDS/IPS, detection and prevention methods, monitoring result analysis, SIEM, and continuous monitoring) and security tests and assessments (vulnerability assessments and penetration tests).

1. Your organization's IT team just identified a new high-severity vulnerability in your systems. After careful review, you decide that it isn't as severe as initially mentioned and can actually be classified as medium. This is an example of:

   A. Risk mitigation

   B. Risk avoidance

   C. Risk transference

   D. Risk recasting

2. Each laptop costs $1,000 to your company, and two machines need to be replaced annually per employee due to loss or theft. Based on these figures, the SLE is:

   A. $500

   B. $2,000

   C. $1,000

   D. 2

3. Which of the following focuses on using impact and likelihood for risk categorization?

   A. Qualitative analysis

   B. Quantitative analysis

   C. CVSS

   D. RMF

4. A script kiddie uses an FTP exploit to attack a company's FTP server, which uses default administrator credentials. In this scenario, the exploit is classified as a:

   A. Threat event

   B. Threat source

   C. Vulnerability

   D. Risk

5. An administrator wants to install a system on an e-mail server with the goal of preventing attacks. Which of the following would be most suitable for that purpose?

   A. HIDS

   B. HIPS

   C. NIDS

   D. NIPS

6. You are working as head of security for a high-profile investment bank, which just created a new web banking application. Prior to its release, you would like to hire a company to do a penetration test of that application to review how secure it is. Which of these types of test would you choose?

   A. White box

   B. Black box

   C. Gray box

   D. Internal testing

7. What is the first step of any vulnerability assessment?

   A. Discovery.

   B. Remediation.

   C. Identify and recommend methods to reduce the vulnerabilities.

   D. Gain permission from management.

8. Which of these statements about sharing threat intelligence is inaccurate?

   A. The best method is to share as much internal information as possible.

   B. It's recommended to set rules about what information can be shared.

   C. One often-used standard for threat intelligence sharing is STIX.

   D. Identify appropriate threat intelligence information sources.

9. What is the major advantage of using a honeynet versus using a honeypot?

   A. Allows security personnel to observe how attackers act

   B. Uses multiple physical machines

   C. Simulates a live network

   D. Diverts an attack from the production network

10. Which of these statements regarding honeypots is accurate?

    A. A honeypot includes two or more servers.

    B. Security administrators can use honeypots to learn how attackers work.

    C. A honeypot contains about 40 percent valid company data and 60 percent dummy data.

    D. Honeypot administrators try to make honeypot access more appealing by deactivating as much security as possible so attackers can access honeypots more easily.

11. Which of these tools would be most suitable to detect an attempt to modify a registry key on a web server?

    A. Stateful inspection firewall

    B. Web proxy

    C. NIDS

    D. HIPS

12. An SQL injection attack is launched against a server, but the IDS placed to protect it fails to generate an alert. This is an example of a:

   A. True positive

   B. True negative

   C. False positive

   D. False negative

13. An attacker replaces a system .dll file in a Windows machine with another .dll file that seemingly performs the same function but also logs user keystrokes. Which of these tools is more appropriate to protect from this type of attack?

   A. File integrity checker

   B. SIEM

   C. Application whitelisting

   D. HIDS

14. A system administrator wants to be able to ensure that host access and audit log files are still available for inspection after an attacker gains access to the company's infrastructure and is able to delete or alter the related files. Which of these tools/methods is more appropriate for that purpose?

   A. File integrity checker

   B. Host weekly backup

   C. SIEM tool

   D. Password-protect the host log files

15. Which of these risk treatment approaches is not a valid option?

   A. Risk ignorance

   B. Risk avoidance

   C. Risk acceptance

   D. Risk transference

16. Which of these statements about NIDS is not accurate?

   A. Can be used to detect port scans.

   B. Require a lot of CPU power to function properly.

   C. Port mirroring is required for them to operate.

   D. Work transparently within the network.

17. Which of the following is an example of an accidental threat source?

   A. HVAC failure

   B. Cable fire at a data center

C. Secretary deleting one of the CEO's board meeting e-mails

D. Server room power outage

18. Which of the following is an evaluation that tries to predict when an attack will take place?

    A. Quantitative analysis

    B. Qualitative analysis

    C. Risk register

    D. Threat modelling

19. A company's single e-commerce server has gone down. The estimation of loss for each day it's not online is $500, and a technician charges $400 per day to repair it, with an initial estimation of repair time being one day. The monthly likelihood of such incidents is estimated at three. What is the ALE?

    A. $32,400

    B. $64,800

    C. $15,600

    D. $53,700

20. The following definition, "a policy violation resulting in an adverse event," defines which of these terms?

    A. Malware

    B. Security incident

    C. Threat

    D. Vulnerability

21. Events that an organization often wants to monitor for are described by the term:

    A. Security alerts

    B. Security incidents

    C. Events of interest

    D. Intrusions

22. An IPS is placed in front of the DMZ segment housing an FTP and a web server. Suddenly, the network administrator receives a report of traffic from a specific external IP address not being received by the web server. However, a packet capture right before the IPS suggests that web traffic is passing properly. What is the most likely reason for this?

    A. Malformed web request.

    B. Packet capture has not been set to capture web traffic properly.

    C. Physical link failure.

    D. IPS dropping the traffic in question.

23. John is working extended hours these last two days in order to prepare a PowerPoint presentation for an upcoming board meeting. A security analyst just received an alert from the IDS system that John's machine is exhibiting suspicious behavior. Which of the following is the most likely reason for this?

    A. Blacklisted application was executed.

    B. IDS malicious signature was triggered.

    C. Malicious macro was executed.

    D. IDS anomaly-based detection was triggered.

24. Which of the following is the most important consideration for a new SIEM implementation?

    A. Configure time synchronization.

    B. Adjust appropriate alert thresholds.

    C. Ensure all available logs are ingested.

    D. Provide security analyst access to individual log sources.

25. Which of the following is a feature that only a vulnerability scanning tool (like Nessus or Qualys) would have in comparison to a port scanning tool (like Nmap or Unicornscan)?

    A. ICMP sweep.

    B. Perform password auditing.

    C. Scan a system for specific services.

    D. OS fingerprinting.

26. The process of disabling nonrequired services on a host is called:

    A. Border security

    B. Vulnerability scanning

    C. Host hardening

    D. Host boosting

27. A vulnerability scanner indicated an unpatched version of Windows running on one of the network hosts. However, when the system administrator inspected the machine in question, he noticed that the host had been properly patched. What is the most probable reason for this?

    A. Misconfigured scan profile.

    B. The host owner patched the machine after the vulnerability scan took place.

    C. False positive report finding.

    D. Scan signature needs to be updated.

28. Gemma has been asked to create a new Wi-Fi subnet at a medium-size law firm. This will be used as a guest network for external consultants and clients to use when coming into the office to attend meetings. Which of these security mechanisms would be most suitable for this new network?

  A. WIDS

  B. NIDS

  C. NIPS

  D. Web proxy

29. Which of these vulnerabilities constitutes the greatest risk for a security-mature organization?

  A. Exploit using a macro

  B. Uneducated user

  C. Antivirus that hasn't been updated for a week

  D. Vulnerability relating to CentOS

30. You are the head of security and your company is running a core finance application on a legacy Windows 2003 server. A recent vulnerability scan flagged the machine in question as being out of support (extended support for Windows 2003 ended in 2015). After contacting the application vendor, they alert you to the fact that the application is quite old and supported only on a Windows 2003 operating system. Which of these options do you choose?

  A. Upgrade the server to the latest version.

  B. Migrate the application to a new server.

  C. Identify a new application that can be safely used.

  D. Accept the risk.

31. Which of the following is a great advantage of qualitative risk analysis?

  A. Uses impact rating

  B. Demonstrates risk cost

  C. Clearly shows what risks are more important

  D. Demonstrates control cost

32. What is the easiest and most accurate way for an organization to check if it's PCI compliant?

  A. Perform a penetration test.

  B. Use a vulnerability scanner.

  C. Use nmap.

  D. Check with the compliance team.

33. Which of the following would a vulnerability scanner use to detect the operating system of a target system?

    A. TCP window size

    B. Closed ports

    C. Reply (or lack of reply) to an ICMP request

    D. TTL incrementation

34. How can an organization best check if vulnerabilities identified by a vulnerability scan have been remediated or not?

    A. Perform a penetration test.

    B. Check with the system administrators.

    C. Manually verify if they are present.

    D. Run another vulnerability scan.

35. A penetration tester is trying to identify what level of patching a target system currently has. During which phase would that activity take place?

    A. Discovery

    B. Reconnaissance

    C. Fingerprinting

    D. Exploitation

36. Which of these terms indicates an attack?

    A. Security incident

    B. Security alert

    C. Event of interest

    D. Threshold

37. James is a security manager who has been tasked with identifying attack trends in his organization. He is looking for an easy and quick way to provide some constructive feedback as to what those are. Which of these would be best suited for this purpose?

    A. IDS

    B. UTM

    C. Honeypot

    D. Proxy

38. Which of the following can be classified as a vulnerability?

    A. Insider

    B. Tailgating

    C. Lack of turnstiles

    D. CCTV monitoring

1. D	**11.** D	**21.** C	**31.** C
2. C	**12.** D	**22.** D	**32.** B
3. A	**13.** A	**23.** D	**33.** A
4. A	**14.** C	**24.** A	**34.** D
5. B	**15.** A	**25.** B	**35.** C
6. B	**16.** B	**26.** C	**36.** A
7. D	**17.** C	**27.** C	**37.** B
8. A	**18.** D	**28.** A	**38.** C
9. C	**19.** A	**29.** B	
10. B	**20.** B	**30.** D	

1. Your organization's IT team just identified a new high-severity vulnerability in your systems. After careful review, you decide that it isn't as severe as initially mentioned and can actually be classified as medium. This is an example of:

   A. Risk mitigation

   B. Risk avoidance

   C. Risk transference

   D. Risk recasting

   ☑ **D.** Risk recasting refers to a risk being reclassified to a different severity level (which might be higher or lower than the initial one).

   ☒ **A, B,** and **C** are incorrect. **A** is incorrect because risk mitigation can only be achieved by implementing appropriate controls that aim to reduce it. **B** is incorrect because risk avoidance refers to avoiding the risk by not pursuing the related activity (i.e., if malware analysis poses a high risk for a security team, the team manager might choose not to allow the team to perform that activity, thus avoiding the related risk). **C** is incorrect because risk transference entails having the risk transferred to another party and is usually achieved by purchasing insurance, which will offer coverage to an organization in the event of a related risk materializing (i.e., a company can purchase ransomware insurance so it can have coverage in case a ransomware attack takes place).

2. Each laptop costs $1,000 to your company, and two machines need to be replaced annually per employee due to loss or theft. Based on these figures, the SLE is:

   A. $500

   B. $2,000

   C. $1,000

   D. 2

   ☑ **C.** The SLE (Single Loss Expectancy) expresses how much a single occurrence of a risk would cost, meaning how much it would cost the business each time a risk materializes (calculated per annum). Since each laptop costs $1,000, each time one is lost or stolen, the business has to pay $1,000 to acquire a new one.

   ☒ **A, B,** and **D** are incorrect. **A** is incorrect because $500 is the result of dividing $1,000 (which is the cost of obtaining a new machine) by 2 (which is the number of machines stolen or lost each year, also known as ARO, or Annual Rate of Occurrence). But that's incorrect, as the SLE is used to express the cost of a single occurrence and doesn't need to be divided by the number of occurrences. **B** is incorrect because multiplying the SLE (which is $1,000) with the ARO (which is 2) yields the ALE (also known as Annual Loss Expectancy), which is used to express the annual cost for the business if the risk in question materializes. **D** is incorrect because 2 is used to express the ARO, as two machines are lost or stolen each year.

3. Which of the following focuses on using impact and likelihood for risk categorization?

A. Qualitative analysis

B. Quantitative analysis

C. CVSS

D. RMF

☑ **A.** Qualitative analysis mostly uses the impact and likelihood of a risk and usually classifies risks in three to four categories, such as low, medium, high, and critical.

☒ **B, C,** and **D** are incorrect. **B** is incorrect because quantitative analysis uses cost figures and calculations to perform risk analysis. It includes terms like SLE (Single Loss Expectancy), ARO (Annual Rate of Occurrence), and ALE (Annual Loss Expectancy) to make decisions on what controls to implement in order to minimize organizational risk. **C** is incorrect because CVSS (Common Vulnerability Scoring System) doesn't focus on impact and likelihood for risk categorization. It's a standard referring to computer system vulnerabilities that is often used by companies and focuses on a variety of metrics such as attack vector, confidentiality impact, attack complexity, and various others. **D** is incorrect because RMF (Risk Management Frameworks) refers to NIST and ISO documents (usually 800-37 and 31000:2018), which use a multistep approach for risk management but don't particularly focus on likelihood and impact.

4. A script kiddie uses an FTP exploit to attack a company's FTP server, which uses default administrator credentials. In this scenario, the exploit is classified as a:

A. Threat event

B. Threat source

C. Vulnerability

D. Risk

☑ **A.** A threat event is initiated by a threat source. In this scenario, the threat source (i.e., the script kiddie) is trying to leverage an exploit towards the FTP server, thus constituting a threat event.

☒ **B, C,** and **D** are incorrect. **B** is incorrect because the script kiddie (i.e., the attacker) is a threat source, as he is the one initiating a threat event. **C** is incorrect because a vulnerability is defined as a system flaw or weakness that could result in a security breach if properly exploited. In this case, the default administrator login credentials that the FTP server is configured to use are the vulnerability, which the attacker is trying to exploit to gain unauthorized entry to the system. **D** is incorrect because risk is related to how probable it is that a vulnerability will be exploited by a threat.

5. An administrator wants to install a system on an e-mail server with the goal of preventing attacks. Which of the following would be most suitable for that purpose?

A. HIDS

B. HIPS

C. NIDS

D. NIPS

☑ **B.** In order for the e-mail server to be able to protect itself against various attacks, a host-based system will be required to have the ability to block any type of offending traffic it identifies. A HIPS (host intrusion prevention system) is the best answer, as it can be installed on the e-mail server and has the ability to not only identify but also drop any malicious traffic.

☒ **A, C,** and **D** are incorrect. **A** is incorrect because although a HIDS (host intrusion detection system) can be installed on an e-mail server, it only offers the ability to alert when an attack takes place but is not able to block offending traffic. **C** is incorrect because a NIDS (network intrusion detection system) would be placed at a specific network location and monitor traffic that passes through that point, in addition to not being able to block any attack that it identifies. **D** is incorrect because a NIPS (network intrusion prevention system) can be placed at a specific network location and monitor (and block) traffic that passes through that point but wouldn't be installed on an endpoint.

6. You are working as head of security for a high-profile investment bank, which just created a new web banking application. Prior to its release, you would like to hire a company to do a penetration test of that application to review how secure it is. Which of these types of test would you choose?

   A. White box

   B. Black box

   C. Gray box

   D. Internal testing

   ☑ **B.** Prior to the launch of this new product, it would be highly recommended for the bank to perform a black box penetration test, as the testers would have no knowledge of the system. That way, a real-world scenario of the application being released to the public and an attacker obtaining it and attempting to exploit it can be simulated.

   ☒ **A, C,** and **D** are incorrect. **A** is incorrect because a white box test entails the tester having full knowledge of the system, which wouldn't be the case with a banking application being offered to the public. **C** is incorrect because a gray box test implies at least some basic knowledge about the application, which isn't something that an external attacker would easily get. **D** is incorrect because "internal testing" is another term used for white box testing, which implies full knowledge of the application and wouldn't be suitable in this case.

7. What is the first step of any vulnerability assessment?

   A. Discovery.

   B. Remediation.

C. Identify and recommend methods to reduce the vulnerabilities.

D. Gain permission from management.

☑ **D.** Before any type of vulnerability assessment commences, the most important step is to ensure that management has provided permission to begin the activity. A common mistake is for someone to be hosting a service or platform on a cloud provider (like Amazon AWS) and think that because of that fact, permission is not required to perform a vulnerability scan. However, a review of the terms and conditions will verify that proper permission for any type of such engagement is required prior to a test being performed.

☒ **A, B,** and **C** are incorrect. **A** is incorrect because discovery is the step that follows after proper permission has been provided. During this phase, related scans are performed with the aim of acquiring information about the various vulnerabilities that might exist within the target network. **B** is incorrect because remediation would take place at the end, after the related vulnerabilities have been identified and recommendations have been accepted by the target company about how to mitigate them. **C** is incorrect because identification and recommendation of methods to reduce the vulnerabilities would take place after running and analyzing the results of the vulnerability scan but certainly not as a first step within the process.

8. Which of these statements about sharing threat intelligence is inaccurate?

A. The best method is to share as much internal information as possible.

B. It's recommended to set rules about what information can be shared.

C. One often-used standard for threat intelligence sharing is STIX.

D. Identify appropriate threat intelligence information sources.

☑ **A.** Sharing all related information is hardly ever useful for any given organization. Usually, a company will identify what internal information (if any) it is willing to share so it can be reduced to a minimum. Sharing internal information should be done very carefully so as to not release any proprietary or confidential organizational data to the wider public.

☒ **B, C,** and **D** are incorrect. **B** is incorrect because the parties with which the organization's information is allowed to be shared should be very specific so any unintentional data leakage can be avoided. **C** is incorrect because STIX (Structured Threat Information eXpression) is indeed used for threat intelligence sharing, as it allows for a common language to share related data. **D** is incorrect because identifying appropriate sources (i.e., data sharing tools, procedures, platforms, etc.) is key to efficient data sharing.

9. What is the major advantage of using a honeynet versus using a honeypot?

A. Allows security personnel to observe how attackers act

B. Uses multiple physical machines

C. Simulates a live network

D. Diverts an attack from the production network

☑ **C.** The greatest advantage of using a honeynet versus a honeypot is that it offers more machines and gives the attacker the impression of a full production network with multiple devices and services running. Sometimes, experienced attackers can identify honeypots by the way they are configured or the services they are running. This becomes more difficult in the case of a honeynet, where a whole network of devices seems to exist.

☒ **A, B,** and **D** are incorrect. **A** is incorrect because observing how an attacker acts is something that can be achieved with both a honeypot and a honeynet, so it's not a unique advantage of one or the other. **B** is incorrect because a honeynet doesn't need to use multiple physical machines. One physical machine can be used (as long as it has enough resources), which will have multiple virtual machines to simulate a variety of other devices within the honeynet. **D** is incorrect because diverting an attack from the production network is something that would happen with both a honeypot and a honeynet.

10. Which of these statements regarding honeypots is accurate?

   A. A honeypot includes two or more servers.

   B. Security administrators can use honeypots to learn how attackers work.

   C. A honeypot contains about 40 percent valid company data and 60 percent dummy data.

   D. Honeypot administrators try to make honeypot access more appealing by deactivating as much security as possible so attackers can access honeypots more easily.

   ☑ **B.** One of the primary goals of a honeypot is to observe attacker TTPs (tactics, techniques, and procedures) so that the organizational defenses are then adjusted appropriately against future attacks.

   ☒ **A, C,** and **D** are incorrect. **A** is incorrect because a honeypot doesn't include two or more servers. That is actually the definition of a honeynet (which is composed of two or more honeypots). **C** is incorrect because a honeypot only contains dummy data to lure attackers into attacking it but doesn't have any real organizational data that would be in danger of getting stolen. **D** is incorrect because although honeypots need to be accessible by attackers, they also need to be appealing to them. In order for that to happen, they need to simulate a real system as much as possible. As such, some services need to be deactivated (mimicking a more hardened system), and access to a honeypot should be fairly straightforward but without being too direct, which might give away its true nature to a skilled attacker.

11. Which of these tools would be most suitable to detect an attempt to modify a registry key on a web server?

   A. Stateful inspection firewall

   B. Web proxy

   C. NIDS

   D. HIPS

☑ **D.** A HIPS (host intrusion prevention system) would be the best tool to detect a registry key modification at the server level. A HIPS is installed on the host and aims to monitor for suspicious activity. Once something malicious is detected, it can take further steps to mitigate that activity.

☒ **A, B,** and **C** are incorrect. **A** is incorrect because a stateful inspection firewall's goal is to filter inbound (and outbound) communications based on access control lists and a stateful inspection table. However, it won't be able to detect a registry key modification taking place at the server, as it is unable to monitor for that type of change. **B** is incorrect because a web proxy aims to filter web traffic and won't have any visibility of a change taking place on a particular host. **C** is incorrect because a NIDS (network intrusion detection system) is installed at a specific network location and monitors traffic that passes through that point, which wouldn't allow it to detect host registry key modifications.

12. An SQL injection attack is launched against a server, but the IDS placed to protect it fails to generate an alert. This is an example of a:

A. True positive

B. True negative

C. False positive

D. False negative

☑ **D.** A "false negative" occurs when the IDS fails to generate an alert although a valid attack is taking place (meaning it is unable to detect it). In this case, the attacker launched an SQL injection attack but the IDS didn't generate any type of alert about that activity.

☒ **A, B,** and **C** are incorrect. **A** is incorrect because a "true positive" occurs when the IDS correctly identifies an attack that is occurring and raises an alert to notify the security team or administrator of that fact (in the example of the SQL injection attack, the IDS should have raised an appropriate alert to notify of an attack taking place). **B** is incorrect because a "true negative" event means that there was no suspicious traffic worthy of raising an alert, and the IDS correctly didn't raise any alert. **C** is incorrect because a "false positive" event means that the IDS raises an alert without an attack being present (i.e., if a user sends the server some other type of request that the IDS considers an SQL injection attack and raises an alert for that traffic).

13. An attacker replaces a system .dll file in a Windows machine with another .dll file that seemingly performs the same function but also logs user keystrokes. Which of these tools is more appropriate to protect from this type of attack?

A. File integrity checker

B. SIEM

C. Application whitelisting

D. HIPS

☑ **A.** File integrity checking tools create a list of file hashes, which they safely store on the local or remote system. Their goal is to generate hashes of the files they are tasked with protecting and then compare those with the values that exist on the file that was stored earlier. If the values match, it means no tampering took place.

☒ **B, C,** and **D** are incorrect. **B** is incorrect because a SIEM (security information and event management) platform works by ingesting various log files and performing correlations across data but won't be able to check for any specific file manipulation. **C** is incorrect because application whitelisting aims to identify if a program or process that is executed on a system at any given moment in time matches a prepopulated list of applications and processes. If it's not in the list, then it won't be allowed. **D** is incorrect because although IDS systems sometimes offer file integrity checking, they usually do that by employing some file integrity checking tool, while the primary purpose of an IDS tool is to monitor the network or host (depending on if it's a NIDS or HIDS) for any suspicious traffic and alert upon it once it is identified.

14. A system administrator wants to be able to ensure that host access and audit log files are still available for inspection after an attacker gains access to the company's infrastructure and is able to delete or alter the related files. Which of these tools/methods is more appropriate for that purpose?

   A. File integrity checker

   B. Host weekly backup

   C. SIEM tool

   D. Password-protect the host log files

   ☑ **C.** SIEM (security information and event management) tools store log data centrally (similar to any centrally logging platform), which means that once a copy of the logs is forwarded to a SIEM tool, that data is locally stored on the SIEM and remains there based on the retention period that has been configured. Typical log retention periods can be from three to five years (for highly critical or sensitive environments, like banking and military systems).

   ☒ **A, B,** and **D** are incorrect. **A** is incorrect because a file integrity checker will alert when a file is modified but won't be able to provide an up-to-date copy of the log file so the administrator can review its content. **B** is incorrect because a system backup is a good way of obtaining a copy of the host log files; however, as that takes place on a given period (i.e., weekly), it's not enough to ensure that up-to-date information exists, as it might be even a week old in the case where an attacker gains access close to when a backup was taken. **D** is incorrect, as password protecting the host log files will ensure that a file won't be tampered with (assuming the attacker is not able to brute force the file password) but doesn't offer any protection against file deletion, so the attacker can still delete the file altogether.

15. Which of these risk treatment approaches is not a valid option?

   A. Risk ignorance

   B. Risk avoidance

C. Risk acceptance

D. Risk transference

☑ **A.** Sometimes companies tend to ignore risks rather than following various valid risk treatment approaches. However, risk ignorance is not a valid risk strategy. If a company doesn't wish to mitigate or otherwise handle an identified risk, it would be prudent to accept that risk.

☒ **B, C,** and **D** are incorrect. **B** is incorrect because risk avoidance is an option that can be followed in the event that an activity is not performed. That is, if there's a high risk associated with selling laptops in an area with high levels of theft, not opening a shop in that area will avoid the associated risk. **C** is incorrect because sometimes accepting the risk is the best option, especially in cases where the cost associated with risk reduction is greater than the asset value. For example, assume that a home office includes two laptops with a total cost of $4,000. The best way to protect it is to install a state-of-the-art security system and physical guards that would cost $8,000. In that case, the owner might decide to accept the risk, since applying appropriate protection would cost double the amount of the assets (without, of course, considering the value of the data of those two machines). **D** is incorrect, as transferring the risk (usually to an insurance company) is a commonly accepted risk treatment approach. Buying cyber insurance is very common (especially for medium to large companies) in order to be protected in the event of a cyber attack.

16. Which of these statements about NIDS is not accurate?

A. Can be used to detect port scans.

B. Require a lot of CPU power to function properly.

C. Port mirroring is required for them to operate.

D. Work transparently within the network.

☑ **B.** NIDS don't require substantial CPU power to operate, as that is a characteristic requirement of HIDS. Because a HIDS is installed on a given host, it requires significant amounts of processing power to be able to monitor for all host activities and generate appropriate alerts.

☒ **A, C,** and **D** are incorrect. **A** is incorrect because a NIDS can be used to detect port scans. (Traffic generated by different types of port scans is fairly distinctive, so most NIDS tools have predefined signatures that will identify it. However, attackers attempt to use methods to go undetected, like trying to fragment packets or perform slow scans to evade IDS systems). **C** is incorrect, as port mirroring is required for a NIDS to be able to monitor traffic. With port mirroring enabled, the NIDS will get a copy of the network traffic and be able to monitor it for suspicious patterns, which will cause it to generate appropriate alerts. **D** is incorrect because NIDS are placed at specific network segments and monitor traffic passing through them. That function is transparent to an attacker that manages to gain access to a file server, as the NIDS is not installed on the server and thus can't be switched off or manipulated by the attacker.

17. Which of the following is an example of an accidental threat source?

   A. HVAC failure

   B. Cable fire at a data center

   C. Secretary deleting one of the CEO's board meeting e-mails

   D. Server room power outage

   ☑ **C.** A secretary deleting one of the CEO's e-mails relating to a board meeting is an example of an accidental threat source. In this case, the secretary was able to accidentally perform this action due to the level of access she has to her manager's mailbox.

   ☒ **A, B,** and **D** are incorrect. **A** is incorrect because an HVAC (heating, ventilation, and air conditioning) failure would be classified as a structural threat source, similar to any IT, software, or other environmental control failure. **B** is incorrect because a cable fire at a data center would be classified as an environmental threat source, like a hurricane or a tornado. **D** is incorrect because a server room power outage would be classified as an environmental threat source (external service failures, such as power outages or satellite disk failures, can be classified as environmental threat sources).

18. Which of the following is an evaluation that tries to predict when an attack will take place?

   A. Quantitative analysis

   B. Qualitative analysis

   C. Risk register

   D. Threat modelling

   ☑ **D.** Threat modelling tries to estimate when an attack will take place by using various methods with which it models attack parameters about any given system.

   ☒ **A, B,** and **C** are incorrect. **A** is incorrect because quantitative analysis uses cost figures and calculations to perform risk analysis. **B** is incorrect because qualitative analysis mostly uses the impact and likelihood of a risk and usually classifies risks in three to four categories. **C** is incorrect because a risk register is used to record all organizational risks and related impact, as well as the progress of placing controls to mitigate those.

19. A company's single e-commerce server has gone down. The estimation of loss for each day it's not online is $500, and a technician charges $400 per day to repair it, with an initial estimation of repair time being one day. The monthly likelihood of such incidents is estimated at three. What is the ALE?

   A. $32,400

   B. $64,800

   C. $15,600

   D. $53,700

☑ **A.** In order to calculate the ALE, the following formula will be required: ALE = SLE × ARO. Furthermore, the SLE can be found by adding all related server costs, which are daily loss and repair cost. Based on that, the SLE will be $500 + ($400 × 1 day) = $500 + $400 = $900. The ARO is 3 monthly occurrences × 12 months = 36 occurrences per year. ALE = SLE × ARO = $900 × 36 = $32,400.

☒ **B, C,** and **D** are incorrect. All those figures are distractors, as none of them is correct.

20. The following definition, "a policy violation resulting in an adverse event," defines which of these terms?

    A. Malware

    B. Security incident

    C. Threat

    D. Vulnerability

☑ **B.** A security incident can be defined as "a policy violation resulting in an adverse event" (i.e., privilege escalation or data exfiltration).

☒ **A, C,** and **D** are incorrect. **A** is incorrect because the term "malware" is used to describe malicious software and is one example of a security incident. However, there are various examples of security incidents that don't have any relation to malware, like tailgating, identity theft, and many more. **C** is incorrect because a threat is any action that can pose a danger to an organizational asset. **D** is incorrect because a vulnerability is a weakness in a system (which is something that attackers often try to exploit to gain unauthorized access).

21. Events that an organization often wants to monitor for are described by the term:

    A. Security alerts

    B. Security incidents

    C. Events of interest

    D. Intrusions

☑ **C.** The term "events of interest" is used to describe any event of particular interest (usually logged in a database or registered in some type of application/system log) that an organization wants to keep track of. It is worth mentioning that it doesn't necessarily refer to a suspicious action, as sometimes a system administrator might be interested in receiving confirmations of activities that have been successfully completed (i.e., antivirus updates or a new Windows policy push).

☒ **A, B,** and **D** are incorrect. **A** is incorrect because the term "security alerts" usually refers to some type of activity that warrants the attention of a security analyst or system administrator and is usually produced when a related rule is triggered within some type of security tool (usually an IDS, firewall, router, SIEM, or similar device). **B** is incorrect because a security incident can be defined as a policy violation resulting in an adverse event (i.e., privilege escalation or data exfiltration). **D** is incorrect because the term "intrusion" refers to some type of unwarranted access into a system, database, or tool.

22. An IPS is placed in front of the DMZ segment housing an FTP and a web server. Suddenly, the network administrator receives a report of traffic from a specific external IP address not being received by the web server. However, a packet capture right before the IPS suggests that web traffic is passing properly. What is the most likely reason for this?

A. Malformed web request.

B. Packet capture has not been set to capture web traffic properly.

C. Physical link failure.

D. IPS dropping the traffic in question.

☑ **D.** Since the packet capture shows web traffic being received by the web server without traffic from a specific source passing through the IPS, it seems that the traffic in question is being identified as malicious and thus is blocked from traversing the rest of the network.

☒ **A, B,** and **C** are incorrect. **A** is incorrect because although a malformed web request could have been sent, there's not enough information to suggest that this is the case and is the specific reason for dropping traffic from the IP in question. **B** is incorrect because there's no actual indication that web traffic is not being captured properly. In addition, the fact that only traffic from a specific IP is not seen by the web server suggests that packet capturing has been properly configured but some part of the traffic is just not passing through the IPS. **C** is incorrect because a physical link failure would result in no traffic reaching any of the servers in the DMZ, which is not the case here.

23. John is working extended hours these last two days in order to prepare a PowerPoint presentation for an upcoming board meeting. A security analyst just received an alert from the IDS system that John's machine is exhibiting suspicious behavior. Which of the following is the most likely reason for this?

A. Blacklisted application was executed.

B. IDS malicious signature was triggered.

C. Malicious macro was executed.

D. IDS anomaly-based detection was triggered.

☑ **D.** Other than the fact that John started working extended hours, there doesn't seem to be any other deviation in his behavior nor any suspicious activity. However, it is likely that the IDS (using anomaly-based detection) has considered the nonstandard hours a malicious deviation for his machine, thus triggering the related alert.

☒ **A, B,** and **C** are incorrect. **A** is incorrect because John is using a presentation program (PowerPoint), which in all likelihood he has used in the past (the question doesn't state this was the first use and doesn't mention anything that could be considered an illegitimate application execution); hence, this doesn't suggest that a blacklisted application was executed. **B** is incorrect because there's no indication of a malicious IDS signature being triggered or an activity that could suggest malicious activity taking place. **C** is incorrect because there's no indication that any macro was used.

24. Which of the following is the most important consideration for a new SIEM implementation?

   A. Configure time synchronization.

   B. Adjust appropriate alert thresholds.

   C. Ensure all available logs are ingested.

   D. Provide security analyst access to individual log sources.

   ☑ **A.** In order for proper analysis to take place, a SIEM needs accurate data synchronization. If an analyst tries to track an attacker's actions through various device logs that are in different time zones, the analysis can become unmanageable. In addition, it becomes very difficult for cooperating third parties to track any reports that are produced when data from different time zones is referenced in various parts of the report.

   ☒ **B, C,** and **D** are incorrect. **B** is incorrect because although adjusting the alert thresholds is important to ensure that related teams are only engaged in the event of a valid security incident, this is something that can happen during the initial stages of the SIEM operation and usually happens gradually as more log sources are added and analyst teams become more familiar with its operation. It's difficult to ensure that thresholds are properly adjusted right at the beginning, as this takes substantial effort and time. **C** is incorrect because adding all available log sources to the SIEM (depending on their amount and volume) would result in overwhelming the tool as well as the analyst team supporting it. Organizations usually start by on-boarding the basic log sources that are required to achieve their goals and gradually adding more devices as they grow, while at the same time performing fine-tuning. **D** is incorrect because a SIEM works as a central logging and correlation platform. It allows analysts to view all the basic information to perform their tasks. Although having access to individual log sources can sometimes be beneficial (i.e., the analyst can review the raw logs that haven't been normalized within the SIEM, meaning all initial information is present), the whole point of the SIEM is to offer log storage and correlation without needing to access the end devices.

25. Which of the following is a feature that only a vulnerability scanning tool (like Nessus or Qualys) would have in comparison to a port scanning tool (like Nmap or Unicornscan)?

   A. ICMP sweep.

   B. Perform password auditing.

   C. Scan a system for specific services.

   D. OS fingerprinting.

   ☑ **B.** A password audit can be performed by vulnerability scanning tools, as those have the ability to identify accounts that use default or empty passwords or a password that matches the username of the account and other similar conditions that indicate a weak or noncompliant password being used.

☒ **A, C,** and **D** are incorrect. **A** is incorrect because both a port scanner and a vulnerability analysis tool can perform an ICMP sweep to check what hosts are active within a given network. **C** is incorrect because a service scan can be performed by both categories of tools. It is common for attackers to use nmap to perform reconnaissance and identify specific services that might be running on a target host with the intention of finding an exploit that can be used against those. **D** is incorrect because OS fingerprinting can be performed by both vulnerability and port scanners. Attackers often use open port scanners to identify any old or unpatched OS versions running on a target host, while security analysts use vulnerability scanning tools to identify the same hosts and report them to the IT team for patching or upgrading.

26. The process of disabling nonrequired services on a host is called:

    A. Border security

    B. Vulnerability scanning

    C. Host hardening

    D. Host boosting

    ☑ **C.** The term "host hardening" is used to describe the process during which a host is configured to only run the required set of services that support its role (i.e., a web server doesn't necessarily need to be running an FTP service). Nonessential services should be disabled so they can't be exploited by an attacker, thus reducing the host's attack surface.

    ☒ **A, B,** and **D** are incorrect. **A** is incorrect because "border security" entails reviewing the various routes to the network from any external source. Any device that is placed in the network path should be checked (i.e., switches, routers, firewalls, IDS/IPS, etc.). **B** is incorrect because vulnerability scanning entails using a tool like Qualys or Nessus to scan a network or a specific host for any vulnerabilities and flag those to the system administrators so they can be appropriately dealt with. **D** is incorrect because the term "host boosting" is a distractor and doesn't have any real meaning.

27. A vulnerability scanner indicated an unpatched version of Windows running on one of the network hosts. However, when the system administrator inspected the machine in question, he noticed that the host had been properly patched. What is the most probable reason for this?

    A. Misconfigured scan profile.

    B. The host owner patched the machine after the vulnerability scan took place.

    C. False positive report finding.

    D. Scan signature needs to be updated.

    ☑ **C.** Vulnerability scanners may sometimes produce inaccurate results, which is the most probable reason why lack of a certain patch or system update would be reported by the scanner without it actually being absent in reality.

    ☒ **A, B,** and **D** are incorrect. **A** is incorrect because there's no indication that the scan profile was somehow misconfigured. **B** is incorrect because the system administrator would be responsible for deploying new patches within the environment, and he would know what the patching schedule is. Hence, it is improbable that such an activity took place after the initial scan without him realizing. **D** is incorrect because although a problem with the signature might be causing an issue, there's not enough information in the question to deduce that. Furthermore, the question does state "What is the most probable reason," which again suggests a false positive is the correct answer.

28. Gemma has been asked to create a new Wi-Fi subnet at a medium-size law firm. This will be used as a guest network for external consultants and clients to use when coming into the office to attend meetings. Which of these security mechanisms would be most suitable for this new network?

    A. WIDS

    B. NIDS

    C. NIPS

    D. Web proxy

    ☑ **A.** A WIDS (wireless intrusion detection system) would be most suitable to monitor traffic to this new subnet. Since a new wireless segment is being implemented, installing a WIDS will allow Gemma to monitor the wireless network for suspicious activity that she can be alerted for.

    ☒ **B, C,** and **D** are incorrect. **B** is incorrect because even though a NIDS can also be used to monitor traffic to this new subnet, since it's a wireless one, the best option is to use a wireless IDS (aimed specifically at Wi-Fi), not a traditional NIDS. **C** is incorrect because although a NIPS could also be employed for the purposes of monitoring and acting upon malicious traffic that is present with the network in question, a WIDS is still the best option (aiming at the wireless aspect). In addition, since this is a guest network and not a critical internal network, there's a small probability that automatically blocking traffic will be required (which is what an IPS can do). Gemma can review any suspicious activity and take appropriate action, thus leaving the option of a WIDS as the best one. **D** is incorrect because a web proxy is a great solution for filtering web traffic but is unable to monitor any other type of traffic that traverses the network, which is why using an IDS is highly recommended.

29. Which of these vulnerabilities constitutes the greatest risk for a security-mature organization?

    A. Exploit using a macro

    B. Uneducated user

    C. Antivirus that hasn't been updated for a week

    D. Vulnerability relating to CentOS

    ☑ **B.** An uneducated user is usually the greatest risk, as an attacker can use social engineering tactics to gain valuable information just by asking for it over a phone or an SMS message. No matter how efficient and elaborate the company's security architecture might be, all of that can be easily defeated by a user who provides a username and a password for remotely accessing a system to someone posing as a valid IT employee.

☒ **A, C,** and **D** are incorrect. **A** is incorrect because a macro exploit can have severe consequences, but in order for it to run properly, macro execution needs to be allowed and on top of that, any endpoint monitoring tool needs to allow that action. In a security-mature organization, macro execution would usually be disabled, and often some type of endpoint protection tool would be enabled to monitor for malicious macro execution. **C** is incorrect because an antivirus that has not been updated does pose a risk, but judging by the fact that only a week has gone by with no update, an uneducated user still poses a greater risk. **D** is incorrect because a vulnerability relating to a specific OS (no matter how severe it might be) can only have serious side effects if that OS is being actively used in the organization. If the company doesn't have any CentOS machines (something that the question doesn't mention), then this is not a concern.

30. You are the head of security and your company is running a core finance application on a legacy Windows 2003 server. A recent vulnerability scan flagged the machine in question as being out of support (extended support for Windows 2003 ended in 2015). After contacting the application vendor, they alert you to the fact that the application is quite old and supported only on a Windows 2003 operating system. Which of these options do you choose?

A. Upgrade the server to the latest version.

B. Migrate the application to a new server.

C. Identify a new application that can be safely used.

D. Accept the risk.

☑ **D.** Accepting the risk may sometimes be the only way to move forward (that's why risk acceptance is a valid risk strategy, although it is not recommended to follow it unless all other avenues have been exhausted). As this is a core finance application, meaning its operation is crucial to the business, a way to continue using it must be identified. If upgrading the server (due to being out of support) or reverting to the application's vendor for a solution (i.e., if the application is only supported on a Windows 2003 system) are both nonviable options, accepting the risk seems the only viable solution.

☒ **A, B,** and **C** are incorrect. **A** is incorrect because upgrading the server to the latest version (which is several versions after the current one that the server is running) might disrupt the application's normal operation or even disrupt the functionality of the legacy application (only supported in Windows 2003). **B** is incorrect because migrating the application to a new server (judging by the fact that the application is old and not supported anymore) might again result in not being able to use it further. **C** is incorrect because although identifying a new application (given the age of the current one being used) might take some time, it seems like a viable way moving forward. However, this will possibly take several weeks or months, as the new application will need to be identified, then reviewed from the finance team to ensure that it fulfills all related needs, and then tested and accepted. However, that won't solve the challenge at hand (i.e., the machine being flagged as out of support and a core application being run on it), so this can only be a viable long-term approach.

31. Which of the following is a great advantage of qualitative risk analysis?

    A. Uses impact rating

    B. Demonstrates risk cost

    C. Clearly shows what risks are more important

    D. Demonstrates control cost

    ☑ **C.** The greatest advantage of using qualitative analysis is that it can provide a clear depiction of the most important organizational risks that need immediate attention.

    ☒ **A, B,** and **D** are incorrect. **A** is incorrect because although qualitative analysis uses impact ratings, that doesn't constitute its greatest advantage, but rather is a part of how it operates. The benefit of using impact rating (as well as likelihood rating) is being able to prioritize organizational risks appropriately. **B** is incorrect because the risk of a cost is depicted using quantitative risk analysis. **D** is incorrect because control cost (similar to risk cost) is also depicted using quantitative risk analysis.

32. What is the easiest and most accurate way for an organization to check if it's PCI compliant?

    A. Perform a penetration test.

    B. Use a vulnerability scanner.

    C. Use nmap.

    D. Check with the compliance team.

    ☑ **B.** A vulnerability scanner offers the option of configuring an appropriate profile, allowing you to scan for specific types of compliance (like PCI-DSS, HIPAA, etc.). Depending on the results, a report usually can be generated showing a compliance percentage (e.g., 60 percent), thus tracking how compliant the organization is and what steps are required to reach full compliance.

    ☒ **A, C,** and **D** are incorrect. **A** is incorrect because a penetration test would be more suitable to check if vulnerabilities can be exploited by attackers. **C** is incorrect because nmap would commonly be used to check for active hosts or open ports within a given network or specific host. **D** is incorrect because checking with the compliance team might not produce accurate results. Even though someone might think that the company is compliant, some network, hardware, or any other type of change might have created an issue that needs to be addressed before the organization is fully compliant.

33. Which of the following would a vulnerability scanner use to detect the operating system of a target system?

    A. TCP window size

    B. Closed ports

    C. Reply (or lack of reply) to an ICMP request

    D. TTL incrementation

☑ **A.** Most OS fingerprinting tools use the TCP window size to gain information about the OS a remote system is running. Depending on the remote system response, a result can be reached as to what OS it's running.

☒ **B, C,** and **D** are incorrect. **B** is incorrect because closed ports don't help identify an OS, as some might be closed because they are not used. **C** is incorrect because an ICMP request might not be replied to due to the fact that a firewall is filtering that type of traffic and doesn't allow for a reply to be sent. **D** is incorrect because TTL is decremented as packets pass through various systems (also note that tools commonly use the initial TTL to perform OS fingerprinting, as that varies in different systems).

34. How can an organization best check if vulnerabilities identified by a vulnerability scan have been remediated or not?

    A. Perform a penetration test.

    B. Check with the system administrators.

    C. Manually verify if they are present.

    D. Run another vulnerability scan.

    ☑ **D.** Running a new vulnerability scan is the easiest and most accurate way to check if previously identified vulnerabilities are still present within a given system. The same scanning profile as before can be used in order to verify which of the vulnerabilities are still present.

    ☒ **A, B,** and **C** are incorrect. **A** is incorrect because a penetration test should only be performed after any vulnerabilities have been successfully remediated, as the penetration testers would exploit any existing ones. **B** is incorrect because checking with a system administrator doesn't guarantee accurate results (the individual might not be in a position to properly verify the vulnerability's existence or sometimes might feel like being questioned about the level of his work). **C** is incorrect because manual verification might not be possible in large environments where a vulnerability scan might show 1,000 vulnerabilities in need of remediation.

35. A penetration tester is trying to identify what level of patching a target system currently has. During which phase would that activity take place?

    A. Discovery

    B. Reconnaissance

    C. Fingerprinting

    D. Exploitation

    ☑ **C.** Trying to identify patching levels, open ports, and OS versions would all take place during the "fingerprinting" phase.

    ☒ **A, B,** and **D** are incorrect. **A** is incorrect because "discovery" entails identifying what hosts are active within the target network, as well as obtaining as much information about the target as possible that can be later used to exploit its systems. **B** is incorrect because "reconnaissance" is just a different term for "discovery." **D** is incorrect because during "exploitation," the penetration tester would try to exploit any of the vulnerabilities that were identified in previous steps.

36. Which of these terms indicates an attack?

    A. Security incident

    B. Security alert

    C. Event of interest

    D. Threshold

    ☑ **A.** The term "security incident" can be defined as "a policy violation resulting in an adverse event." Usually, some type of monitoring will be in place to notify a team or a security administrator of an event of interest or an alert. After further investigation, that may prove to be nothing substantial or may be an actual security incident (i.e., privilege escalation or data exfiltration) that requires more in-depth investigation and possibly escalation to other organizational teams or third parties.

    ☒ **B, C,** and **D** are incorrect. **B** is incorrect because a "security alert" isn't an indication of an actual attack. However, it does show that a rule has been triggered in a tool or system and has generated an alert for someone to investigate. For example, an administrator entering a wrong remote access password five consecutive times might generate an alert but that doesn't mean that an actual brute-force attack is taking place. **C** is incorrect because an "event of interest" describes an event (usually logged in a database or registered in some type of application/system log) that an organization wants to keep track of. **D** is incorrect because a "threshold" is a limit that, when surpassed, an alert is generated to draw attention to the activity in question. However, more investigation is required to decide if an actual attack is taking place.

37. James is a security manager who has been tasked with identifying attack trends in his organization. He is looking for an easy and quick way to provide some constructive feedback as to what those are. Which of these would be best suited for this purpose?

    A. IDS

    B. UTM

    C. Honeypot

    D. Proxy

    ☑ **B.** A UTM (Unified Threat Management) device combines a variety of functions, which may include IDS/IPS, spam filtering, proxy, firewall, and antivirus. Performing trend analysis based on data from such a device would provide James with a wealth of information that can be filtered to show attack patterns, failed attack attempts versus successful ones, attacker IPs of interest, targeted services, and a lot more.

    ☒ **A, C,** and **D** are incorrect. **A** is incorrect because IDS logs (although quite valuable) will only show a part of the picture (and that would heavily depend on how logging has been configured and what type of IDS is being used as well as what signatures it is currently employing). **C** is incorrect because a honeypot is great for gathering data for trend analysis and allows security personnel to monitor attacker activities and obtain a lot of detail on how they operate. However, efficiently setting up a honeypot may take a substantial amount of time. (In large organizations, this will require a request to be submitted and may take a lot of time to be reviewed—a separate subnet or even a whole network might need to be set up to maintain appropriate segregation from the corporate network, and several tests might need to be performed before this actually goes live, so this approach can't be classified as quick and easy.) **D** is incorrect because a proxy would only provide insight to the specific type of data that is being proxied (i.e., if it's a web proxy, then trend analysis around web browsing patterns can be provided).

38. Which of the following can be classified as a vulnerability?

    A. Insider

    B. Tailgating

    C. Lack of turnstiles

    D. CCTV monitoring

    ☑ **C.** A vulnerability is defined as "a system flaw or weakness that could result in a security breach if properly exploited." In this case, the lack of turnstiles can be exploited by an attacker, who can perform tailgating due to this fact.

    ☒ **A, B,** and **D** are incorrect. **A** is incorrect because an insider would be classified as the threat source, which is someone who can exploit a vulnerability. **B** is incorrect because tailgating is the threat event that a threat source (i.e., insider or outsider) can initiate. **D** is incorrect because the CCTV monitoring option is a distractor, as it doesn't pose a vulnerability, but rather enhances physical security at any given situation.

Incident Response and Recovery

This chapter includes questions from the following objectives:

- 4.1 Support incident lifecycle
- 4.2 Understand and support forensic investigations
- 4.3 Understand and support Business Continuity Plan (BCP) and Disaster Recovery Plan (DRP) activities

This chapter contains a complete set of questions and answers regarding support of an incident's lifecycle (preparation, detection, analysis and escalation, containment, eradication, recovery, lessons learned/implementation of new countermeasure), understanding fault tolerance (RAID, failover clusters, load balancing, redundant connections), and backups. It also contains questions and answers about understanding BCP and DRP activities (BIA, DRP, BCP, restoration planning, testing plans, and establishing alternative locations), as well as computer forensics (evidence handling and computer forensics investigations).

1. In which of these phases of the incident response lifecycle would the identification of an appropriate tool for memory forensics fall into?

   A. Containment

   B. Detection, Analysis and Escalation

   C. Preparation

   D. Recovery

2. Which of the following provides no fault tolerance?

   A. RAID 0

   B. RAID 1

   C. RAID 5

   D. RAID 6

3. Which of these statements regarding a "hot site" is inaccurate?

   A. It is commonly usable within a few hours.

   B. It includes network infrastructure.

   C. Cost is quite significant.

   D. Contains up-to-date organizational data.

4. If a company server is unavailable for more than 45 minutes, core business functions are affected. That means that 45 minutes is the:

   A. RPO

   B. BIA

   C. DRP

   D. MAO

5. A security analyst identified outbound command and control traffic towards a malicious IP address. Which of these steps would most likely follow?

   A. Investigate why there's traffic towards the malicious IP address.

   B. Block the IP at the firewall.

   C. Take a forensic image of the affected machine's memory.

   D. Reimage the asset using a previous backup.

6. A forensic investigator needs to capture data for later analysis. Which one of these types of data should be captured first?

   A. Remote logs

   B. Local drive

C. Swap file

D. Backup tape

7. Which of the following does forensic software use to ensure no data tampering has taken place?

   A. Serial numbers

   B. Hashing

   C. Digital signatures

   D. Encryption

8. A company's client database is stored on a server so that online purchases can take place. The database needs to be accessible constantly even if the server goes down. Which of the following would be more suitable for that purpose?

   A. Failover cluster

   B. Load balancing

   C. Full backup

   D. Differential backup

9. A company is hosting an SQL, cloud, and web server at its own premises. Which of these backup locations would you recommend as the safest option for backup storage and later retrieval of the web server's data?

   A. A backup server placed in the server room, along with the web server

   B. A magnetic tape stored on the premises but in a different building

   C. An encrypted copy of the data backed up on the company cloud server

   D. Backup of the data stored on Amazon AWS

10. A DRP's goal is to:

    A. Identify monetary losses that a critical organizational function may suffer because of an incident.

    B. Detail how to restore critical functions after an incident.

    C. Provide a plan on how a company can continue running once an incident takes place.

    D. Provide a risk evaluation at a specific moment in time.

11. An organization wants to test the existing DRP plan. Which of these methods is less intrusive but able to identify gaps in the plan?

    A. Parallel test

    B. Live test

    C. Tabletop exercise

    D. Warm site

12. Using a proprietary forensic tool for investigation relates to which of these reliability factors?

    A. Clarity

    B. Error rate

    C. Credibility

    D. Testability

13. Which of these tools is not an open source forensic application/suite?

    A. SIFT

    B. Sleuth Kit

    C. FTK

    D. Coroner's Toolkit

14. An online sports retailer is experiencing an increased volume of client web requests, as it just released new products with a heavy discount. The company is considering some options to cope with these requests. Which of these options is the best one?

    A. WAF

    B. RAID

    C. Failover cluster

    D. Load balancing cluster

15. A company's backup policy states that a full backup is performed every Monday at 9:00 P.M. Incremental backups are performed daily at 12:00 P.M. If a server goes down at 8:30 P.M. on Thursday evening, how many backups in total will be required to restore the server?

    A. 1

    B. 2

    C. 3

    D. 4

16. Which of the following is not one of the three forensic investigation phases?

    A. Acquire

    B. Validate

    C. Analyze

    D. Authenticate

17. A security administrator is reviewing corporate SIEM logs regarding possible incidents for a company using BYOD. Which of these activities is most likely a valid security incident?

    A. Playing an online game

    B. Browsing to Facebook

C. Downloading a movie

D. Using Google Drive

18. A type of malware has been identified on the corporate network. It has the ability to record keystrokes, and it is known to open TCP port 52145 on an infected system and receive command-and-control traffic from its creator using IP address 10.10.10.10. (Please note that this IP is private and is used specifically for the purposes of the question. In a real-life scenario, the attacker would be using a public IP address.) Which of these actions would most likely be taken during the "containment" phase of an incident response plan?

A. Block communication to 10.10.10.10 at the perimeter firewall.

B. Close TCP port 52145 on all infected systems.

C. Create an IDS rule for traffic to 10.10.10.10.

D. Use a web proxy to block offending traffic.

19. Source address affinity is used to direct traffic according to the:

A. User's source address

B. Server's source address

C. User's source address and port combination

D. User's geographical source location

20. In which phase would chain of custody be present?

A. Acquire

B. Authenticate

C. Analyze

D. All of the above

21. A company's backup policy states that a full backup is performed every Friday at 9:00 P.M. Differential backups are performed daily at 8:00 P.M. If a server goes down at 11:00 P.M. on Tuesday evening, how many backups in total will be required to restore the server?

A. 1

B. 2

C. 3

D. 4

22. What is one of the most important challenges of a "lessons learned" session?

A. Ensure all systems are working normally after an incident.

B. Verify no traces of malicious activity are present within the company network.

C. Refrain from blaming specific individuals about the incident or its investigation.

D. Ensure that processes are improved to deal with future incidents.

23. A company wants to select a dedicated alternative location for continuing its operations in the event of an incident, while minimizing operational downtime. Which of the following would be most appropriate for that purpose?

    A. Hot site

    B. Warm site

    C. Cold site

    D. Mobile site

24. Which of the following is the last phase of incident response?

    A. Recovery

    B. Eradication

    C. Containment

    D. Implementation of new countermeasures

25. A company's backup policy states that a full backup is performed every Tuesday at 8:00 A.M. Incremental backups are performed daily at 6:00 P.M. If a server goes down at 4:30 P.M. on the following Sunday evening, how many full backups will be required to restore the server?

    A. 1

    B. 2

    C. 3

    D. 4

26. An organization performs a full weekly backup and is considering combining that with a differential or incremental one. Why would a full/differential backup be preferred over a full/incremental backup?

    A. A full/differential backup takes less time to complete during the week.

    B. When restoring a system, recovery time is reduced.

    C. A full/incremental backup takes less time to complete during the week.

    D. Differential backups are smaller in size.

27. If a company wants to ensure it maintains constant Internet connectivity, which of these options would be most appropriate?

    A. Failover cluster

    B. Load balancing

    C. Redundant connection

    D. Optical fiber

28. Which of the following is the definition of RTO?

   A. How much data (at most) a business can sustain losing (i.e., three days of data)

   B. How much time it takes (at most) for a system or service to be restored after an outage (i.e., three days to restore the web server after crashing)

   C. How much time (at most) a crucial application or function can be unavailable without severe business impact

   D. Identifying what the business impact of an incident is to the organization

29. Which of the following isn't a phase of the incident lifecycle?

   A. Analyze evidence

   B. Preparation

   C. Eradication

   D. Containment

30. Anything of particular interest that may be identified in a system is classified as a(n):

   A. Alert

   B. Threshold

   C. Event

   D. Baseline

31. A company's RPO is set at three days, while the MAO is four days. Which of these values indicates a realistic RTO?

   A. 3

   B. 5

   C. 7

   D. 9

32. A company wants to select a dedicated alternative location for continuing its operations in the event of an incident. They have some budget limitations and can cope with operating from an alternative location within 24 to 48 hours of any major incident that might compromise the primary location. Which of the following would be most appropriate for that purpose?

   A. Hot site

   B. Warm site

   C. Cold site

   D. Mobile site

33. A police chief appointed John to lead a high-profile case involving organized crime, which requires the investigation of 100 machines with various forensic artifacts. John has been working as a senior forensic investigator for the last six years and has been teaching advanced forensics at the local police college. Which of these factors is the chief trying to support by appointing John on this case?

    A. Testability

    B. Error rate

    C. Acceptance

    D. Credibility

1. C	10. B	19. A	28. B
2. A	11. C	20. B	29. A
3. A	12. D	21. B	30. C
4. D	13. C	22. C	31. A
5. B	14. D	23. A	32. B
6. C	15. D	24. D	33. D
7. B	16. B	25. A	
8. A	17. C	26. B	
9. D	18. A	27. C	

1. In which of these phases of the incident response lifecycle would the identification of an appropriate tool for memory forensics fall into?

   A. Containment

   B. Detection, Analysis and Escalation

   C. Preparation

   D. Recovery

   ☑ **C.** Software and hardware identification would normally take place in the preparation phase. During that phase, the team would highlight the appropriate hardware and software tools (i.e., write blockers, USB flash drives, evidence bags, field kits, incident handling platforms, memory forensics and data erasure software) that are required to adequately respond to any given incident.

   ☒ **A, B,** and **D** are incorrect. **A** is incorrect because "containment" refers to using appropriate methods, tools, and processes (already identified and/or created during the preparation phase) to contain an incident already taking place in an organization. **B** is incorrect because "Detection, Analysis, and Escalation" would follow the preparation phase. At this point, an incident would be discovered (usually by some alert or report that the security team might receive) and then further investigated and escalated as appropriate. **D** is incorrect because "Recovery" refers to the processes and steps that are required in order to mitigate the incident and return to business as usual. In the case of a crypto-ransomware encrypting 100 machines, during the "Recovery" phase, those would most likely be reimaged and restored from backups so they can once again be used by the company employees.

2. Which of the following provides no fault tolerance?

   A. RAID 0

   B. RAID 1

   C. RAID 5

   D. RAID 6

   ☑ **A.** RAID 0 uses two or more disks and is primarily used for read/write operation improvement but is unable to provide any fault tolerance.

   ☒ **B, C,** and **D** are incorrect. **B** is incorrect because RAID 1 has two disks using mirror configuration so if one of the disks fails, data is still retrievable from the copy that exists on the second disk. **C** is incorrect because RAID 5 is able to offer fault tolerance as long as only a single drive fails. **D** is incorrect because RAID 6 provides fault tolerance. It is similar to RAID 5, but the main difference is that parity data is written on two drives (using at least four drives in total), extending the fault tolerance of the model to two drives.

3. Which of these statements regarding a "hot site" is inaccurate?

    A. It is commonly usable within a few hours.

    B. It includes network infrastructure.

    C. Cost is quite significant.

    D. Contains up-to-date organizational data.

    ☑ **A.** A hot site is available in a very short time. Usually that is within one hour or even less, but not a few hours, as the organization using a hot site wants to be able to switch from the primary site to the alternative location in as little time as possible (often even in minutes).

    ☒ **B, C,** and **D** are incorrect. **B** is incorrect because a "hot site" includes network infrastructure, water, and heating, allowing it to be usable immediately in case of any failure to the organization's primary site. **C** is incorrect because cost is very high for a hot site. If a company wants to lower that, it could go with the option of a warm site, which would be more cost-efficient but takes more time to transfer operations to the alternative location. **D** is incorrect because the data contained in a "hot site" is usually constantly updated so it can be immediately available for use when it is required.

4. If a company server is unavailable for more than 45 minutes, core business functions are affected. That means that 45 minutes is the:

    A. RPO

    B. BIA

    C. DRP

    D. MAO

    ☑ **D.** The MAO (maximum acceptable outage) is the time that a crucial application or service can be unavailable without severe business impact. For example, a private health provider might determine that patients queuing up to be served at their branch usually leave for a competitor if a doctor doesn't triage them in the first 15 minutes of a visit. In that case, the MAO might be set to 15 minutes, as the provider starts losing business after that.

    ☒ **A, B,** and **C** are incorrect. **A** is incorrect because the RPO (recovery point objective) is used to express how much data a business can sustain losing. For example, in the case of a military environment, the RPO may be set to 0 (or something close to it) if the related system controls troop deployment and personnel tracking. **B** is incorrect because BIA (business impact analysis) refers to identifying what the business impact of an incident is to the organization. **C** is incorrect because DRP (disaster recovery plan) details how to restore key business functions after an incident (or outage) takes place.

5. A security analyst identified outbound command and control traffic towards a malicious IP address. Which of these steps would most likely follow?

A. Investigate why there's traffic towards the malicious IP address.

B. Block the IP at the firewall.

C. Take a forensic image of the affected machine's memory.

D. Reimage the asset using a previous backup.

☑ **B.** After identifying and analyzing the threat, containment would follow. That can be achieved by blocking the offending IP at the firewall level so no outbound or inbound malicious traffic can pass through the firewall.

☒ **A, C,** and **D** are incorrect. **A** is incorrect because investigating why there is traffic towards the malicious IP should happen after the threat is contained. Once the block is implemented, additional investigation can take place to identify the reason for that traffic being generated. **C** is incorrect because containing the threat should be the first step. Since a malicious IP address has been identified, blocking traffic to and from that is key to ensure that no additional malicious traffic is present on the network. In addition, if that IP address is being used to exfiltrate data, then implementing a block is crucial so no organizational information is exfiltrated. **D** is incorrect because reimaging the asset would normally take place during the recovery stage. Once the investigation has been concluded, the assets can be reimaged and returned to the employees so they can be used again.

6. A forensic investigator needs to capture data for later analysis. Which one of these types of data should be captured first?

A. Remote logs

B. Local drive

C. Swap file

D. Backup tape

☑ **C.** The swap file data is the most volatile from the options provided in the question. A swap file is a form of memory (an extension of the machine's RAM) that is stored on the machine's hard drive. When it's powered off, that file is deleted.

☒ **A, B,** and **D** are incorrect. **A** is incorrect because any remote logs are stored at a remote location and shouldn't be affected by any activity taking place on the primary machine being investigated. **B** is incorrect because the machine's local hard disk contains data that can survive a system shutdown, which is not the case with the swap file. **D** is incorrect because a backup tape is a form of removable backup media and is certainly less volatile than the swap file data.

7. Which of the following does forensic software use to ensure no data tampering has taken place?

A. Serial numbers

B. Hashing

C. Digital signatures

D. Encryption

☑ **B.** Forensic tools use hashing algorithms (commonly MD5 and SHA) to create a unique signature of the captured data. This can be later used to prove no data tampering has occurred since the hash of the original data has remained unaltered.

☒ **A, C,** and **D** are incorrect. **A** is incorrect because a serial number can't be used to prove data tampering hasn't taken place. Forensic tools use serial numbers to identify the different devices being analyzed so an analyst can switch between those during an investigation. **C** is incorrect because forensic tools don't use digital signatures for file tampering purposes. **D** is incorrect because encryption isn't used to ensure evidence hasn't been altered. Encryption can only be used to allow for safe data storage by ensuring that if data is obtained by an unauthorized third party, it will remain inaccessible.

8. A company's client database is stored on a server so that online purchases can take place. The database needs to be accessible constantly even if the server goes down. Which of the following would be more suitable for that purpose?

A. Failover cluster

B. Load balancing

C. Full backup

D. Differential backup

☑ **A.** A failover cluster is the most appropriate solution, as it can allow the database to be accessible if the server goes down. For that purpose, at least two servers are required, which can then be configured into a pair. One of them can be set to operate as the primary instance, while the other will be the secondary one. Once the secondary server detects any type of failure on the primary instance, it can assume its place as primary, thus guaranteeing minimal database downtime.

☒ **B, C,** and **D** are incorrect. **B** is incorrect because load balancing is primarily used for performance improvement, not for fault tolerance. **C** is incorrect because a full backup will not guarantee that the database will be accessible all the time. If a server goes down, an administrator would need to intervene and manually restore that backup in addition to containing only accurate information up until the moment the backup was taken. If a full backup was taken a week ago, then after a server failure, the backup that is restored will contain data that is a week old, so all other transactions would have been lost. **D** is incorrect because a differential backup won't be able to ensure constant access to the server database, as any type of restoration would need to be manually performed by an administrator, with substantial associated time if any failure occurs out of normal business hours, in addition to any transactions that are not contained in the backup that was lost.

9. A company is hosting an SQL, cloud, and web server at its own premises. Which of these backup locations would you recommend as the safest option for backup storage and later retrieval of the web server's data?

   A. A backup server placed in the server room, along with the web server

   B. A magnetic tape stored on the premises but in a different building

   C. An encrypted copy of the data backed up on the company cloud server

   D. Backup of the data stored on Amazon AWS

   ☑ **D.** A backup of the data on a third-party cloud is the safest option, as that ensures the data survives any physical disaster that the main server room faces.

   ☒ **A, B,** and **C** are incorrect. **A** is incorrect because if the backup is placed in the server room, any physical disaster will destroy both the primary server and its backup. **B** is incorrect because a magnetic tape stored in a different building provides some assurance, but if a major physical disaster takes place (i.e., an earthquake or a tornado), that would most likely destroy the backup as well. **C** is incorrect because although the encrypted copy of the data stored on the company cloud might initially look like a good solution, the question mentions that the cloud is hosted on a server located in the server room, meaning the primary location of the web server. Hence, any physical disaster would result in losing that data.

10. A DRP's goal is to:

    A. Identify monetary losses that a critical organizational function may suffer because of an incident.

    B. Detail how to restore critical functions after an incident.

    C. Provide a plan on how a company can continue running once an incident takes place.

    D. Provide a risk evaluation at a specific moment in time.

    ☑ **B.** The primary goal of a DRP (disaster recovery plan) is to provide a plan on how key business functions of an organization can continue to operate after an incident takes place.

    ☒ **A, C,** and **D** are incorrect. **A** is incorrect because the identification of monetary losses from an incident is a primary deliverable of the BIA (business impact analysis). **C** is incorrect because a BCP (business continuity plan) depicts how a company can continue to operate once an incident takes place. **D** is incorrect because an evaluation of organizational risks at a specific moment in time is the goal of risk assessment.

11. An organization wants to test the existing DRP plan. Which of these methods is less intrusive but able to identify gaps in the plan?

    A. Parallel test

    B. Live test

    C. Tabletop exercise

    D. Warm site

☑ **C.** A tabletop exercise is the least intrusive method but still quite capable of identifying any procedural gaps that may exist. During such an activity, personnel from various teams are gathered in a room, and a hypothetical incident is presented and analyzed, while each team describes the actions that would be performed. If there's any issue, it can be flagged for later review so it's appropriately addressed.

☒ **A, B,** and **D** are incorrect. **A** is incorrect because a parallel test requires a lot of preparation as well as infrastructure resources. During such a test, primary business systems are still responsible for handling all traffic, while recovery systems are built and tested to review if production traffic can properly flow through them. **B** is incorrect because a live test requires the most preparation and is the riskiest approach. During such a test, primary systems are not used to handle traffic, as that will be directed to any redundant systems that exist. This is the most accurate method of determining how well a DRP plan can perform, but the risk of downtime is present since the secondary systems might not work as expected. **D** is incorrect because a warm site test entails substantial preparation, and if an organization intends to fully test the secondary location, it might decide to divert all (or the majority) of the production traffic through that location, which can be quite intrusive should something not go as planned.

12. Using a proprietary forensic tool for investigation relates to which of these reliability factors?

    A. Clarity

    B. Error rate

    C. Credibility

    D. Testability

    ☑ **D.** Testability relates to how much a tool or technique has been tested before being used in an investigation. Using a proprietary tool will not allow a variety of people from different industries to test the tool, hence its testability would be very low.

    ☒ **A, B,** and **C** are incorrect. **A** is incorrect because clarity refers to how easy it is to explain the tool or technique and its results to the court. **B** is incorrect because error rate refers to the tool's statistics regarding errors. **C** is incorrect because credibility refers to the individual handling a tool or using a method and how credible he or she is, as well as how reproducible the technique is by similar specialists.

13. Which of these tools is not an open source forensic application/suite?

    A. SIFT

    B. Sleuth Kit

    C. FTK

    D. Coroner's Toolkit

    ☑ **C.** FTK (Forensic Toolkit) is a tool developed by Access Data for forensic investigations. It provides the ability to capture a device (i.e., server, laptop, desktop, mobile) and acquire a forensic image of it for later analysis.

☒ **A, B,** and **D** are incorrect. **A** is incorrect because SIFT (SANS Investigative Forensic Toolkit) is an open source suite of forensic tools developed by the SANS Institute that is based on Ubuntu 14.04. **B** is incorrect because the Sleuth Kit is an open source collection of CLI tools used for disk imaging and analysis. **D** is incorrect because the Coroner's Toolkit is a collection of open source tools aiding data recovery and system data analysis.

14. An online sports retailer is experiencing an increased volume of client web requests, as it just released new products with a heavy discount. The company is considering some options to cope with these requests. Which of these options is the best one?

    A. WAF

    B. RAID

    C. Failover cluster

    D. Load balancing cluster

    ☑ **D.** A load balancing cluster is the best option for this scenario, as it is completely scalable and allows for large load optimization. When the organization experiences increased web requests, it can add more web servers to handle those accordingly. If traffic decreases with time, some servers can be powered down to reduce operational costs.

    ☒ **A, B,** and **C** are incorrect. **A** is incorrect because a WAF (web application firewall) would be used for security (i.e., to filter web traffic), not for load optimization. **B** is incorrect because any type of RAID (Redundant Array of Independent Disks) would mainly be used for fault tolerance, not for performance optimization. **C** is incorrect because a failover cluster would be used to ensure continuous operation of the web server, allowing for an additional server (or more) to be used and handle the traffic in case the primary machine is unavailable.

15. A company's backup policy states that a full backup is performed every Monday at 9:00 P.M. Incremental backups are performed daily at 12:00 P.M. If a server goes down at 8:30 P.M. on Thursday evening, how many backups in total will be required to restore the server?

    A. 1

    B. 2

    C. 3

    D. 4

    ☑ **D.** As per the organizational backup policy, a full backup will take place on Monday at 9:00 P.M. Following that, an incremental backup will take place on Tuesday at 12:00 P.M., as well as Wednesday and Thursday at the same time. After the last incremental backup (Thursday at 12:00 P.M.), the server goes down (8:30 P.M. on Thursday). That means all previously mentioned backups will need to be used to restore the server to its most current state, meaning all four (one full and three incremental ones).

    ☒ **A, B,** and **C** are incorrect, as these are distractors.

16. Which of the following is not one of the three forensic investigation phases?

    A. Acquire

    B. Validate

    C. Analyze

    D. Authenticate

    ☑ **B.** There is no forensic phase known as "validate." Any type of required data validation would be performed during the "authenticate" phase.

    ☒ **A, C,** and **D** are incorrect. **A** is incorrect because "acquire" is the phase where evidence from the scene is gathered (i.e., hard disk/memory capture, mobile phone acquisition). **C** is incorrect because "analyze" is the last phase of the process (following acquisition and authentication) where all captured data is analyzed in detail. It is worth noting that analysis is performed on copies of the original data (which should have been obtained during the "acquire" phase) so that no tampering of the original evidence takes place. **D** is incorrect because the "authenticate" phase includes evidence control and proof that it hasn't been modified (i.e., by using proper chain of custody forms).

17. A security administrator is reviewing corporate SIEM logs regarding possible incidents for a company using BYOD. Which of these activities is most likely a valid security incident?

    A. Playing an online game

    B. Browsing to Facebook

    C. Downloading a movie

    D. Using Google Drive

    ☑ **C.** Depending on how strict the organizational policies are, it is possible that all mentioned activities constitute a security incident (although this is highly unlikely in the case of BYOD, or bring your own device). However, regardless of that, most companies would consider any user downloading a movie while in the corporate network a genuine security incident indicating a policy violation, as the user is most probably downloading copyrighted material.

    ☒ **A, B,** and **D** are incorrect. **A** is incorrect because playing an online game is not necessarily a security incident (especially in the case of BYOD), as that may be allowed by the corporate policy. **B** is incorrect because browsing to social media is often allowed by most companies (although sometimes access hours may be restricted). In addition, when using BYOD, companies are aware that users using their personal devices would most likely be accessing their social media or using personal applications to some extent but tend to focus on the benefits of BYOD. **D** is incorrect because using Google Drive doesn't necessarily indicate a security incident, especially because some companies use Google Drive for business purposes.

18. A type of malware has been identified on the corporate network. It has the ability to record keystrokes, and it is known to open TCP port 52145 on an infected system and receive command-and-control traffic from its creator using IP address 10.10.10.10. (Please note that this IP is private and is used specifically for the purposes of the question. In a real-life scenario, the attacker would be using a public IP address.) Which of these actions would most likely be taken during the "containment" phase of an incident response plan?

A. Block communication to 10.10.10.10 at the perimeter firewall.

B. Close TCP port 52145 on all infected systems.

C. Create an IDS rule for traffic to 10.10.10.10.

D. Use a web proxy to block offending traffic.

   ☑ **A.** The primary goal of the "containment" phase is to stop further malicious activity. Since the malware is communicating with its creator via IP address 10.10.10.10, blocking that traffic at the perimeter firewall will ensure that all such communication ceases. Even if there are multiple malware instances within different machines in the company network, none of them will be able to communicate with the malware's creator to exfiltrate information or receive instructions.

   ☒ **B, C,** and **D** are incorrect. **B** is incorrect because closing TCP port 52145 will not necessarily stop communication with the malicious IP address, which might also be used as a source for other attacks (not necessarily using the same port). **C** is incorrect because creating an IDS rule for traffic to 10.10.10.10 is beneficial for receiving alerts regarding offending traffic but will not contain it, as the IDS doesn't have an ability to block that communication. **D** is incorrect because a web proxy will only be able to filter web traffic, which will have no effect in this case, as the traffic in question is not reported to be web related.

19. Source address affinity is used to direct traffic according to the:

A. User's source address

B. Server's source address

C. User's source address and port combination

D. User's geographical source location

   ☑ **A.** Source address affinity uses the source IP address of a user. It is used for load balancing and allows the load balancer to redirect requests originating from the same client IP address to be served by the same server.

   ☒ **B, C,** and **D** are incorrect. **B** is incorrect because requests will originate from the client, not the server side. **C** is incorrect because source affinity only works by identifying a request from the same client IP, but the client source port isn't relevant. **D** is incorrect because the user's geographical location doesn't change anything, as source affinity only uses the client IP address, regardless of its physical location.

20. In which phase would chain of custody be present?

    A. Acquire

    B. Authenticate

    C. Analyze

    D. All of the above

    ☑ **B.** Chain of custody refers to controlling evidence from the moment of collection, which is something that would happen during the "authenticate" phase. The purpose of a chain of custody is to demonstrate that adequate control has been enforced to ensure that the evidence hasn't been tampered with and has been properly handled.

    ☒ **A, C,** and **D** are incorrect. **A** is incorrect because "acquire" is the phase where evidence from the scene is gathered (i.e., hard disk/memory capture, mobile phone acquisition). **C** is incorrect because "analyze" is the last phase of the process (following acquisition and authentication), where all captured data is analyzed in detail. It is worth noting that the analysis is performed on copies of the original data (which should have been obtained during the "acquire" phase) so that no tampering of the original evidence takes place. **D** is incorrect because chain of custody starts being used at the "authenticate" phase.

21. A company's backup policy states that a full backup is performed every Friday at 9:00 P.M. Differential backups are performed daily at 8:00 P.M. If a server goes down at 11:00 P.M. on Tuesday evening, how many backups in total will be required to restore the server?

    A. 1

    B. 2

    C. 3

    D. 4

    ☑ **B.** As per the company policy, a full backup will first be taken on Friday at 9:00 P.M. Following that, differential backups will be taken on Saturday, Sunday, Monday, and Tuesday at 8:00 P.M. Finally, after those are taken, the server goes down. As you may remember, when a differential backup is taken, all changes from the previous full backup are recorded. Since the server went down at 11:00 P.M. on Tuesday and a differential backup was taken three hours prior to that, a restoration process will only require that backup in addition to the full backup taken last Friday. Hence, a total of two backups will be required.

    ☒ **A, C,** and **D** are incorrect, as these are distractors.

22. What is one of the most important challenges of a "lessons learned" session?

    A. Ensure all systems are working normally after an incident.

    B. Verify no traces of malicious activity are present within the company network.

    C. Refrain from blaming specific individuals about the incident or its investigation.

    D. Ensure that processes are improved to deal with future incidents.

☑ **C.** After any given incident, most company employees involved with the investigation always have concerns about how they performed and if the incident could have been avoided altogether if they had acted differently. However, a "lessons learned" session should focus on how to improve things for future responses and not dwell on blaming specific people for how they performed and if they were solely responsible for the incident taking place.

☒ **A, B,** and **D** are incorrect. **A** is incorrect because during the "recovery" phase, all systems would be brought back to normal either by reverting any damage caused by the incident or by restoring them from a previous backup (which is a common method to ensure that nothing might have been overlooked). **B** is incorrect because ensuring all threats have been neutralized would normally take place during the "eradication" phase, where the goal is to ensure the components of any given threat are removed from the environment. **D** is incorrect because ensuring that processes are improved to deal with future incidents is the actual goal of a "lessons learned" session, but the challenge is to do that without focusing on blaming specific individuals for the incident or how it was investigated.

23. A company wants to select a dedicated alternative location for continuing its operations in the event of an incident, while minimizing operational downtime. Which of the following would be most appropriate for that purpose?

   A. Hot site

   B. Warm site

   C. Cold site

   D. Mobile site

☑ **A.** A "hot site" is the best choice for this purpose, as it offers a dedicated alternative location for continuing operations in the event of any incident rendering the primary location unusable. Such a site has everything in place (i.e., HVAC, network infrastructure, hardware) so the organization can continue operating.

☒ **B, C,** and **D** are incorrect. **B** is incorrect because a "warm site" offers some of the capabilities of a hot site but not all of them (i.e., commonly the data from the primary location is not up to date and a synchronization needs to take place before commencing operations). In addition, it takes some time before a warm site is fully activated for use, meaning that it won't offer minimal operational downtime, which is what is required here. **C** is incorrect because a "cold site" will take substantial resources and time to activate, as it doesn't have any hardware or software set up. **D** is incorrect because a mobile site is used when an organization doesn't require a dedicated alternative location. In addition, it usually consists of necessary hardware, but software and data are not kept up to date, which means that some time for setting it up is required, thus it does not offer minimal operational downtime.

24. Which of the following is the last phase of incident response?

   A. Recovery

   B. Eradication

C. Containment

D. Implementation of new countermeasures

☑ **D.** The last incident response phase is called "lessons learned/implementation of new countermeasure" (most commonly known as "lessons learned"). The goal of this phase is to review if current processes are adequate or need to be amended in order to respond to any future incidents more efficiently. In addition, evaluation of current countermeasures takes place, as new ones might need to be introduced to protect the environment from future attacks.

☒ **A, B,** and **C** are incorrect. **A** is incorrect because during "recovery," actions are taken to restore system operation to a known good state, like the one prior to the incident. **B** is incorrect because during "eradication," the root cause of the issue is identified and eliminated. **C** is incorrect because during "containment," the incident will be contained and further damage to the business stopped.

25. A company's backup policy states that a full backup is performed every Tuesday at 8:00 A.M. Incremental backups are performed daily at 6:00 P.M. If a server goes down at 4:30 P.M. on the following Sunday evening, how many full backups will be required to restore the server?

A. 1

B. 2

C. 3

D. 4

☑ **A.** Full backups are performed on a weekly basis (every Tuesday). Since the server went down on the following Sunday, only one full backup is available for the restoration. Note that the question refers to the number of full backups, not the total number of backups required.

☒ **B, C,** and **D** are incorrect, as these are distractors.

26. An organization performs a full weekly backup and is considering combining that with a differential or incremental one. Why would a full/differential backup be preferred over a full/incremental backup?

A. A full/differential backup takes less time to complete during the week.

B. When restoring a system, recovery time is reduced.

C. A full/incremental backup takes less time to complete during the week.

D. Differential backups are smaller in size.

☑ **B.** Using a full/differential backup results in reduced recovery time, as the differential backup captures any changes from the last full backup. That means that at any given moment, a total of two backups will be required to perform system restoration: the most recent full weekly backup and the most recent differential one.

☒ **A, C,** and **D** are incorrect. **A** is incorrect because a full/differential backup takes more time to be completed during the week, as all changes from the moment the full weekly backup was taken need to be recorded. **C** is incorrect because a full/incremental backup does take less time to complete during the week (i.e., if taken daily, it records daily database transactions, which takes a relatively short time). However, that won't be a reason for choosing a full/differential backup solution over a full/incremental one. It's rather a statement regarding how the full/differential backup method works. **D** is incorrect because differential backups are larger in size (not smaller) because they include all changes since the last full weekly backup was taken, which may require substantial space.

27. If a company wants to ensure it maintains constant Internet connectivity, which of these options would be most appropriate?

   A. Failover cluster

   B. Load balancing

   C. Redundant connection

   D. Optical fiber

   ☑ **C.** The best method to maintain "close to constant" Internet connectivity is to have multiple connections (at least two) in order to be able to use an alternative connection in the event of any issue. Many organizations use leased lines to get constant connectivity at very good upload and download speeds. Having a second leased line as a redundant connection is a great option, but since the cost of those is quite high, more cost-effective options are usually preferred (like a very low-end leased line or very good-rate ADSL option, which is significantly cheaper) so they can efficiently cope when the primary line goes down.

   ☒ **A, B,** and **D** are incorrect. **A** is incorrect because a failover cluster is used to provide fault tolerance (usually relating to servers and services), not connection redundancy. **B** is incorrect because load balancing is used to distribute load efficiently among different servers (i.e., file or web servers) and doesn't aim to address network connection redundancy. Although it may offer redundancy from an aspect of a server or service going down (i.e., when having three servers and one goes down, the load balancer would distribute remaining requests to the two remaining servers), network connectivity to the load balancer is still required in order to make that happen. **D** is incorrect because using optical fiber would offer great speeds, would support longer distances, would be resistant to electromagnetic interference, and would offer great security, but all those advantages don't have anything to do with maintaining constant connectivity. This means that an optical fiber may still become unavailable, hence the company needs to have an alternative connection available when that happens.

28. Which of the following is the definition of RTO?

   A. How much data (at most) a business can sustain losing (i.e., three days of data)

   B. How much time it takes (at most) for a system or service to be restored after an outage (i.e., three days to restore the web server after crashing)

C. How much time (at most) a crucial application or function can be unavailable without severe business impact

D. Identifying what the business impact of an incident is to the organization

☑ **B.** The definition of RTO (recovery time objective) is the time it takes (at most) for a system or service to be restored after an outage (i.e., three days to restore the web server after going down). This is what usually drives business processes and administrators to architect proper systems that can support service restoration at the level that is required for a company to properly function.

☒ **A, C,** and **D** are incorrect. **A** is incorrect because the amount of data a business can sustain losing (i.e., three days of data) expresses the RPO (recovery point objective). This may vary but in critical environments can be quite challenging to achieve (i.e., a SCADA [supervisory control and data acquisition] system controlling water pressure might have an RPO of minutes in order for operations to properly continue). **C** is incorrect because the time a crucial application or function can be unavailable without severe business impact taking place refers to the MAO (maximum acceptable outage), also known as MTD (maximum tolerable downtime). **D** is incorrect because identification of the business impact of an incident to the organization is the definition of BIA (business impact analysis).

29. Which of the following isn't a phase of the incident lifecycle?

A. Analyze evidence

B. Preparation

C. Eradication

D. Containment

☑ **A.** "Analyze evidence" (also known as "analyze") is one of the phases of a computer forensics investigation, during which all previously acquired data is fully analyzed to investigate the incident that took place.

☒ **B, C,** and **D** are incorrect. **B** is incorrect because during "preparation" the team would highlight the appropriate tools that are required to adequately respond to any given incident and review any processes the organization has in place, as well as enforce the company defenses to ensure adequate preparation is in place prior to an incident. **C** is incorrect because "eradication" is when the root cause of the issue is identified and eliminated. **D** is incorrect because "containment" refers to using appropriate methods, tools, and processes (which were already identified and/or created during the preparation phase) to contain an incident already taking place in an organization.

30. Anything of particular interest that may be identified in a system is classified as a(n):

A. Alert

B. Threshold

C. Event

D. Baseline

☑ **C.** An "event" can be classified as any activity that may be identified in a system. A user named James logging on a system might be classified as an event.

☒ **A, B,** and **D** are incorrect. **A** is incorrect because an "alert" (usually identified on an IDS/IPS, SIEM, or some other similar system or tool) is a notification for a particular activity of interest that someone (i.e., security analyst or administrator) would like to be informed of and usually is created after a rule of some kind is triggered, which is set to look for the activity in question. **B** is incorrect because a "threshold" can be defined as a specific limit configured in a rule or tool that, once surpassed, an appropriate action is taken. **D** is incorrect because a "baseline" is a known initial state and is commonly used in configuration management to describe an initial image of an operating system that an organization may be using, or it may refer to security tools that require a baseline to be set before performing related analysis (i.e., anomaly-based IDS, which needs to have a baseline of the network created in order to alert on what events might be valid security incidents).

31. A company's RPO is set at three days, while the MAO is four days. Which of these values indicates a realistic RTO?

    A. 3

    B. 5

    C. 7

    D. 9

    ☑ **A.** The time a crucial application or function can be unavailable without severe business impact refers to the MAO (maximum acceptable outage), which is stated as four days. The RTO is the time it takes (at most) for a system or service to be restored after an outage. Since the business can cope for up to four days (MAO set at four days), the RTO needs to be less than the MAO in order for the business to successfully recover and continue operations. From the provided options, only the first one (three days) allows for a viable RTO.

    ☒ **B, C,** and **D** are incorrect, as these are distractors.

32. A company wants to select a dedicated alternative location for continuing its operations in the event of an incident. They have some budget limitations and can cope with operating from an alternative location within 24 to 48 hours of any major incident that might compromise the primary location. Which of the following would be most appropriate for that purpose?

    A. Hot site

    B. Warm site

    C. Cold site

    D. Mobile site

☑ **B.** A "warm site" would be most suitable in this case. It offers some of the capabilities of a "hot site" but not all of them (i.e., commonly the data from the primary location is not up to date and synchronization needs to take place before commencing operations). However, the cost of maintaining a "warm site" is significantly lower than that of a "hot site." In addition, such a site would be usually available within a matter of hours, commonly up to 24, which aligns with the organization's requirements.

☒ **A, C,** and **D** are incorrect. **A** is incorrect because a "hot site," although available in a very short time, would require a substantial budget, and the company in this scenario only has a limited budget to spend, thus making this option not suitable for what is required. **C** is incorrect because a "cold site" (although quite affordable) will take substantial resources and time to activate, as it doesn't have any hardware or software set up. **D** is incorrect because a "mobile site" is used when an organization doesn't require a dedicated alternative location.

33. A police chief appointed John to lead a high-profile case involving organized crime, which requires the investigation of 100 machines with various forensic artifacts. John has been working as a senior forensic investigator for the last six years and has been teaching advanced forensics at the local police college. Which of these factors is the chief trying to support by appointing John on this case?

A. Testability

B. Error rate

C. Acceptance

D. Credibility

☑ **D.** The police chief is trying to ensure that the individual who handles the case has adequate credibility, which will aid John when the case goes to court. Credibility refers to the individual handling a tool or using a method and how credible he or she is, as well as how reproducible the technique is by similar specialists. Since John has been working at the police force as a senior forensic investigator for six years and has been teaching forensics at the police academy, he should be credible enough to lead the investigation in question.

☒ **A, B,** and **C** are incorrect. **A** is incorrect because testability relates to how much a tool or technique has been tested before being used in an investigation, but the focus of the question is the investigator, not a tool or technique. **B** is incorrect because the error rate refers to a tool's statistics regarding errors, but the question focuses on the investigator and his qualifications. **C** is incorrect because acceptance refers to a scientific theory or technique and how much that has been peer reviewed, not the actual investigator handling a case.

CHAPTER 5

Cryptography

This chapter includes questions from the following objectives:

- 5.1 Understand fundamental concepts of cryptography
- 5.2 Understand reasons and requirements for cryptography
- 5.3 Understand and support secure protocols
- 5.4 Understand Public Key Infrastructure (PKI) systems

This chapter contains a complete set of questions and answers regarding the fundamental principles of cryptography (necessary terminology, hashing, symmetric and asymmetric encryption, steganography, IPSEC) and why cryptography is used, as well as its key requirements (types of data, handling techniques, data protection). It also includes questions about secure protocol operation (basic protocol ports and operation, remote access solutions) and PKI (certificates, certificate authorities, key escrow, and certificate trust).

1. Consider two text files: The first one contains the sentence "this is an SSCP example" and the second one contains the sentence "this is another SSCP example with different text". The MD5 hash of the first file is 063ba1995095c95c2e2184837fd47067, and the MD5 hash of the second file is 063ba1995095c95c2e2184837fd47067. What is this an example of?

   A. Work factor

   B. Collusion

   C. Rainbow tables

   D. Collision

2. Which of these data labels would be most suitable for client information that a company is storing?

   A. Confidential

   B. Private

   C. Sensitive

   D. Public

3. James is the head of sales and needs to send a proposal regarding a new product to the CEO. He changes its value by adding 10 percent with the intent of getting that for himself afterwards. Which of these terms describes this scenario?

   A. Data inference

   B. Deduplication

   C. Data diddling

   D. Data interference

4. Consider the command shown in the following illustration. Which of these statements is accurate?

```
[nick:~ Nick$ ping www.google.com
PING www.google.com (216.58.204.4): 56 data bytes
64 bytes from 216.58.204.4: icmp_seq=0 ttl=53 time=4.352 ms
64 bytes from 216.58.204.4: icmp_seq=1 ttl=53 time=3.001 ms
64 bytes from 216.58.204.4: icmp_seq=2 ttl=53 time=3.739 ms
64 bytes from 216.58.204.4: icmp_seq=3 ttl=53 time=4.043 ms
64 bytes from 216.58.204.4: icmp_seq=4 ttl=53 time=4.080 ms
64 bytes from 216.58.204.4: icmp_seq=5 ttl=53 time=4.420 ms
64 bytes from 216.58.204.4: icmp_seq=6 ttl=53 time=3.031 ms
^C
--- www.google.com ping statistics ---
7 packets transmitted, 7 packets received, 0.0% packet loss
round-trip min/avg/max/stddev = 3.001/3.809/4.420/0.542 ms
```

A. The operating system in use is a version of Windows.

B. The command shows echo reply packets.

C. The remote host is unreachable.

D. The command completed its execution and terminated automatically.

5. A company wants to ensure bandwidth is preserved for business-related traffic (related to the internal company network) while employees access the corporate network remotely. Which of the following would be the most appropriate option?

A. Split tunneling

B. Tunnel mode

C. Transport mode

D. RADIUS

6. Which of the following is the most accurate statement regarding what TLS uses for key exchange and session encryption?

A. Symmetric encryption

B. Asymmetric encryption

C. Both symmetric and asymmetric encryption

D. SSL

7. Which of the following can't be achieved with digital signatures?

A. Integrity

B. Confidentiality

C. Nonrepudiation

D. Authentication

8. A key escrow is used for storing:

A. Public keys

B. Digital certificates

C. WOT certificates

D. Private keys

9. Which of these algorithms provides integrity in addition to authenticity?

A. MD5

B. RSA

C. SHA-3

D. HMAC-MD5

10. Jane is a system administrator and wants to download a new tool from a third-party website (the official vendor's server doesn't have enough bandwidth, and Jane achieves a very slow download speed, and the file is quite large). After downloading the tool, she calculates an MD5 hash of it. When attempting to compare the calculated MD5 hash with the official vendor's hash as stated on the vendor website, she notices they are different. After repeating the whole process, she still doesn't see the hashes matching. What would be the most probable reason for this?

    A. The file that was downloaded from the third-party server is corrupted.

    B. The file that was downloaded from the third-party server contains malware.

    C. The file that was downloaded from the third-party server doesn't seem to be the official vendor file.

    D. This is an example of a collision.

11. Which of the following would be most suitable to protect files stored on a hard drive?

    A. AES-128

    B. TLS 1.1

    C. RSA-512

    D. 3-DES

12. Which of these ports would be used when a user attempts to send an e-mail?

    A. TCP 110

    B. TCP 25

    C. UDP 53

    D. TCP 443

13. Which person is responsible for defining a company's data classification scheme?

    A. Data owner

    B. Data custodian

    C. User

    D. Management

14. Which of the following would be used for a new certificate registration request?

    A. WOT

    B. RA

    C. CRL

    D. OCSP

15. Which of these authentication protocols would you use to support mutual authentication?

    A. CHAP

    B. PAP

    C. MS-CHAPv2

    D. MS-CHAPv3

16. You want to ensure your company's e-mails are encrypted to maintain communication confidentiality. Which of these options would you choose for that purpose?

    A. DKIM

    B. SPF

    C. S/MIME

    D. DMARC

17. Consider this cipher suite:

    TLS_ECDHE_RSA_WITH_CAMELLIA_256_CBC_SHA384

What key exchange algorithm is being used?

    A. TLS

    B. ECDHE_RSA

    C. CAMELIA_256_CBC

    D. SHA384

18. Your company wants to simplify the process of employees remotely connecting to the company network via VPN. The main requirement is to be able to connect using a web browser. Which of these methods would be most appropriate for that goal?

    A. TLS VPN

    B. Transport mode

    C. Tunnel mode

    D. SSH

19. Which of these attacks would be most suitable to an attacker who has samples of the plaintext and ciphertext messages?

    A. Rainbow table attack

    B. Dictionary attack

    C. Chosen plaintext

    D. Known plaintext

20. An attacker is using a text file's spaces and tabs to store information. Which of the following is this an example of?

    A. Encoding

    B. Hashing

    C. Steganography

    D. Encryption

21. You have a file containing the sentence "This is the plaintext". You use a key of "This is my first key" and generate the following ciphertext: "yu9+m0/mY7rF/6dv6SXNVC7D69Q7b1N4". You encrypt the same file again but with a different key: "This is my second key". The result is "yu9+m0/mY7rF/6dv6SXNVC7D69Q7b1N4". What is this an example of?

    A. Key clustering

    B. Collision

    C. Collusion

    D. Work factor

22. You just received an e-mail from your bank account manager that your account has been breached. She kindly asks you to reset your password and emphasizes not to disclose it to anyone who may be posing as a bank employee over the phone. You follow the URL contained in her e-mail, and your browser presents you with the following message: "This connection is untrusted." What is the most likely reason for that?

    A. Certificate has expired.

    B. You have received a phishing e-mail.

    C. Bank website experiencing technical issues.

    D. A self-signed certificate is being used.

23. Which of the following would you use to check if a certificate has been revoked, using the least amount of network resources?

    A. CRL

    B. CLR

    C. RA

    D. OCSP

24. James wants to communicate with Dianne. For that purpose, he encrypts a message with Dianne's public key before sending it to her. Which of the following is he trying to enforce?

    A. Integrity

    B. Authentication

    C. Confidentiality

    D. Nonrepudiation

25. If a group of eight people uses symmetric key cryptography, how many keys are required to ensure that everyone's communications are secured while each pair uses a different encryption key?

   A. 8

   B. 28

   C. 32

   D. 64

1. D	**8.** D	**15.** C	**22.** B
2. B	**9.** D	**16.** C	**23.** D
3. C	**10.** C	**17.** B	**24.** C
4. B	**11.** A	**18.** A	**25.** B
5. A	**12.** B	**19.** D	
6. C	**13.** D	**20.** C	
7. B	**14.** B	**21.** A	

1. Consider two text files: The first one contains the sentence "this is an SSCP example" and the second one contains the sentence "this is another SSCP example with different text". The MD5 hash of the first file is 063ba1995095c95c2e2184837fd47067, and the MD5 hash of the second file is 063ba1995095c95c2e2184837fd47067. What is this an example of?

   A. Work factor

   B. Collusion

   C. Rainbow tables

   D. Collision

   ☑ **D.** The two MD5 file hashes are identical; however, the content of the two files is different. This is known as a collision and relates to one of the basic principles of a hashing algorithm, which is to be collision free, meaning that two different files should never generate the same hash value. Even a slight change in a file that is used as input in a hashing algorithm should generate a different output.

   ☒ **A, B,** and **C** are incorrect. **A** is incorrect because the work factor relates to cryptography and expresses the time and effort that it would take to decrypt an encrypted message. **B** is incorrect, as it refers to the act of one or more individuals or companies conspiring to commit fraud. Although the syntax might be similar to the correct answer, this term has actually nothing to do with hashing algorithms. **C** is incorrect, as rainbow tables contain precomputed hash values intended to provide a reverse lookup resource for hash values.

2. Which of these data labels would be most suitable for client information that a company is storing?

   A. Confidential

   B. Private

   C. Sensitive

   D. Public

   ☑ **B.** Client information would most probably be labeled private, which is a label reserved for data that is to be used strictly internally. If such data is released to the public domain, serious damage may be caused to the organization. In addition, some client data would most probably be PII (personally identifiable information), and disclosure of it would be an offense that needs to be reported to the appropriate regulating body, which may impose related fines.

   ☒ **A, C,** and **D** are incorrect. **A** is incorrect because data labeled confidential would most likely be used to indicate important information that is crucial to the organization and its operation (i.e., may include internal processes, proprietary research information about new products, incident response protocols, etc.). **C** is incorrect because sensitive information does require a degree of protection (because any sensitive data leak might result in damage for the company) but its nature is not as crucial as private or confidential information. Examples may include company presentations and organizational structure information. **D** is incorrect because public data is publicly available information, and client information wouldn't be classified as such.

3. James is the head of sales and needs to send a proposal regarding a new product to the CEO. He changes its value by adding 10 percent with the intent of getting that for himself afterwards. Which of these terms describes this scenario?

    A. Data inference

    B. Deduplication

    C. Data diddling

    D. Data interference

    ☑ **C.** Data diddling is a term used to describe any unauthorized data change before or while information is entered into a system. In this scenario, James altered the product price before the CEO reviewed it, with the goal of getting 10 percent for himself once that purchase is finally approved.

    ☒ **A, B,** and **D** are incorrect. **A** is incorrect because data inference is used to describe the case where an individual is able to gain knowledge about restricted data (usually labelled secret or classified) by accessing public information. **B** is incorrect because deduplication is used to describe a file being stored in a system without any duplicates existing. It's a concept commonly used to ensure that only one file copy is kept and anyone requiring access to its contents is always able to access the most up-to-date information, while saving valuable storage space. **D** is incorrect because there's no associated term named data interference. This option is a distractor.

4. Consider the command shown in the following illustration. Which of these statements is accurate?

```
[nick:~ Nick$ ping www.google.com
PING www.google.com (216.58.204.4): 56 data bytes
64 bytes from 216.58.204.4: icmp_seq=0 ttl=53 time=4.352 ms
64 bytes from 216.58.204.4: icmp_seq=1 ttl=53 time=3.001 ms
64 bytes from 216.58.204.4: icmp_seq=2 ttl=53 time=3.739 ms
64 bytes from 216.58.204.4: icmp_seq=3 ttl=53 time=4.043 ms
64 bytes from 216.58.204.4: icmp_seq=4 ttl=53 time=4.080 ms
64 bytes from 216.58.204.4: icmp_seq=5 ttl=53 time=4.420 ms
64 bytes from 216.58.204.4: icmp_seq=6 ttl=53 time=3.031 ms
^C
--- www.google.com ping statistics ---
7 packets transmitted, 7 packets received, 0.0% packet loss
round-trip min/avg/max/stddev = 3.001/3.809/4.420/0.542 ms
```

    A. The operating system in use is a version of Windows.

    B. The command shows echo reply packets.

    C. The remote host is unreachable.

    D. The command completed its execution and terminated automatically.

☑ **B.** The output is from the execution of a ping command where echo request packets are being sent to www.google.com, which in turn replies with a number of echo reply messages.

☒ **A, C,** and **D** are incorrect. **A** is incorrect because, by default, a ping command execution in Windows will send four packets to the target host. However, here there are seven echo reply packets, thus indicating that another operating system is in use. **C** is incorrect because the remote host isn't unreachable. ICMP echo reply messages are being successfully received, indicating the remote host is up and running and responding with echo reply. If it wasn't reachable, a response of "Request timeout" would be present in the response messages. Also, at the end of the command output there's a statement of "*0.00% packet loss.*" If the host was unreachable, that would be stating some percentage of packet loss (in the case where the host was completely unreachable to echo request packets, that would state "100.00% packet loss"). **D** is incorrect because the command didn't terminate automatically, as it can be seen that the user used ^C to manually terminate its execution.

5. A company wants to ensure bandwidth is preserved for business-related traffic (related to the internal company network) while employees access the corporate network remotely. Which of the following would be the most appropriate option?

   A. Split tunneling

   B. Tunnel mode

   C. Transport mode

   D. RADIUS

   ☑ **A.** A split tunnel is a common method of preserving bandwidth for any organization, as it ensures only the interesting traffic traverses the corporate VPN tunnel. Any traffic that doesn't need to be encrypted will reach its destination directly, without going through that VPN tunnel. A classic example is websites like social media. When a user connects to the company VPN, any organization-related traffic is encrypted via the VPN tunnel. However, when the user browses to Facebook, that traffic doesn't go through the VPN tunnel.

   ☒ **B, C,** and **D** are incorrect. **B** is incorrect because tunnel mode is a IPSEC mode in which the whole packet is encrypted. This can't be configured in such a way as to allow only business-related traffic to go through the VPN, which is something that split tunneling can achieve. However, split tunneling can be configured with different tunneling protocols. **C** is incorrect because transport mode is a IPSEC mode in which only the packet payload is encrypted (not the packet header). Split tunneling can also be configured for use with this tunneling protocol, but it's not transport mode that fulfils the requirement, but rather split tunneling. **D** is incorrect because RADIUS provides authentication, authorization, and accounting but wouldn't be suitable in this scenario, as the question focuses on bandwidth consumption when the traffic relates to business.

6. Which of the following is the most accurate statement regarding what TLS uses for key exchange and session encryption?

   A. Symmetric encryption

   B. Asymmetric encryption

   C. Both symmetric and asymmetric encryption

   D. SSL

   ☑ **C.** TLS (Transport Layer Security) uses both symmetric and asymmetric encryption. More specifically, it initially uses asymmetric encryption to share a secret (symmetric) key. Once that has been achieved, it uses that symmetric key to encrypt all further communications.

   ☒ **A, B,** and **D** are incorrect. **A** is incorrect because it uses symmetric encryption to encrypt the session after the secret key has been exchanged. **B** is incorrect because it uses asymmetric encryption for key exchange, but after that, symmetric encryption is used to encrypt all further communications. **D** is incorrect because TLS doesn't use SSL. SSL was the first name that the protocol had, and after SSLv3 the name changed to TLS (with version 1.1 being the first one out).

7. Which of the following can't be achieved with digital signatures?

   A. Integrity

   B. Confidentiality

   C. Nonrepudiation

   D. Authentication

   ☑ **B.** A digital signature is a message's encrypted hash. The purpose of using a digital signature is to provide message integrity as well as sender authentication and nonrepudiation. However, in order to enforce confidentiality, the message would need to be encrypted, but as stated earlier it is the hash of the message that is being encrypted, not the message itself. A third party can still intercept and read that message.

   ☒ **A, C,** and **D** are incorrect. **A** is incorrect because a digital signature provides integrity. Since the e-mail's content is hashed prior to being sent, the recipient would be able to identify any unauthorized modification that a third party may have made if the message was intercepted and altered. **C** is incorrect because nonrepudiation is something that a digital signature can provide. That is because in order for the digital signature to be created, the sender's private key needs to be used, which is something that only the sender should have. **D** is incorrect because digital signatures provide authentication, since they are a form of proof to the recipient that any message actually came from a valid sender (being the digital signature's owner).

8. A key escrow is used for storing:

A. Public keys

B. Digital certificates

C. WOT certificates

D. Private keys

☑ **D.** A key escrow is used for safely keeping private keys in order to be able to retrieve them in the event the company's private key is lost or damaged. Only specific people usually have permission to retrieve private keys from a key escrow facility due to the sensitivity of their nature.

☒ **A, B,** and **C** are incorrect. **A** is incorrect because public keys are publicly available and are contained in an individual's digital certificate. **B** is incorrect because any digital certificates would be issued and managed by the certificate authority. Please note that a CA (certificate authority) may be external (i.e., Symantec or VeriSign) or internal to the organization (i.e., when a certificate is needed for a system that is used only internally). **C** is incorrect because there's no such term as WOT certificate. WOT (web of trust) is a decentralized trust model with the goal of allowing a system to establish authenticity between a public key and its owner.

9. Which of these algorithms provides integrity in addition to authenticity?

A. MD5

B. RSA

C. SHA-3

D. HMAC-MD5

☑ **D.** HMAC (Hash-based Message Authentication Code) uses a secret key only known to the sender and recipient of a message. As such, it is used in combination with other hashing algorithms (like MD5 or SHA). When a sender wants to send a message (hashed with MD5), the first step is to create that message's MD5 hash. After that, the secret key is used to create the HMAC-MD5, which is what will be sent to the recipient. Since only the sender and recipient know that key, it is possible to follow the process at the recipient's side and establish that the message originated from the sender it was expected from in addition to not having been modified.

☒ **A, B,** and **C** are incorrect. **A** is incorrect because MD5 can only provide message integrity, but no authenticity is supported (unless combined with HMAC). **B** is incorrect because RSA (Rivest Shamir Adleman) is an asymmetric encryption algorithm and is not used to enforce integrity or authenticity. **C** is incorrect because SHA-3 can only provide message integrity, but no authenticity is supported. That can only be achieved by combining it with HMAC.

10. Jane is a system administrator and wants to download a new tool from a third-party website (the official vendor's server doesn't have enough bandwidth, and Jane achieves a very slow download speed, and the file is quite large). After downloading the tool, she calculates an MD5 hash of it. When attempting to compare the calculated MD5 hash with the official vendor's hash as stated on the vendor website, she notices they are different. After repeating the whole process, she still doesn't see the hashes matching. What would be the most probable reason for this?

A. The file that was downloaded from the third-party server is corrupted.

B. The file that was downloaded from the third-party server contains malware.

C. The file that was downloaded from the third-party server doesn't seem to be the official vendor file.

D. This is an example of a collision.

☑ **C.** A mismatch of the two hashes would commonly point to the files being different. If the file that was downloaded from the third-party website was the original file that is hosted on the official vendor's web server, the same hash should have been calculated. Since that is not the case, it mostly likely points to two different files being present.

☒ **A, B,** and **D** are incorrect. **A** is incorrect because Jane downloaded the file for a second time, as the question states the whole process was repeated. The odds of the file being corrupted in transit two times in a row are fairly slim, and as such, it is more likely that the two files are different. **B** is incorrect because although this may be a possibility, there's not enough information in the question to be certain that the file contains malware. The only thing that can be deduced with relative certainty is that the file from the third-party website seems to be different from the one on the vendor's website. **D** is incorrect because a collision would only take place if two different files had the same file hash. However, the hashes here are different so this isn't an example of collision.

11. Which of the following would be most suitable to protect files stored on a hard drive?

A. AES-128

B. TLS 1.1

C. RSA-512

D. 3-DES

☑ **A.** From the available options, AES (Advanced Encryption Standard) is the most suitable one. AES-128 is stronger than both 3-DES and RSA-256.

☒ **B, C,** and **D** are incorrect. **B** is incorrect because TLS 1.1 is used for encrypting data in motion (commonly to establish a secure communication between a client and a server for online transactions), not data at rest (like hard drive files). Even for the purpose of protecting data in motion, version 1.1 is considered obsolete and a later version should be used. The latest version is 1.3 (released in August 2018), which various companies have started adopting in their systems. **C** is incorrect because RSA is commonly used for key exchange. In addition, a key of 512 bits is not considered secure enough to provide adequate encryption (researchers suggest that an RSA-2048-bit key will be secure enough until 2030). **D** is incorrect because AES is considered 3-DES's successor, as it performs very well, whereas 3-DES is very slow, especially when implemented in software. In addition, AES offers 192- and 256-bit keys, which provide stronger encryption than the 168-bit key that 3-DES offers.

12. Which of these ports would be used when a user attempts to send an e-mail?

    A. TCP 110

    B. TCP 25

    C. UDP 53

    D. TCP 443

    ☑ **B.** Outgoing e-mail would commonly use the SMTP protocol (using TCP port 25). If its secure version was used (SMTP over TLS/SSL), then TCP port 465 would be used.

    ☒ **A, C,** and **D** are incorrect. **A** is incorrect because TCP port 110 (POP3) would be used for receiving e-mails. If its secure version was used (POP3 over TLS/SSL), then TCP port 995 would be used. **C** is incorrect because UDP port 53 is used by the DNS protocol, which facilitates the resolution of host names to IP addresses. **D** is incorrect because TCP port 443 is used by HTTPS (which is HTTP over TLS/SSL).

13. Which person is responsible for defining a company's data classification scheme?

    A. Data owner

    B. Data custodian

    C. User

    D. Management

    ☑ **D.** Management is responsible for defining an organization's data classification scheme. Not only that, the management team is also responsible for clarifying the security requirements that data of each classification level requires.

    ☒ **A, B,** and **C** are incorrect. **A** is incorrect because data owners have the responsibility of ensuring that data in each classification level is adequately protected as per what is stated in the related security policy. **B** is incorrect because a data custodian would commonly have administrative tasks relating to the data (i.e., performing regular data backups or granting data access to appropriate individuals). **C** is incorrect because a user would commonly be the one accessing data. However, note that users do have the responsibility of protecting the data they handle.

14. Which of the following would be used for a new certificate registration request?

    A. WOT

    B. RA

    C. CRL

    D. OCSP

    ☑ **B.** An RA (registration authority) can be used for an organization's certificate registration request. It is tasked with data verification, and after that is completed the request would be passed to the CA (certificate authority). Note that it is not mandatory to use an RA, but large companies do often use one. However, a request can also still just reach the CA directly.

    ☒ **A, C,** and **D** are incorrect. **A** is incorrect because a WOT (web of trust) is a decentralized trust model with the goal of allowing a system to establish authenticity between a public key and its owner. **C** is incorrect because a CRL (certificate revocation list) is a list of revoked certificates that the CA maintains and is used by clients to check a certificate's validity. **D** is incorrect because OCSP (Online Certificate Status Protocol) is another method of checking if a certificate has been revoked. The difference is that instead of a revocation list being provided (like in the case of CRL), the client would just send a request to the OCSP server asking if a certificate of interest is valid or not, and the server would return a verdict.

15. Which of these authentication protocols would you use to support mutual authentication?

    A. CHAP

    B. PAP

    C. MS-CHAPv2

    D. MS-CHAPv3

    ☑ **C.** MS-CHAPv2 is a CHAP (Challenge-Handshake Authentication Protocol) implementation by Microsoft that supports mutual authentication between client and server. This ensures that the client doesn't provide login credentials to a malicious entity that might be posing as the authentication server.

    ☒ **A, B,** and **D** are incorrect. **A** is incorrect because CHAP only supports verification of the client. **B** is incorrect because PAP uses a two-way handshake to only identify the client, so no mutual authentication is supported. **D** is incorrect because there's no MS-CHAPv3. This option is a distractor.

16. You want to ensure your company's e-mails are encrypted to maintain communication confidentiality. Which of these options would you choose for that purpose?

    A. DKIM

    B. SPF

    C. S/MIME

    D. DMARC

☑ **C.** S/MIME (Secure/Multipurpose Internet Mail Extensions) is a protocol that allows one to encrypt and digitally sign e-mails. This works by using the recipient's public key to encrypt an outgoing message. After that has been received, only the recipient can decrypt it (as that would require the recipient's private key), which ensures the security of that transaction. Furthermore, as S/MIME also supports digital signatures, a sender can sign the message that is sent so that the recipient knows it originated from a valid entity.

☒ **A, B,** and **D** are incorrect. **A** is incorrect because DKIM (Domain Keys Identified Mail) is a method of authenticating e-mail and identifying any attempt to spoof a valid sender. It doesn't support e-mail encryption; hence, it wouldn't be used to secure e-mail communications. **B** is incorrect because SPF (Sender Policy Framework) is used to authenticate e-mails and identify e-mail spoofing, not to encrypt them. Assume that you receive an e-mail originating from your bank (which is called amazing bank), sourced from e-mail account security@amazing-bank.com, asking you to change your password to a new value that is provided in the e-mail. If that e-mail is not actually sourced from "amazing bank" but is just an attempt by an attacker to spoof the source header so you are tempted to change your password to what is provided, that would be identified as forged e-mail. **D** is incorrect because DMARC (Domain-based Message Authentication, Reporting, and Conformance) is a protocol that allows organizations to specify if SPF or DKIM (or neither of them) is used and what action to take if validation fails (i.e., mark the message as spam) by publishing the relevant policy through DNS records. However, this protocol wouldn't be used for encrypting messages.

17. Consider this cipher suite:

    TLS_ECDHE_RSA_WITH_CAMELLIA_256_CBC_SHA384

    What key exchange algorithm is being used?

    A. TLS

    B. ECDHE_RSA

    C. CAMELIA_256_CBC

    D. SHA384

    ☒ **B.** A cipher suite is a collection of algorithms that ensure a network connection is secure. It consists of the communication protocol (SSL or TLS), a key exchange algorithm (accompanied by an authentication algorithm), an encryption algorithm, and an algorithm for message authentication. According to this, the key exchange algorithm is ECDHE, which means that elliptic curve Diffie-Hellman is being used for key exchange (while RSA is being used as an authentication algorithm to sign the server's ephemeral keys). A full description of ECDHE_RSA can be found in RFC 4492.

☒ **A, C,** and **D** are incorrect. **A** is incorrect because TLS states the communication protocol being used. **C** is incorrect because CAMELIA_256_CBC is the encryption algorithm being used. Camelia is a symmetric encryption block cipher with possible keys of 128, 192, and 256 bits. Here, a 256-bit key is specified. Also note that CBC indicates the encryption algorithm's mode of operation. Here, Cipher Block Chaining (CBC) is being used. **D** is incorrect because SHA384 indicates the message authentication algorithm being used, which is an SHA algorithm with a 384-bit key.

18. Your company wants to simplify the process of employees remotely connecting to the company network via VPN. The main requirement is to be able to connect using a web browser. Which of these methods would be most appropriate for that goal?

    A. TLS VPN

    B. Transport mode

    C. Tunnel mode

    D. SSH

    ☑ **A.** A TLS VPN would be the simplest way of connecting to a VPN via a web browser. Some of the advantages of this approach are the ease of use (an employee can use the company VPN from any system that has a web browser), ease of configuration (it doesn't require anything specific to be configured, since most organizations already allow HTTPS [TCP 443] traffic within their environment) and cost-efficiency (doesn't tend to require a lot of support due to the simple operation).

    ☒ **B, C,** and **D** are incorrect. **B** is incorrect because transport mode is a IPSEC mode in which only the packet payload is encrypted (not the packet header). As such, it wouldn't be used in a TLS VPN; a IPSEC VPN is a different implementation. **C** is incorrect because tunnel mode is also a IPSEC mode of operation in which the whole packet is encrypted and would only be used in a IPSEC VPN, not in a TLS VPN. **D** is incorrect because SSH (Secure Shell) isn't an option commonly used for VPNs. It is often used to encrypt communications between a client and a server (i.e., for administrative purposes) and to encrypt other protocols that are not secure by design (i.e., FTP).

19. Which of these attacks would be most suitable to an attacker who has samples of the plaintext and ciphertext messages?

    A. Rainbow table attack

    B. Dictionary attack

    C. Chosen plaintext

    D. Known plaintext

    ☑ **D.** A known plaintext attack would be preferred once an attacker is able to get samples of both the plaintext and ciphertext. During this attack, the attacker would commonly try to identify the original key used for encrypting communications.

☒ **A, B,** and **C** are incorrect. **A** is incorrect because a rainbow table attack uses precomputed hashes and is mostly used for offline attacks where the attacker has managed to obtain a copy of a system's hashed password file. **B** is incorrect because a dictionary attack would most commonly be used to try and break a user's password by trying a variety of common words contained in a dictionary. This technique is often used to access system accounts by using automated tools, which can utilize various dictionary files and try multiple combinations until a match has been identified. **C** is incorrect because during a chosen-plaintext attack, an attacker would select random plaintexts that would need to be encrypted so the corresponding ciphertexts can be obtained (but the question states that the attacker has both the plaintext and ciphertext messages already).

20. An attacker is using a text file's spaces and tabs to store information. Which of the following is this an example of?

    A. Encoding

    B. Hashing

    C. Steganography

    D. Encryption

    ☑ **C.** Steganography can be defined as a technique allowing information to be hidden within a file. In this scenario, the attacker is attempting to take advantage of the natural properties of a text file (i.e., the spaces and tabs) in order to hide information within the file without drastically changing its format. If that file is intercepted and viewed by any third party during transit, it would be very difficult at first glance to determine there's anything hidden within it. Usually, special-purpose tools are used (i.e., steganalysis suites), which can scan a file and try to identify if there's any information hidden within it.

    ☒ **A, B,** and **D** are incorrect. **A** is incorrect because encoding means that the initial information is represented in a different way after being encoded. Consider base64 encoding; the phrase "This is an SSCP book" becomes "VGhpcyBpcyBhbiBTU0NQIGJvb2s=". As you can see, the encoded output bears no resemblance to the initial phrase. **B** is incorrect because hashing uses a one-way function to generate a fixed-length output and is used for data integrity, not for concealing information. The MD5 output of the previous phrase is "efdc6672bef132dd47a4a7bc0eb8f89d". **D** is incorrect because encryption entails scrambling data in such a way that only specifically authorized individuals (i.e., that possess the decryption key) can decode it. Although this is sometimes confused with encoding, the difference is that when a simple encoding technique is used (i.e., base64), the original information is still retrievable by using the same technique to reverse the process. With encryption, the technique becomes much more complicated, as the ultimate goal is to thwart anyone from uncovering the original information. In addition to encryption being more complicated, even if the algorithm used is known, retrieving the original information without the encryption key would be very difficult. When encoding is used, decoding information when the encoding scheme is known (i.e., base64) is fairly trivial.

21. You have a file containing the sentence "This is the plaintext". You use a key of "This is my first key" and generate the following ciphertext: "yu9+m0/mY7rF/6dv6SXNVC7D69Q7b1N4". You encrypt the same file again but with a different key: "This is my second key". The result is "yu9+m0/mY7rF/6dv6SXNVC7D69Q7b1N4". What is this an example of?

A. Key clustering

B. Collision

C. Collusion

D. Work factor

☑ **A.** Key clustering takes place when the same plaintext is encrypted with two different keys and yields the same ciphertext. In this case, the plaintext is "This is the plaintext". The two keys are "This is my first key" and "This is my second key". They both yield the same ciphertext of "yu9+m0/mY7rF/6dv6SXNVC7D69Q7b1N4".

☒ **B, C,** and **D** are incorrect. **B** is incorrect because collision refers to hashing and happens when two different files generate the same file hash. MD5 is known to generate a lot of collisions, which makes it a weak hashing algorithm. **C** is incorrect because collusion refers to the act of one or more individuals or companies conspiring to commit fraud. **D** is incorrect because work factor relates to cryptography and expresses the time and effort it would take to decrypt an encrypted message.

22. You just received an e-mail from your bank account manager that your account has been breached. She kindly asks you to reset your password and emphasizes not to disclose it to anyone who may be posing as a bank employee over the phone. You follow the URL contained in her e-mail, and your browser presents you with the following message: "This connection is untrusted." What is the most likely reason for that?

A. Certificate has expired.

B. You have received a phishing e-mail.

C. Bank website experiencing technical issues.

D. A self-signed certificate is being used.

☑ **B.** The account manager should refrain from placing URL links in the e-mail and should state something like "please log in to your account and ensure that you change your password." As the question states, once the link was followed, an error about the legitimacy of the secure connection was displayed (which shouldn't normally happen with your bank's valid website). Although you can choose to disregard that error and continue to the target website (sometimes attackers will even include details of how to do that in the phishing e-mail, stating known errors are being experienced currently with a series of steps on how to bypass the browser warnings), but you should refrain from taking such actions with your banking website. If you are not sure, you should report this to your bank and ask for further guidance.

☒ **A, C,** and **D** are incorrect. **A** is incorrect because the odds of a bank having its certificate being expired are very slim. This is the primary means of verifying the validity of the bank to the clients and then establishing an encrypted connection for data transaction, so the bank should know better and not allow its certificate to expire. **C** is incorrect because if the bank's website was experiencing technical issues, that wouldn't translate to the connection being untrusted. The message points to a certificate issue or an illegitimate connection. Also, consider that when a bank faces any technical issues, it would usually alert its clients so they know about it (either directly or via an announcement on the website). **D** is incorrect because no legitimate bank would ever use a self-signed certificate for interacting with its clients. Organizations sometimes use self-signed certificates for interorganization activities, but if such activities are publicly facing, it is a poor policy to have self-signed certificates in use.

23. Which of the following would you use to check if a certificate has been revoked, using the least amount of network resources?

    A. CRL

    B. CLR

    C. RA

    D. OCSP

    ☑ **D.** From the options provided, only two relate to certificate revocation, which are A and D. OCSP (Online Certificate Status Protocol) is a protocol used to check if a certificate has been revoked, which consumes very few network resources. The client sends a request to the OCSP server containing a certificate's serial number, asking if the certificate of interest is valid or not, and the server comes back with a verdict (i.e., revoked).

    ☒ **A, B,** and **C** are incorrect. **A** is incorrect because when a CRL (certificate revocation list) is used, a full list of revoked certificates that the CA maintains would need to be sent to the client, taking more time and network resources than using OCSP. **B** is incorrect because there's no term known as CLR in use in the context of digital certificates. **C** is incorrect because an RA (registration authority) is used when an organization needs to submit a certificate registration request for a new certificate to be issued.

24. James wants to communicate with Dianne. For that purpose, he encrypts a message with Dianne's public key before sending it to her. Which of the following is he trying to enforce?

    A. Integrity

    B. Authentication

    C. Confidentiality

    D. Nonrepudiation

    ☑ **C.** When James encrypts his message with Dianne's public key, he ensures that the only person who can read the message is Dianne. As such, he's protecting the message from unauthorized disclosure, which means confidentiality is being enforced.

☒ **A, B,** and **D** are incorrect. **A** is incorrect because integrity can't be ensured by encrypting the message with Dianne's public key. Any third party that intercepts this message can still alter it in transit, and Dianne will have no way of verifying its integrity. However, integrity could be maintained if James used HMAC. **B** is incorrect because authentication can't be ensured, as anyone can send Dianne a message and encrypt it with her public key. That doesn't mean James was the one who sent her the message. If a digital certificate was used, Dianne would know this message came from James. **D** is incorrect because nonrepudiation can't be ensured, as there's no way to prove that James took the action of sending the message to Dianne. If required, a digital signature could be used in order to provide nonrepudiation.

25. If a group of eight people uses symmetric key cryptography, how many keys are required to ensure that everyone's communications are secured while each pair uses a different encryption key?

    A. 8

    B. 28

    C. 32

    D. 64

    ☑ **B.** Each pair of people will need a different key to secure all communications and ensure there's no key repetition. Here's a quick formula to find how many keys are required: If k is the number of people in the group, then the total number of keys is: Total = $[k \times (k - 1)]/2$. Since $k = 8$, that means: Total = $8 \times (8 - 1)/2 = 8 \times 7/2 = 28$.

    ☒ **A, C,** and **D** are incorrect. These are all distractors.

CHAPTER 6

Network and Communications Security

This chapter includes questions from the following objectives:

- 6.1 Understand and apply fundamental concepts of networking
- 6.2 Understand network attacks and countermeasures (e.g., DDoS, man-in-the-middle, DNS poisoning)
- 6.3 Manage network access controls
- 6.4 Manage network security
- 6.5 Operate and configure network-based security devices
- 6.6 Operate and configure wireless technologies (e.g., Bluetooth, NFC, Wi-Fi)

This chapter contains a complete set of questions and answers regarding basic and advanced networking and communications (OSI model, network topologies, basic protocols and ports, remote access solutions, and virtual environments); attacks and defenses (attack types and related countermeasures in addition to monitoring and analysis); and network access controls (network access control management and remote access solutions). It also contains questions regarding network security management (LAN security management and firewall concepts), monitoring systems, and network-based detection, as well as wireless security (types of wireless technologies and security protocols).

1. What is a datagram at the Data Link layer called?

   A. Bit

   B. Packet

   C. Frame

   D. Segment

2. Which of the following is not a part of the TCP/IP model?

   A. Application

   B. Network

   C. Transport

   D. Link

3. Which topology is the least resilient?

   A. Star

   B. Tree

   C. Mesh

   D. Bus

4. If you want to receive information about a domain's mail servers, which of these DNS records would you use?

   A. MX

   B. PTR

   C. A

   D. AAAA

5. Which of these commands doesn't use ICMP (by default)?

   A. Ping

   B. Tracert

   C. Pathping

   D. Traceroute

6. You have recently been asked to manage the network security infrastructure of your organization. As a first step, you want to implement a mechanism that can be used to obtain performance-related information (CPU and memory status) from your routers and firewalls. Which of the following would you use for that purpose?

   A. ICMP

   B. SNMP

   C. Telnet

   D. FTP

7. When an attacker sends a phishing e-mail, which of these fields would be spoofed to make it resemble a legitimate message?

   A. From

   B. To

   C. Source headers

   D. MAC address

8. During a SYN flood, an attacker first sends multiple SYN packets, while the target system responds with SYN/ACK. What does the source (attacker) respond with after that?

   A. SYN

   B. ACK

   C. SYN/ACK

   D. Nothing

9. During which of these attacks would the attacker try to capture data from a specific system?

   A. Salami attack

   B. Spoofing

   C. Active MiTM

   D. Passive MiTM

10. You receive a text message on your mobile phone stating your new phone bill has been issued, but you don't use the mobile provider that was mentioned in the message. What type of attack is this?

    A. Vishing

    B. Whaling

    C. Smishing

    D. Spear phishing

11. Which of these statements about the benefits of VLANs is inaccurate?

    A. Increased security

    B. Excellent physical segmentation

    C. Enhanced performance

    D. No additional equipment required for configuration

12. Which of these attacks uses UDP packets and requires spoofing the source IP address so it becomes the address of the victim?

    A. Fraggle

    B. Smurf

    C. LAND

    D. Ping of death

13. You are a network administrator and want to ensure connectivity between two of your internal subnets so that traffic can flow properly. Which of these devices would you most likely use?

    A. Hub

    B. Repeater

    C. Switch

    D. Router

14. A company wants to protect against employees accessing suspicious URLs. Which of the following would be the most suitable solution?

    A. WAF

    B. AV

    C. Web proxy

    D. E-mail gateway

15. You are a security architect designing a security solution for your network. You want to use a combination of firewalls from different vendors to defend the internal network and separate it from the rest of the infrastructure. Based on this description, which of the following are you trying to enforce?

    A. Defense in depth

    B. Defense diversity

    C. Multivendor approach

    D. Next-generation firewalls

16. Which of the following wouldn't be possible when using a stateful inspection firewall?

    A. Allow access to 10.10.10.0/24.

    B. Allow access to 192.168.2.5 only over port 80.

    C. Deny traffic from a host initialing a connection with an ACK packet.

    D. Deny traffic relating to video.

17. Consider a firewall that has the following ruleset (note that rules have been simplified to make it easier for the reader):

```
deny icmp any any
permit tcp any 10.2.2.2 eq 22
deny tcp any 10.2.2.2 eq www
```

    Which of these statements is inaccurate?

    A. Telnet is allowed to 10.2.2.2.

    B. ICMP is not allowed.

    C. Web traffic is not allowed to 10.2.2.2.

    D. FTP is not allowed to 10.2.2.2.

18. Which of the following would be performed by NAC?

A. Authenticate a remote client.

B. Create audit logs about the actions a machine performed while on the network.

C. Check a client machine against an organizational health policy.

D. Allow a client machine to issue specific commands.

19. Which of the following would you use to adequately secure the wireless network of a small office with ten employees, without any excessive administrative burden?

A. WEP (with AES)

B. WPA2 (with AES)

C. WEP-Enterprise

D. WPA2-Enterprise

20. You enter the subway and want to use your mobile phone to touch the reader and pay for your fare. Which protocol would you most likely use for that transaction?

A. 4G

B. WiMAX

C. RFID

D. NFC

21. Which of the following is the least effective method of securing a wireless network?

A. Hiding the SSID

B. Using MAC address filtering

C. Using WEP for security

D. Using NFC

22. Which of these attacks would allow an attacker to intercept communications?

A. Bluesnarfing

B. Bluejacking

C. Bluebugging

D. Bluetagging

23. Which of these methods for mobile device protection wouldn't be performed before a device is lost or stolen?

A. MDM

B. Full device encryption

C. Enable PIN protection

D. Remote deletion

24. You have a network composed of a hundred endpoints, ten firewalls, five routers, five IPS sensors, and three proxies across two geographical regions. Data from all of those devices is being forwarded to a SIEM platform. What would be the most crucial element for any type of security investigation you perform?

    A. Log integrity

    B. Verbose logging across all devices

    C. Appropriate alert thresholds

    D. Time synchronization

25. Which of these media types is most susceptible to electromagnetic interference?

    A. Shielded twisted pair

    B. UTP

    C. Optical fiber

    D. STP cat 6

26. In a full mesh topology consisting of ten devices, how many connections would be required?

    A. 10

    B. 20

    C. 45

    D. 90

27. Which of the following is a valid IPv6 address representation?

    A. 0:0:0:0:0:ffff:a0a:a0a

    B. 0:0:0:0:0:gggg:a0a:a0a

    C. 0:0:0:0:0:ffff:a0a

    D. ::ffff:a0a::

28. As a network administrator of a small law firm you get a call from John stating that he's unable to access the law firm's website, http://www.which-is-best-law-firm-ever.com, hosted at 10.10.10.10. (Please note that the scenario uses a private IP address but in a real-world situation this address would be a public one.) Hannah, one of John's colleagues sitting next to him, is able to access the web page just fine. You ask John to try accessing http://10.10.10.10, and the webpage loads fine, and an attempt to ping 10.10.10.10 is also successful. What is most likely the problem?

    A. DHCP server issue.

    B. Website is temporarily unavailable.

    C. The web server is blocking John's IP address.

    D. DNS server issue.

29. For management purposes, you need to ensure that administrators only use secure protocols to log-in to devices. Which of the following would be most appropriate for that?

A. SFTP

B. HTTPS

C. SSH

D. Telnet

30. You use your browser to navigate to a web page located at internal IP address 192.168.1.2, which is a web server listening on TCP port 8080. Your machine has an IP address of 10.10.10.16 and a source port of TCP 500. During the first stage of the communication (when your machine is sending the initial SYN packet to the web server), which of this information given is most probably wrong?

A. Source IP address of 10.10.10.16

B. Source TCP port 500

C. Destination IP address of 192.168.1.2

D. Destination TCP port 8080

31. Which of these methods would you choose to protect a Windows 2003 physical server that needs to directly communicate with critical infrastructure?

A. Hardening

B. VM isolation

C. Patching

D. User awareness

32. You have enhanced your network security by adding MAC address filtering. Which of these attacks can be used against that in order to gain unauthorized network access?

A. Sniffing

B. MiTM

C. Spoofing

D. Session hijacking

33. Which of the following would you use to prevent an SQL injection attack?

A. NIDS

B. Stateful inspection firewall

C. Disallow stored procedures

D. Input validation

34. Which of the following devices uses MAC addresses?

    A. Hub

    B. Switch

    C. Repeater

    D. Router

35. In which of the following would you configure ERSPAN so you mirror traffic to your NIDS?

    A. Riverbed switch.

    B. Cisco Catalyst switch.

    C. MikroTik router.

    D. None of the above support ERSPAN.

36. As a network administrator you are asked to select the most cost-effective security device that can filter based on the following criteria:

    • IP addresses/subnets

    • Specific ports

    Which of these devices would be more suitable in this case?

    A. Router

    B. Stateful inspection firewall

    C. Packet-filtering firewall

    D. IDS

37. Which of these types of attackers would probably target a military installation to obtain new research and development (R&D) plans?

    A. APT

    B. Script kiddie

    C. Hacktivist

    D. White hat

38. During a DDoS attack, who would be responsible for issuing commands?

    A. Botnet

    B. Zombie

    C. Victim

    D. Bot herder

39. Which of the following needs to take place so your machine can capture all the wireless transmissions within your device's range?

    A. An external USB-wireless adapter is required.

    B. Wireless NIC set to nonpromiscuous mode.

    C. Wireless NIC set to promiscuous mode.

    D. Wireless network needs to be open (i.e., not have any security protocol enabled).

40. Which of the following is a valid WPA-PSK preshared key?

    A. KsIA349

    B. AK09EYei

    C. £jh85418

    D. RΣ98*6Te

1. C	11. B	21. A	31. A
2. B	12. A	22. C	32. C
3. D	13. D	23. D	33. D
4. A	14. C	24. D	34. B
5. D	15. B	25. B	35. B
6. B	16. D	26. C	36. C
7. A	17. A	27. A	37. A
8. D	18. C	28. D	38. D
9. C	19. B	29. C	39. C
10. C	20. D	30. B	40. B

1. What is a datagram at the Data Link layer called?

   A. Bit

   B. Packet

   C. Frame

   D. Segment

    ☑ **C.** Each OSI layer adds more information to the original data. When data initially arrives at a machine, it comes in the form of binary 0 and 1 (reaching the Physical layer, where it is known as "bit"), but once that is passed to the Data Link layer, it is then called a "frame." At that layer MAC (media access control) addresses are used, which uniquely identify a NIC (network interface card).

    ☒ **A, B,** and **D** are incorrect. **A** is incorrect because a datagram is called a bit at the Physical layer, where data is converted from binary 0 and 1 to streams of bits. **B** is incorrect because a datagram is called a packet at the Network layer. In this layer, IP addresses are used and routing takes place to ensure packets are appropriately routed to their final destination. **D** is incorrect because a datagram is known as a segment at the Transport layer, which is where error detection and establishment of reliable communications take place.

2. Which of the following is not a part of the TCP/IP model?

   A. Application

   B. Network

   C. Transport

   D. Link

    ☑ **B.** The Network layer is a term used in the OSI model, not TCP/IP. TCP/IP uses Internet layer to refer to the respective Network layer of the OSI model.

    ☒ **A, C,** and **D** are incorrect. **A** is incorrect because TCP/IP uses the Application layer to map three of the OSI model layers (Application, Presentation, and Session). **C** is incorrect because OSI's Transport layer is named Transport in the TCP/IP model (note that it is also known as Host-to-Host layer). **D** is incorrect because TCP/IP uses the Link layer (also known as Network Access layer) to map OSI's Physical and Data Link layers.

3. Which topology is the least resilient?

   A. Star

   B. Tree

   C. Mesh

   D. Bus

☑ **D.** When using a bus topology, any issue with one of the connected devices will bring the whole network to a halt. A bus topology uses T connectors for connectivity. That means that one end of a computer is connected to the bus and the other is connected to the next computer. If one of the computers or T connectors experiences an issue, the whole network stops working. In addition, if a lot of machines are connected to that network, identifying the issue may require vast amounts of time. This means the network will not be usable until the issue is resolved.

☒ **A, B,** and **C** are incorrect. **A** is incorrect because a star topology commonly uses a switch to allow the various machines to connect, which means that any issue with one machine doesn't affect the network's overall operation. **B** is incorrect because a tree topology uses a combination of a bus and a star, where multiple star networks connect over a common bus. If the bus experiences an issue, all the star networks are disconnected until the issue is resolved. **C** is incorrect because in a mesh topology, all machines are individually connected with each other, meaning that any issues with one connection don't affect the operation of the network.

4. If you want to receive information about a domain's mail servers, which of these DNS records would you use?

   A. MX

   B. PTR

   C. A

   D. AAAA

   ☑ **A.** "MX" (mail exchange) is the type of record responsible for providing information about mail servers. A security analyst will often use a command like "nslookup," in which a specific parameter for MX records can be specified (which is set q = MX) to only return mail server–related information.

   ☒ **B, C,** and **D** are incorrect. **B** is incorrect because "PTR" (pointer) records are used to resolve an IP address to a corresponding host name, which is what a reverse lookup would use. **C** is incorrect because an "A" (host) record would normally be used for a DNS request trying to resolve a host name to an IPv4 address. **D** is incorrect because an "AAAA" (host) record would normally be used for a DNS request trying to resolve a host name to an IPv6 address.

5. Which of these commands doesn't use ICMP (by default)?

   A. Ping

   B. Tracert

   C. Pathping

   D. Traceroute

   ☑ **D.** Traceroute is a Linux/UNIX command that uses UDP by default. It is used for checking the route of the traffic towards a destination.

☒ **A, B,** and **C** are incorrect. **A** is incorrect because ping uses ICMP packets and is used to check if there's connectivity between two hosts. **B** is incorrect because tracert is used for checking the route of the traffic towards a destination, but the difference is that tracert uses ICMP to accomplish this. **C** is incorrect because pathping also uses ICMP to track the intermediate hops between a source and destination and provides network latency information.

6. You have recently been asked to manage the network security infrastructure of your organization. As a first step, you want to implement a mechanism that can be used to obtain performance-related information (CPU and memory status) from your routers and firewalls. Which of the following would you use for that purpose?

   A. ICMP

   B. SNMP

   C. Telnet

   D. FTP

   ☑ **B.** SNMP (Simple Network Management Protocol) is used extensively for network device management. It can be used to communicate with a monitored device for a variety of tasks, like to query about its current state (i.e., current CPU utilization or free disk and memory levels).

   ☒ **A, C,** and **D** are incorrect. **A** is incorrect because ICMP is mostly used for diagnostic purposes by commands like ping and tracert. **C** is incorrect because Telnet is commonly used for connecting remotely to a system using basic commands via command line. **D** is incorrect because FTP (File Transfer Protocol) is used for file transfers.

7. When an attacker sends a phishing e-mail, which of these fields would be spoofed to make it resemble a legitimate message?

   A. From

   B. To

   C. Source headers

   D. MAC address

   ☑ **A.** In order for any attacker to be able to resemble a legitimate message, the "From" field would need to be spoofed to include a legitimate sender. Think of an example in which you receive an e-mail from someone claiming to be your account manager at Magic Bank. The "From" field might be something like "account-management@magic-bank .com," which would entice you to open it and follow any instructions (like navigating to a URL) it contains, thinking it's from your legitimate account manager.

   ☒ **B, C,** and **D** are incorrect. **B** is incorrect because there's no point in spoofing the "To" field, as the recipient would be the true victim of the phishing attack. **C** is incorrect because a message's headers will have information about what "path" the message used to reach you. In this example, the actual "Received" header field would not state "account-management@magic-bank.com," but rather the actual e-mail account that was used to send this message. **D** is incorrect because the MAC address isn't displayed to the victim so it wouldn't make any difference if it's real or not.

8. During a SYN flood, an attacker first sends multiple SYN packets, while the target system responds with SYN/ACK. What does the source (attacker) respond with after that?

   A. SYN

   B. ACK

   C. SYN/ACK

   D. Nothing

   ☑ **D.** A SYN flood aims to overwhelm the target system with half-open connections. In order for that to happen, after a source sends a SYN packet and a destination responds with SYN/ACK, no other packet is sent. However, the target system will still have the connection information in its connection table, thus occupying space, and will wait for a completion of that connection with a final ACK from the source (which never comes).

   ☒ **A, B,** and **C** are incorrect. **A** is incorrect because a SYN packet would have been sent when the connection was initiated. **B** is incorrect because an ACK packet would normally be sent from the source to complete the three-way handshake in the case that this wasn't a SYN flood but a legitimate connection request. **C** is incorrect because a SYN/ACK would only be sent from the target after receiving a request for a connection (SYN packet) from the source.

9. During which of these attacks would the attacker try to capture data from a specific system?

   A. Salami attack

   B. Spoofing

   C. Active MiTM

   D. Passive MiTM

   ☑ **C.** During an active MiTM (man in the middle) attack, an attacker would use a sniffing tool (i.e., Wireshark) to capture traffic of interest from one specific system (or systems).

   ☒ **A, B,** and **D** are incorrect. **A** is incorrect because a salami attack aims at taking advantage of small actions that may lead to a large outcome when combined—for example, an attacker using DNS to exfiltrate small chunks of data and after several days or weeks of effort managing to extract a rather large file with proprietary organizational data. **B** is incorrect because during a spoofing attack, the attacker would attempt to spoof the IP or MAC address he or she has been assigned to make it look like his or her machine is a legitimate network device. **D** is incorrect because during a passive MiTM attack, the attacker would try to capture traffic from any system (contrary to an active MiTM, where specific systems would be targeted).

10. You receive a text message on your mobile phone stating your new phone bill has been issued, but you don't use the mobile provider that was mentioned in the message. What type of attack is this?

   A. Vishing

   B. Whaling

   C. Smishing

   D. Spear phishing

   ☑ **C.** Smishing is a type of attack that uses text messages as an attack vector. Typically, a text message would be sent to the victim about a utility bill or online purchase confirmation or even a contest with a prize. Regardless of the context, the message will usually contain a URL, which the victim is requested to navigate to for an action to be completed, which, of course, is used to have the victim enter personal details or run a possible exploit.

   ☒ **A, B,** and **D** are incorrect. **A** is incorrect because vishing doesn't use text messages, but rather the actual phone to place a call to the victim (or notify the victim to call the attacker) and convince them to provide personal details or perform a specific action. **B** is incorrect because whaling is a type of phishing attack where an executive is targeted and a phishing e-mail is sent to that victim. However, no text messages are used to deliver the attack. **D** is incorrect because a spear phishing attack uses e-mail as an attack vector. This message is sent to various individuals (commonly working in the same company or team) in the hope that a URL that is included in the message will be followed and credentials provided or a specific file (attached to the message) run for an action to be invoked.

11. Which of these statements about the benefits of VLANs is inaccurate?

   A. Increased security

   B. Excellent physical segmentation

   C. Enhanced performance

   D. No additional equipment required for configuration

   ☑ **B.** VLANs (virtual local area networks) work by virtually segmenting the network and not providing physical segmentation. The way a VLAN operates is by allowing a network administrator to configure specific devices (connected to one or more switches) as parts of a VLAN. The devices can be in the same room or in different floors of a building and still be able to communicate with each other as if they were physically connected.

   ☒ **A, C,** and **D** are incorrect. **A** is incorrect because VLANs offer increased security, as they separate broadcast domains (similar to a router). That means no other devices can intercept the traffic of a specific VLAN, allowing for greater security. **C** is incorrect because VLANs offer enhanced performance because less broadcast traffic is required, since broadcast traffic will now be sent to the related VLAN only. **D** is incorrect because if existing switches support VLAN configuration, no additional equipment is required to configure them.

12. Which of these attacks uses UDP packets and requires spoofing the source IP address so it becomes the address of the victim?

   A. Fraggle

   B. Smurf

   C. LAND

   D. Ping of death

   ☑ **A.** A fraggle attack works by using UDP packets while spoofing the source IP address so it becomes the address of the victim. It targets UDP 7 (echo protocol, which will make the operation work similarly with ping) or UDP 19 (character generation protocol, which will make the target system respond with a random character when it receives traffic over that port).

   ☒ **B, C,** and **D** are incorrect. **B** is incorrect because a smurf attack uses ICMP packets while sending traffic to various network hosts with a spoofed IP address to match the victim. That way, any ICMP reply packets will go to the victim, thus overwhelming it with traffic. **C** is incorrect because a LAND attack makes a target machine continuously send traffic to itself, since the packets have both the source and destination IP address of the victim. **D** is incorrect because a "ping of death" attack changes the size of a ping packet to 64KB or more, which has been known to cause crashes, especially to older machines.

13. You are a network administrator and want to ensure connectivity between two of your internal subnets so that traffic can flow properly. Which of these devices would you most likely use?

   A. Hub

   B. Repeater

   C. Switch

   D. Router

   ☑ **D.** A router can be used so that traffic between two different subnets can be properly routed to any machine. Routers are used for forwarding packets within different networks by use of internal routing tables (either using static routes or dynamic routing protocols).

   ☒ **A, B,** and **C** are incorrect. **A** is incorrect because a hub is unable to route traffic to different networks and is commonly used to connect machines over a common network. **B** is incorrect because a repeater is used to regenerate the signal in order to allow it to reach longer distances, so it wouldn't be suitable in this scenario. **C** is incorrect because a switch is used to connect devices over a local area network and wouldn't be appropriate for routing traffic between different networks. Please note that there are also layer 3 switches that have a lot of functionality and combine functions of a switch and a router. Those types of devices would be able to route traffic accordingly, but the question doesn't mention layer 3 switches. In addition, the question asks what you would "most likely use," and commonly a router would be used to route traffic between different networks.

14. A company wants to protect against employees accessing suspicious URLs. Which of the following would be the most suitable solution?

   A. WAF

   B. AV

   C. Web proxy

   D. E-mail gateway

   ☑ **C.** A web proxy would be the most suitable solution, as it has the ability to filter all web requests (i.e., the URLs that the employees will navigate to), and if any of them are found to be suspicious, it can block the content from specific websites. Furthermore, browsing categories can be specified for the staff, and if an individual is not authorized to browse a specific category, that won't be allowed, regardless if the destination page is malicious or not.

   ☒ **A, B,** and **D** are incorrect. **A** is incorrect because a WAF (web application firewall) would be suitable to protect the business against any application attack, like an attacker trying to use cross-site scripting or an SQL injection attack, but that wouldn't be used for filtering user web traffic. **B** is incorrect because an AV (antivirus) tool would be useful to identify any malicious activity at an endpoint level (e.g., suspicious file execution or malicious processes running). Although a lot of modern antivirus applications do offer web filtering, that's a different component, and the question doesn't specify if the AV has web filtering capabilities in place, thus not making this the most suitable answer. **D** is incorrect because an e-mail gateway would be used to filter any e-mails for suspicious content (including malicious URLs), but that can only filter e-mail content. It won't help to filter any user's web traffic since that is not associated with e-mail (i.e., user opening a browser and navigating to a malicious website).

15. You are a security architect designing a security solution for your network. You want to use a combination of firewalls from different vendors to defend the internal network and separate it from the rest of the infrastructure. Based on this description, which of the following are you trying to enforce?

   A. Defense in depth

   B. Defense diversity

   C. Multivendor approach

   D. Next-generation firewalls

   ☑ **B.** The term defense diversity describes the use of different vendors in order to provide resiliency in case of any issues with one (or some) of them. That means that if for some reason one of these firewalls fails to provide adequate protection or it is affected by a possible zero-day exploit, the other one(s) can still protect the corporate environment.

☒ **A, C,** and **D** are incorrect. **A** is incorrect because defense in depth describes the use of a layered defense in which several defenses are in place that the attacker would need to penetrate to access any data. For example, there might be a border router at the perimeter (with properly configured access lists), followed by a firewall, an IPS, and other devices, all of which would need to be defeated if an attacker wanted to obtain access to sensitive data. **C** is incorrect because there's no such term as multivendor approach used in security. The correct terms are defense in depth and defense diversity. This option is a distractor. **D** is incorrect because all of the firewalls could very well be next-generation devices but that doesn't mean you are trying to enforce that. You are still trying to enforce defense diversity, and in order to do that you are using next-generation firewalls.

16. Which of the following wouldn't be possible when using a stateful inspection firewall?

    A. Allow access to 10.10.10.0/24.

    B. Allow access to 192.168.2.5 only over port 80.

    C. Deny traffic from a host initialing a connection with an ACK packet.

    D. Deny traffic relating to video.

    ☑ **D.** A stateful inspection firewall can work as a traditional packet-filtering firewall, plus it offers the added benefit of being able to track the state of connections via a stateful inspection table. That means traffic will only be allowed if it relates to an already established session or a valid new connection (assuming the ruleset allows it). However, it's not able to perform protocol inspection, which is what would be required in order to inspect traffic and classify it as video while afterwards taking an appropriate action regarding it (i.e., permit or deny).

    ☒ **A, B,** and **C** are incorrect. **A** is incorrect because it is very easy to allow access to a specific subnet using just features from a traditional packet-filtering firewall. **B** is incorrect because allowing access to a specific host over a specific port is again something that a stateful inspection firewall can perform. **C** is incorrect because a stateful inspection firewall can monitor traffic and drop any malformed packets (i.e., if a client sends a request to start a connection with something other than a SYN packet, the firewall can deny that traffic).

17. Consider a firewall that has the following ruleset (note that rules have been simplified to make it easier for the reader):

    ```
    deny icmp any any
    permit tcp any 10.2.2.2 eq 22
    deny tcp any 10.2.2.2 eq www
    ```

    Which of these statements is inaccurate?

    A. Telnet is allowed to 10.2.2.2.

    B. ICMP is not allowed.

    C. Web traffic is not allowed to 10.2.2.2.

    D. FTP is not allowed to 10.2.2.2.

☑ **A.** Based on the ruleset, Telnet is not allowed to 10.2.2.2. There's no rule relating to Telnet (only one for SSH: TCP port 22). This means that once the firewall applies the current rules to find a match, it will reach the end of the ruleset, where there is an implicit deny rule. That means that whatever traffic was not explicitly allowed earlier, will now be denied.

☒ **B, C,** and **D** are incorrect. **B** is incorrect because ICMP is not allowed as per the first rule. **C** is incorrect because web traffic is not allowed to 10.2.2.2 as per the third rule (denying traffic to 10.2.2.2 over port www, which is web traffic). **D** is incorrect because FTP is not allowed to 10.2.2.2. Because there's no rule allowing FTP, after the existing rules are examined for a match, the implicit deny rule will be applied, which will deny any FTP traffic (since it wasn't explicitly allowed earlier).

18. Which of the following would be performed by NAC?

    A. Authenticate a remote client.

    B. Create audit logs about the actions a machine performed while on the network.

    C. Check a client machine against an organizational health policy.

    D. Allow a client machine to issue specific commands.

    ☑ **C.** A NAC (Network Access Control) device is primarily used to check if a client that is requesting to connect to the corporate network fulfills the minimum requirements to be allowed to join the network. If that is the case, a NAC device will allow the client to connect. If not, the client will usually be restricted to a quarantined network until it achieves the minimum company security requirements.

    ☒ **A, B,** and **D** are incorrect. **A** is incorrect because the authentication of a remote client would happen by an authentication server (i.e., RADIUS or TACACS+). **B** is incorrect because a NAC device wouldn't be able to perform auditing of a network client. That is a task that needs to be performed by the authentication server (i.e., a server supporting AAA, like RADIUS, TACACS+, or Diameter). **D** is incorrect because reviewing a client's permissions to issue specific commands takes place during the authorization process (which typically happens when a client logs on using an AAA server).

19. Which of the following would you use to adequately secure the wireless network of a small office with ten employees, without any excessive administrative burden?

    A. WEP (with AES)

    B. WPA2 (with AES)

    C. WEP-Enterprise

    D. WPA2-Enterprise

    ☑ **B.** The best solution to provide adequate security without added administrative requirements would be WPA2 (with AES). It allows the use of AES encryption, while it ensures that the old and insecure WEP protocol is not used but without going to the extent of using WPA2-Enteprise, which requires an authentication server to be implemented.

☒ **A, C,** and **D** are incorrect. **A** is incorrect because WEP is an insecure wireless protocol that doesn't support AES but actually uses RC-4. **C** is incorrect, as there's no enterprise mode in WEP. This option is a distractor. **D** is incorrect because WPA2-Enterprise could be used as the most secure option from the ones provided (as it supports the use of an authentication server, like RADIUS, which would be used to authenticate clients to the network). However, that comes with an added administrative cost of configuring and maintaining an authentication server, which would possibly be too much overhead for a small office of ten people.

20. You enter the subway and want to use your mobile phone to touch the reader and pay for your fare. Which protocol would you most likely use for that transaction?

    A. 4G

    B. WiMAX

    C. RFID

    D. NFC

    ☑ **D.** NFC (near field communication) is a protocol that allows various devices (including smartphones that support it) to make contactless payments. This is the equivalent of using a contactless debit or credit card. Note that this protocol also allows for devices in close proximity (usually around 3 to 4 inches) to connect and exchange data.

    ☒ **A, B,** and **C** are incorrect. **A** is incorrect because 4G is a protocol that allows mobile devices (like phones and tablets) to perform tasks, like use mobile web browsing, make video calls, and access social and streaming media. **B** is incorrect because WiMAX (Worldwide Interoperability for Microwave Access) is a wireless protocol (also known as Wireless MAN) that allows a wireless network to span large areas (with an approximate radius of 30 miles). **C** is incorrect because RFID (radio frequency identification) is commonly used for tagging and inventory control. You can tag your suitcase with an RFID chip to ensure you are able to locate it in the event that it gets lost or stolen while you travel.

21. Which of the following is the least effective method of securing a wireless network?

    A. Hiding the SSID

    B. Using MAC address filtering

    C. Using WEP for security

    D. Using NFC

    ☑ **A.** Hiding the SSID (service set identifier) means disabling the network's SSID broadcasting feature, with the goal of hiding the network's existence. However, this doesn't really offer actual protection against an attacker with even elementary skills. That's because the SSID name is still part of the control frames being sent, so if anyone attempts to use a packet analyzer (like Wireshark) to capture the traffic, they can identify the network's SSID.

    ☒ **B, C,** and **D** are incorrect. **B** is incorrect because using MAC address filtering is better than hiding the network's SSID. In order for an attacker to gain access to the network, the first thing to do would be to identify a MAC address that is allowed on the network and then take the additional step of spoofing his or her MAC address to pose as one of the legitimate machines. **C** is incorrect because using WEP doesn't offer optimal security (as it is easily defeated) but at least the network doesn't remain open so anyone can connect to it; in addition, in order for someone to crack WEP, basic skills are still required. **D** is incorrect because NFC (near field communication) is a protocol that allows various devices (including smartphones that support it) to make contactless payments or perform data transactions. However, it's unable to secure a wireless network, thus making it an invalid option.

22. Which of these attacks would allow an attacker to intercept communications?

    A. Bluesnarfing

    B. Bluejacking

    C. Bluebugging

    D. Bluetagging

    ☑ **C.** Bluebugging would be used by an attacker in order to control a Bluetooth-enabled device (often used to target phones). Common tasks that can be performed are remotely controlling a device, sending/reading text messages, placing/intercepting calls, and setting call forwarding.

    ☒ **A, B,** and **D** are incorrect. **A** is incorrect because bluesnarfing takes advantage of the fact that some Bluetooth-enabled devices are set to be discovered by default, and if such a device is susceptible to bluesnarfing, the attacker may be able to connect to that device by pairing with it and obtain information like the phone book or calendar files but not intercept communications. **B** is incorrect because bluejacking (being the most harmless Bluetooth attack in comparison to bluesnarfing and bluebugging) allows an attacker to use Bluetooth to send short messages to any neighboring devices susceptible to bluejacking. However, other than sending a short message, this attack doesn't really offer the attacker anything else (certainly not the ability to intercept communications). **D** is incorrect because there's no associated Bluetooth attack known as bluetagging. This term is a distractor.

23. Which of these methods for mobile device protection wouldn't be performed before a device is lost or stolen?

    A. MDM

    B. Full device encryption

    C. Enable PIN protection

    D. Remote deletion

    ☑ **D.** From the provided options, remote deletion is the only method that would be performed after the device is lost or stolen. Obviously, you can remotely delete your device at any moment in time, but clearly that would only make sense after that device has been verified as lost or stolen.

⊠ **A, B,** and **C** are incorrect. **A** is incorrect because an MDM (Mobile Device Management) tool would be used to enroll the device under its supervision once the device is initially handed over to the user (typically an employee of a company implementing the MDM solution). **B** is incorrect because the device's full encryption option (if such an option is supported by the device) would need to be configured before that is lost or stolen. Once the configuration has been made, the device starts being fully encrypted. **C** is incorrect because a PIN (personal identification number) would need to be configured to protect the device before that is lost or stolen. If a company policy is in place, it will commonly force the user to set a four- to six-digit PIN to ensure that the phone never remains unlocked so any sensitive data remains protected at all times.

24. You have a network composed of a hundred endpoints, ten firewalls, five routers, five IPS sensors, and three proxies across two geographical regions. Data from all of those devices is being forwarded to a SIEM platform. What would be the most crucial element for any type of security investigation you perform?

    A. Log integrity

    B. Verbose logging across all devices

    C. Appropriate alert thresholds

    D. Time synchronization

    ☑ **D.** For any effective investigation to take place, appropriate time synchronization needs to be present for all the devices across the network. Even with a handful of devices, like five to six, analysis can become very complicated when those devices are not in a common time zone (i.e., UTC). Imagine you receive an alert from the SIEM with a time stamp of 14:00 UTC-8 (which might be the time zone of the tool or the location where it is installed) and you log in to individual devices to investigate further. Some of them are in UTC+4 and others in UTC-2. How are you going to be able to track a specific attacker's activities across all those time zones?

    ⊠ **A, B,** and **C** are incorrect. **A** is incorrect because log integrity is crucial, but in this scenario the logs are being forwarded to a SIEM tool, which stores copies of them, so a good level of integrity is present. **B** is incorrect because verbose logging across various devices might be too intense (depending on the amount of traffic and device type) and cause issues with them, while it also consumes a lot of network bandwidth. SIEM platforms use EPS (events per second), and as that increases, the cost of the tool grows exponentially—not to mention that a more robust architecture will be required in order to cope with the excessive traffic being forwarded to the SIEM tool. However, if there's no time synchronization, even with an abundance of data, it will be very difficult to identify crucial artifacts of any attack. **C** is incorrect because for any SIEM to work effectively, appropriate alert thresholds need to be configured; however, those can be gradually defined as the tool is being used. Lack of time synchronization will pose a greater challenge when investigating malicious activities across logs of various devices in different regions (and various time zones).

25. Which of these media types is most susceptible to electromagnetic interference?

   A. Shielded twisted pair

   B. UTP

   C. Optical fiber

   D. STP cat 6

   ☑ **B.** UTP (unshielded twisted pair) is a cable type that is very commonly used in computer networks (especially for short to medium distances), CCTV circuits, and telephone systems, as it's very cost effective. However, its greatest disadvantage is that it is susceptible to both electromagnetic and radio frequency interference.

   ☒ **A, C,** and **D** are incorrect. **A** is incorrect because shielded twisted pair (STP) uses additional shielding to reduce the effect of electromagnetic interference. Although it is more expensive as a result, it is often used for outdoors implementations and signal transmissions over large distances. **C** is incorrect because optical fiber cabling uses light to transmit data and as such is not susceptible to electromagnetic interference. It's often used in high-speed networks and can allow high data transmission speeds over large distances, while also offering enhanced security in comparison to traditional media, like copper cables. **D** is incorrect because STP Cat 6 (also known as category 6) is a type of STP cable that is less prone to electromagnetic interference than common UTP cables.

26. In a full mesh topology consisting of ten devices, how many connections would be required?

   A. 10

   B. 20

   C. 45

   D. 90

   ☑ **C.** In a full mesh topology, each device uses multiple connections and is individually connected to every other device, thus offering enhanced availability. In order to identify the appropriate number of connections, you can use one of two options. Either create a diagram with ten nodes and interconnect those while counting how many lines are required for the connections or use a mathematical formula to obtain the result faster. Assuming h is the number of the devices in the model, the formula is $h \times (h - 1)/2$. Since $h = 10$, that makes the total: $10 \times (10 - 1)/2 = 45$ connections.

   ☒ **A, B,** and **D** are incorrect. These are distractors.

27. Which of the following is a valid IPv6 address representation?

   A. 0:0:0:0:0:ffff:a0a:a0a

   B. 0:0:0:0:0:gggg:a0a:a0a

   C. 0:0:0:0:0:ffff:a0a

   D. ::ffff:a0a::

☑ **A.** A valid IPv6 address representation uses only hexadecimal characters in eight groups of four characters each. For display purposes, leading (not trailing) zeros can be omitted, and a group of consecutive zeros can be represented by a "::" character only once. The only answer that fulfills all these requirements is option A.

☒ **B, C,** and **D** are incorrect. **B** is incorrect, as it includes an invalid segment ("gggg") instead of only using appropriate hexadecimal numbers. **C** is incorrect because it uses seven groups of characters, not eight (without any legitimate display compression taking place). **D** is incorrect because the display compression is wrong, as it includes two sets of "::" when only one is allowed.

28. As a network administrator of a small law firm you get a call from John stating that he's unable to access the law firm's website, http://www.which-is-best-law-firm-ever.com, hosted at 10.10.10.10. (Please note that the scenario uses a private IP address but in a real-world situation this address would be a public one.) Hannah, one of John's colleagues sitting next to him, is able to access the web page just fine. You ask John to try accessing http://10.10.10.10, and the webpage loads fine, and an attempt to ping 10.10.10.10 is also successful. What is most likely the problem?

A. DHCP server issue.

B. Website is temporarily unavailable.

C. The web server is blocking John's IP address.

D. DNS server issue.

☑ **D.** Let's summarize the information provided in the question. John is unable to access the law firm's website, but Hannah is able to access that just fine, likely pointing to the fact there's no website issue. At the same time, John is able to access the website using its IP address and manages to ping that IP successfully, indicating communication between John's machine and the web server is also working properly. The difference between accessing the page on a browser and using the web server's IP address in the browser is that in the first case John's machine will use DNS to do a lookup and identify the web server that the web page is hosted at. If the DNS server is not working or the DNS server settings on John's machine are not correct, then this lookup will fail, thus not allowing the web page to be accessed.

☒ **A, B,** and **C** are incorrect. **A** is incorrect because there's no indication of a DHCP server issue. Although the question doesn't specify if a DHCP server is in use, the fact that John is able to ping the web server successfully means that John's machine has a properly configured IP address, so a DHCP issue doesn't seem to be present. **B** is incorrect because Hannah managed to access the website, so there doesn't seem to be any issues with its availability. **C** is incorrect because if something was blocking John's IP address, he wouldn't be able to ping the server successfully. Of course, it's technically possible for a device (i.e., a firewall) to only block specific traffic from John's machine (i.e., web traffic), but it is highly unlikely that the web server would block web traffic from John's machine, as there is no information in the question to support that.

29. For management purposes, you need to ensure that administrators only use secure protocols to log-in to devices. Which of the following would be most appropriate for that?

A. SFTP

B. HTTPS

C. SSH

D. Telnet

☑ **C.** SSH (Secure Shell) is most commonly used for remote administration of devices, as it supports encrypted communication and is capable of protecting any related data transaction (i.e., password exchange or command output).

☒ **A, B,** and **D** are incorrect. **A** is incorrect because SFTP does offer encryption, but it only allows for file transfers to take place, so it's not very useful for device management, which would most likely require various commands to be issued. **B** is incorrect because HTTPS is commonly used to secure a browser communication between a client and server, like in the case of a user logging in to his or her bank account. Although some devices support management over HTTPS, not all of them do, and administrators tend not to use HTTPS to access a device's GUI, as it's often unstable and doesn't allow them to run command scripts to allow for easy maintenance. **D** is incorrect because Telnet is an insecure protocol that doesn't offer encryption, so any communication over Telnet can be easily intercepted by an attacker, who would then be able to obtain sensitive data.

30. You use your browser to navigate to a web page located at internal IP address 192.168.1.2, which is a web server listening on TCP port 8080. Your machine has an IP address of 10.10.10.16 and a source port of TCP 500. During the first stage of the communication (when your machine is sending the initial SYN packet to the web server), which of this information given is most probably wrong?

A. Source IP address of 10.10.10.16

B. Source TCP port 500

C. Destination IP address of 192.168.1.2

D. Destination TCP port 8080

☑ **B.** TCP port 500 falls within the well-known port range 0 to 1023 and as such, it wouldn't be used by a system as a source port. Only a port from the dynamic range (49152 through 65535) would be used for that purpose. Various operating systems may have a slightly different pool of ports that are used as source ports, but they would certainly not use any of the well-known ones.

☒ **A, C,** and **D** are incorrect. **A** is incorrect because a source IP address of 10.10.10.16 is a valid private IP address. **C** is incorrect because a destination IP address of 192.168.1.2 is also a valid address for an internal web server. **D** is incorrect because TCP port 8080 may not be the standard TCP 80 port that a web server listens to by default, but 8080 can be configured for that purpose, as it's not one of the well-known ports.

31. Which of these methods would you choose to protect a Windows 2003 physical server that needs to directly communicate with critical infrastructure?

    A. Hardening

    B. VM isolation

    C. Patching

    D. User awareness

    ☑ **A.** The most effective method to protect a legacy system that requires direct critical infrastructure communication is to perform system hardening. That way, although the operating system is quite old, the attack surface will be reduced to only include required services.

    ☒ **B, C,** and **D** are incorrect. **B** is incorrect because the question states that this machine needs to directly communicate with critical infrastructure, so isolating it by using a virtual machine will not help in that regard. In addition, the question states the server is a physical machine. As this is a legacy device and no support is provided anymore, trying to migrate it to a virtual machine for isolation might create additional issues. **C** is incorrect because there's no support for Windows Server 2003 anymore (extended support ended in 2015), which means that no new patches are available for this operating system. **D** is incorrect because user awareness would entail educating users about browsing habits and what activities to avoid performing, but since this is a server and not a user machine, that will have little effect.

32. You have enhanced your network security by adding MAC address filtering. Which of these attacks can be used against that in order to gain unauthorized network access?

    A. Sniffing

    B. MiTM

    C. Spoofing

    D. Session hijacking

    ☑ **C.** An attacker can use a packet analyzer and identify a legitimate machine's MAC address. Following that, the attacker would spoof the attacking machine's MAC address to a legitimate MAC address in order to be allowed access to the network.

    ☒ **A, B,** and **D** are incorrect. **A** is incorrect because a sniffing attack would commonly be used to obtain data being transferred in an unencrypted format (i.e., Telnet, FTP, and other similar protocols). Although an attacker would typically use sniffing to intercept the traffic and identify a legitimate MAC address that can be used for spoofing the attacking machine's address, it is the actual spoofing that allows the MAC address filtering mechanism to be defeated, not the initial sniffing that would be performed. **B** is incorrect because an MiTM (man in the middle) attack allows data between systems to be intercepted, but that wouldn't be used to defeat MAC address filtering. **D** is incorrect because a session hijacking attack entails an attacker intercepting traffic between systems (similar to an MiTM attack), with the intent of obtaining information about an established session that will be later used to impersonate one of the communication ends. If an attacker manages to steal a user's session cookie during a communication with a server, that could be used later to establish a session with the server and try to impersonate the original user.

33. Which of the following would you use to prevent an SQL injection attack?

A. NIDS

B. Stateful inspection firewall

C. Disallow stored procedures

D. Input validation

☑ **D.** Enforcing input validation is a very good countermeasure against SQL injection attacks. For example, when a website is requesting the age of a user, that field should be restricted to only contain numbers, since nothing else would be included in a user's age. That way, no special characters can be used for SQL injection (i.e., "--", ";").

☒ **A, B,** and **C** are incorrect. **A** is incorrect because a NIDS has the ability to identify an SQL injection attack but is unable to prevent it. It can only provide an alert so a security administrator or analyst can review the event and take further action. **B** is incorrect because a stateful inspection firewall doesn't have the ability to filter web application requests, meaning it wouldn't be able to detect or prevent such an attack. **C** is incorrect because stored procedures can also be used to prevent SQL injection attacks by allowing the stored procedure to accept the user's data as input and then use predefined SQL statements to have that data inserted, thus not allowing a user to manipulate the SQL fields of a website's form, for example. As such, this feature should be enabled in order to prevent an SQL injection attack, but the answer states it shouldn't be allowed, thus making this option incorrect.

34. Which of the following devices uses MAC addresses?

A. Hub

B. Switch

C. Repeater

D. Router

☑ **B.** A switch is used to connect devices over a local area network and is able to direct traffic based on device MAC addresses. That's because the switch maintains a table with device MAC addresses. When two devices on the network need to communicate, the switch does a lookup and forwards traffic from the source to the appropriate destination based on the table entries.

☒ **A, C,** and **D** are incorrect. **A** is incorrect because a hub is commonly used to connect machines over a common network but doesn't have any context of MAC addresses. It is just used to provide device connectivity by copying the packets received and forwarding them on all other interfaces. **C** is incorrect because a repeater is used to regenerate a signal in order to allow it to reach longer distances but is not able to use

MAC addresses, as it works at layer 1 (MAC addresses work at layer 2). **D** is incorrect because a router is used for forwarding packets within different networks by using static or dynamic routing. It uses IP addresses for that purpose and works at layer 3.

35. In which of the following would you configure ERSPAN so you mirror traffic to your NIDS?

   A. Riverbed switch.

   B. Cisco Catalyst switch.

   C. MikroTik router.

   D. None of the above support ERSPAN.

   ☑ **B.** From the provided options, the only device that supports ERSPAN (Encapsulated Remote Switch Port Analyzer) is Cisco Catalyst switches. ERSPAN is a Cisco-proprietary protocol that uses a GRE tunnel and allows traffic to be mirrored to another port of the switch or to another switch within the network.

   ☒ **A, C,** and **D** are incorrect. **A** is incorrect because Riverbed switches don't have the ability to support ERSPAN, as it is a Cisco-proprietary protocol. **C** is incorrect because MikroTik routers don't support ERSPAN (it's a Cisco-proprietary protocol). **D** is incorrect as it's a distractor.

36. As a network administrator you are asked to select the most cost-effective security device that can filter based on the following criteria:

   - IP addresses/subnets

   - Specific ports

   Which of these devices would be more suitable in this case?

   A. Router

   B. Stateful inspection firewall

   C. Packet-filtering firewall

   D. IDS

   ☑ **C.** Since the requirements only describe filtering based on IP addresses/subnets and specific ports, a packet-filtering firewall would be adequate and offer the most cost-effective option.

   ☒ **A, B,** and **D** are incorrect. **A** is incorrect because a router is not considered a security device. Although quite a few models can support access lists, which might fulfill the criteria, the question specifically mentions a "security device able to filter," while a router's purpose is to route traffic between various networks. **B** is incorrect because although a stateful inspection firewall can fulfill the requirements, it would typically be more expensive than a packet-filtering one, and as such it doesn't constitute the most cost-effective option. **D** is incorrect because an IDS would be used to inspect traffic for malicious patterns but wouldn't be used to filter network traffic based on IP addresses/subnets and ports.

37. Which of these types of attackers would probably target a military installation to obtain new research and development (R&D) plans?

    A. APT

    B. Script kiddie

    C. Hacktivist

    D. White hat

    ☑ **A.** An APT (advanced persistent threat) is a well-funded and highly skilled category of attackers, usually nation-state sponsored, that have the ability to launch sophisticated attacks towards rival government and military organizations.

    ☒ **B, C,** and **D** are incorrect. **B** is incorrect because a script kiddie wouldn't have the skill or the tools required to be able to target a military installation. **C** is incorrect because hacktivists launch attacks usually with political or environmental motives and they don't tend to focus on profit. Hence, any information that would be obtained from such an attack would most likely be leaked online for everyone to view. **D** is incorrect because the term white hat is used to describe a penetration tester (also known as an ethical hacker) with no intent to do any harm. Hence, such a person wouldn't target a military installation with the goal of stealing and then selling information.

38. During a DDoS attack, who would be responsible for issuing commands?

    A. Botnet

    B. Zombie

    C. Victim

    D. Bot herder

    ☑ **D.** The bot herder is responsible for controlling the network of victim machines and issuing related instructions to them (i.e., direct them to launch a DDoS attack or send spam e-mails).

    ☒ **A, B,** and **C** are incorrect. **A** is incorrect because the term botnet is used to describe a collection of victim machines under the attacker's control. **B** is incorrect because a zombie is just another term used to describe a compromised machine that is under the control of an attacker. **C** is incorrect because the term "victim" refers to a compromised machine that is now functioning as a part of the bot network (botnet) and is under the bot herder's control.

39. Which of the following needs to take place so your machine can capture all the wireless transmissions within your device's range?

    A. An external USB-wireless adapter is required.

    B. Wireless NIC set to nonpromiscuous mode.

    C. Wireless NIC set to promiscuous mode.

    D. Wireless network needs to be open (i.e., not have any security protocol enabled).

☑ **C.** In order to intercept all wireless transmissions within the machine's range, the wireless NIC (network interface controller) needs to be switched to promiscuous mode. If that doesn't happen, it is not possible to capture wireless traffic from various network devices.

☒ **A, B,** and **D** are incorrect. **A** is incorrect because there's no need for an external USB-wireless adapter. Any wireless NIC would do, as long as it's able to support operation in promiscuous mode. **B** is incorrect because if the wireless NIC is not set in promiscuous mode, only traffic towards your machine can be captured. **D** is incorrect because it doesn't matter if the wireless network is open or a security protocol is in place (like WEP or WPA). Any traffic can still be intercepted. For example, the first step to cracking WEP's encryption is to capture enough wireless traffic for further manipulation.

40. Which of the following is a valid WPA-PSK preshared key?

   A. KsIA349

   B. AK09EYei

   C. £jh85418

   D. RΣ98*6Te

☑ **B.** WPA-PSK keys need to be at least 8 and up to 64 ASCII characters in length. The only answer that fulfills those requirements is option B.

☒ **A, C,** and **D** are incorrect. **A** is incorrect because it's seven characters long, which is less than the minimum of eight. **C** is incorrect because although it's eight characters long, it contains the £ character, which is a non-ASCII character. **D** is incorrect because although it's eight characters long, it contains the Σ character, which is a Greek alphabet letter and not an ASCII character.

Systems and Application Security

This chapter includes questions from the following objectives:

- 7.1 Identify and analyze malicious code and activity
- 7.2 Implement and operate endpoint device security
- 7.3 Operate and configure cloud security
- 7.4 Operate and secure virtual environments

This chapter contains a complete set of questions and answers regarding attacks (attack categories and attacker types, as well as related countermeasures); malicious code (types of malware, delivery methods, and countermeasures); virtual environments; and cloud computing security.

1. In which of these categories would a penetration tester belong?

   A. White hacker

   B. Black hat

   C. Gray hat

   D. White hat

2. A pharmaceutical company was made aware that a competitor is developing a new drug that will result in massive business loss. The lead scientist requires in-depth information about this drug and wants to identify someone who can covertly obtain data from the competitor. Which of these attackers would most likely be able to perform this task?

   A. Script kiddie

   B. Commercial hacker

   C. Hacktivist

   D. Nation-state actor

3. You have submitted a suspicious file for analysis to an AV vendor, but they are experiencing difficulties in understanding the malware's operation. Based on this fact, what type of malware is most likely present?

   A. Polymorphic virus

   B. Worm

   C. Armored virus

   D. Boot sector virus

4. You just received an e-mail from someone stating he has managed to access all your files and get screenshots from your camera. Which of the following is the attacker most likely using?

   A. RAT

   B. Trojan horse

   C. Ransomware

   D. Keylogger

5. During a drive-by download attack, where would the attacker most likely host malware?

   A. Target machine

   B. Attacking machine

   C. Attacker's website

   D. Compromised third-party website

6. If you want to ensure a system is protected against a user who might execute a malicious application from a USB disk, which of these scan types would you choose?

    A. On-demand

    B. Real-time

    C. Scheduled

    D. Signature-based

7. Your company is mainly using Windows and Apple devices and has recently implemented spam filtering and web proxy filtering and installed endpoint antivirus software on all devices. Which of the following presents the greatest risk to the company?

    A. AV with no update for the last month

    B. Unpatched RHEL 6.0 OS

    C. Fully patched Windows Vista OS

    D. Phishing e-mails

8. You browse to a website and receive a pop-up message stating your computer is vulnerable and in immediate need of a missing patch. Which of the following might be present on that website?

    A. PUA

    B. Spyware

    C. Virus

    D. Scareware

9. Which of these types of hardware would most commonly be virtualized to ensure the business reduces the related cost of physical equipment?

    A. Server

    B. Firewall

    C. Router

    D. VLAN

10. Which of these terms is unrelated to virtualization?

    A. Host

    B. VPN

    C. Hypervisor

    D. Guest

11. Which of the following is not characteristic of a worm?

    A. Spreads over the network

    B. Consumes bandwidth

    C. Requires human intervention

    D. May bring a system to a halt

12. Which of these statements regarding virtualization is inaccurate?

    A. Improved elasticity

    B. Easier migration

    C. Better resource management

    D. Less robust system restoration

13. How can you best protect against VM escape?

    A. Patch the hypervisor software.

    B. Patch the guest OS.

    C. Use a next-generation firewall on the host.

    D. Use a host antivirus.

14. Which of the following would be most crucial to investigate and address as soon as possible when attempting to harden a corporate e-mail server that also acts as a DNS server?

    A. Open TCP port 53

    B. OS license expiring soon

    C. Open TCP port 80

    D. Open UDP port 161

15. One of the employees at your company is accessing social media websites. As the information security officer, you have been tasked with forming an appropriate document that prohibits that behavior. Which of the following would be best for that purpose?

    A. Security policy

    B. AUP

    C. Allowed application policy

    D. Related guideline

16. Which of the following provides hardware disk encryption and remote attestation?

    A. BYOD

    B. CYOD

    C. MDM

    D. TPM

17. A friend of yours had her mobile phone stolen. Which of these actions would you recommend next?

    A. Remote wipe

    B. Remote lock

    C. MDM

    D. Encrypt the phone

18. Which of the following would provide an attacker with high-level system permissions and often appear as a legitimate process?

    A. Logic bomb

    B. Trojan horse

    C. Rootkit

    D. Macro virus

19. Which of these attacks allows an attacker access to forbidden file system locations and often targets a system's password file?

    A. XSS

    B. Directory traversal

    C. Buffer overflow

    D. CSRF

20. A new company employee received an e-mail containing a Google Drive URL, which is supposedly used for exchanging data with the company's clients. When he tries to browse to it and log in, his browser presents him with a security warning stating that the connection to that site is not secure. Which term describes this attack more accurately?

    A. Pharming

    B. Phishing

    C. Social network attack

    D. Vishing

21. Which of the following tries to disable or attack the AV software?

    A. Stealth virus

    B. Multipartite virus

    C. Polymorphic virus

    D. Retrovirus

22. Which of the following statements regarding Java applets is incorrect?

    A. Require JRE to be present so they can run.

    B. They're commonly used in web applications.

    C. They execute at the server.

    D. Work on various operating systems.

23. What is the best method to protect against shoulder surfing?

    A. Clean desktop

    B. Privacy filter

    C. User education

    D. Screensaver

24. Which of the following provides the least benefit against phishing e-mails?

    A. Install spam filters on all web servers.

    B. Users shouldn't open unsolicited e-mail attachments.

    C. Scan all e-mails for viruses.

    D. Maintain phishing campaign awareness.

25. Which of the following can't be provided by a TPM?

    A. Boot protection

    B. Encryption key storage

    C. Remote wiping

    D. Device identification

26. A cloud service can be accessed through a variety of operating systems. Which cloud characteristic does that relate to?

    A. Measured service

    B. Resource pooling

    C. Elasticity

    D. Broad network access

27. Which of these cloud operation models would be better for easy storage and access, for a European company that needs to be in full control of sensitive data as well as conform with GDPR?

    A. Public cloud

    B. Private cloud

    C. Community cloud

    D. Hybrid cloud

28. Your company is thinking of migrating to a cloud model for a variety of services. However, security is of paramount importance, so all responsibility for OS and application security should reside with your company. Which of these cloud models would be more suitable?

    A. PaaS

    B. SaaS

    C. IaaS

    D. DaaS

29. Which of these types of attackers would most likely create and use a zero-day exploit?

    A. APT

    B. Insider threat

    C. Script kiddie

    D. Social engineering

30. Which of the following is the best option to ensure secure deletion of data stored on a public cloud?

    A. Use specialized software.

    B. Ask cloud provider to provide the hard disk.

    C. Use cloud provider's tool to securely delete data.

    D. Encrypt data prior to uploading and delete when no longer needed.

31. Which of these attacks would most probably be used by a remote attacker who wants to steal sensitive files from a CEO's machine?

    A. XSS

    B. Trojan

    C. ARP spoofing

    D. SQL injection

32. Which of the following exclusively refers to an illegal operation being present?

    A. Botnet

    B. Backdoor

    C. Adware

    D. None of the above

33. A newly formed company wants to use cloud computing in order to save budget on hardware and administration. Which of the following responsibility models would be most appropriate for that purpose?

    A. PaaS

    B. Private cloud

    C. Public cloud

    D. IaaS

34. Which of these types of data residing in a cloud server would be protected by HIPAA?

    A. Patient first name

    B. Last four digits of patient credit card

    C. Patient year of birth

    D. Healthcare provider

35. Your company requires data to be labeled appropriately so it can be placed in different cloud servers, depending on its importance. How would you classify data relating to company employees?

   A. Confidential

   B. Private

   C. Sensitive

   D. Public

36. Which of these tasks would you avoid performing on a corporate host's virtual machine?

   A. Run another OS.

   B. Develop and test applications.

   C. Reverse-engineer malware.

   D. Host a file server.

37. Which of the following would prevent a zero-day exploit from running on your server?

   A. Signature-based AV

   B. Behavioral-based AV

   C. Network IPS

   D. None of the above

38. Your company wants to develop a new application that will be distributed in a preconfigured VM (containing the application running on a Linux OS). Which of these terms best describes this?

   A. Host

   B. Guest

   C. Virtual appliance

   D. Hypervisor

1. D	**11.** C	**21.** D	**31.** B
2. B	**12.** D	**22.** C	**32.** C
3. C	**13.** A	**23.** B	**33.** A
4. A	**14.** C	**24.** A	**34.** D
5. D	**15.** B	**25.** C	**35.** B
6. B	**16.** D	**26.** D	**36.** C
7. C	**17.** A	**27.** B	**37.** D
8. D	**18.** C	**28.** C	**38.** C
9. A	**19.** B	**29.** A	
10. B	**20.** B	**30.** D	

1. In which of these categories would a penetration tester belong?

   A. White hacker

   B. Black hat

   C. Gray hat

   D. White hat

   ☑ **D.** A penetration tester would be classified as a white hat, which is a term used to describe individuals who perform tests on systems to discover vulnerabilities and alert the system owners to mitigate any associated risks before attackers have a chance to exploit security gaps. Note that another term used is ethical hacker, and sometimes another term used for the process of penetration testing is ethical hacking.

   ☒ **A, B,** and **C** are incorrect. **A** is incorrect because there's no term known as white hacker, as the correct term is white hat. This option is a distractor. **B** is incorrect because a black hat is an individual who intends to identify and exploit vulnerabilities and use that knowledge to perform malicious activities on the target system. **C** is incorrect because a gray hat is someone who has advanced skills in computing (and often in networking, scripting, and penetration testing) and although not primarily using that skillset nefariously, there's an element of going outside the boundaries of the law sometimes, for example, scanning a web server without permission only to alert the system owner of possible open ports that are used by vulnerable services and need to be disabled.

2. A pharmaceutical company was made aware that a competitor is developing a new drug that will result in massive business loss. The lead scientist requires in-depth information about this drug and wants to identify someone who can covertly obtain data from the competitor. Which of these attackers would most likely be able to perform this task?

   A. Script kiddie

   B. Commercial hacker

   C. Hacktivist

   D. Nation-state actor

   ☑ **B.** A commercial hacker is someone who is usually hired to target a particular organization with a very distinct goal. Common goals include data theft, industrial espionage or sabotage, and data alteration or destruction.

   ☒ **A, C,** and **D** are incorrect. **A** is incorrect because a script kiddie is someone who has basic knowledge of attacks and is mostly limited to using already existing tools but is not a sophisticated attacker. As such, a script kiddie wouldn't be suitable for performing a covert operation against a pharmaceutical company. **C** is incorrect because a hacktivist is a type of attacker with a specific ideology, that is, in favor of world peace or against weapons. Stealing data from a pharmaceutical company to provide it to a competitor is not something that a hacktivist would commonly be interested in doing. **D** is incorrect because a nation-state actor refers to an individual or group of people working on behalf of a government to perform hostile activities, commonly against other governments. Such actors possess a high degree of technical skill, have enormous budgets, and perform highly disruptive operations (i.e., attacks on nuclear power plants or military installations).

3. You have submitted a suspicious file for analysis to an AV vendor, but they are experiencing difficulties in understanding the malware's operation. Based on this fact, what type of malware is most likely present?

A. Polymorphic virus

B. Worm

C. Armored virus

D. Boot sector virus

☑ **C.** An armored virus is specifically developed to thwart reverse-engineering attempts. Common techniques include several layers of code obfuscation, use of encryption, and adding code sections that don't serve any real purpose but are just present to create confusion about what the real operation is.

☒ **A, B,** and **D** are incorrect. **A** is incorrect because a polymorphic virus is a type of virus that can change a malicious file in order to make signature detection more difficult; however, the replication and payload mechanisms remain unaltered. **B** is incorrect because a worm's main characteristic is its ability to propagate through a network without any user interaction. When it is first installed on a system, it will usually try to find a way to self-replicate to other neighboring machines, which can result in an increase in network traffic and resource consumption. **D** is incorrect because a boot sector virus is installed on the operating system's MBR (master boot record) and is then loaded into memory when the system starts. If any removable media are inserted on the system (i.e., external hard disks or USB flash drives), the virus can copy itself to those and continue spreading.

4. You just received an e-mail from someone stating he has managed to access all your files and get screenshots from your camera. Which of the following is the attacker most likely using?

A. RAT

B. Trojan horse

C. Ransomware

D. Keylogger

☑ **A.** A RAT (remote access Trojan) can give an attacker full control of a target machine, including the ability to record keystrokes, access all files, use the camera to take screenshots, and install files.

☒ **B, C,** and **D** are incorrect. **B** is incorrect because a Trojan horse is an application that is supposed to have a legitimate function but actually performs other tasks in addition to that. Assume you are looking for software that can compress audio files. You find one through a third-party website and start using it. If this was a Trojan horse, it would compress audio files but do something additional to that, possibly without even your knowing, like log your keystrokes or collect passwords from your browser and then send that to the application's author. **C** is incorrect because ransomware commonly works by not allowing a user access to his or her files before an amount is paid to the attacker. Furthermore, the term crypto-ransomware is used to describe a scenario where the user's files are encrypted and the attacker requires an amount to be paid in order to provide the encryption key to the victim. **D** is incorrect because a keylogger will only record victim keystrokes, which will then be passed to the attacker.

5. During a drive-by download attack, where would the attacker most likely host malware?

   A. Target machine

   B. Attacking machine

   C. Attacker's website

   D. Compromised third-party website

   ☑ **D.** During a drive-by attack, an attacker will place malicious code that the victim needs to download and execute so an action takes place, that is, allow the attacker access to the victim's machine by opening a backdoor or making the target machine part of a botnet. The attacker will need to store the code somewhere that is easily accessible by a victim, so a common practice is to compromise third-party websites and store malicious code there and then redirect an unsuspecting victim to download and execute it.

   ☒ **A, B,** and **C** are incorrect. **A** is incorrect because a target machine (meaning the victim's personal machine) wouldn't allow uninterrupted access to any other future victim. For example, even if the attacker finds a way to store malware on a target machine and installs a web server on it so future victims can download malicious code, that doesn't guarantee availability, as the victim might power off the computer and go on holiday for a month. **B** is incorrect because if the attacker hosts malware on his or her machine, that would be identifiable and easily blocked by law enforcement. Also, it is much more possible that someone will browse to a legitimate third-party website (i.e., a known newspaper or online store) that the attacker has compromised, as the victim would hardly ever consider that malicious. **C** is incorrect because (similarly to the previous point) a website owned by the attacker can be identified and taken down by law enforcement, so it would commonly only be available for a short period.

6. If you want to ensure a system is protected against a user who might execute a malicious application from a USB disk, which of these scan types would you choose?

   A. On-demand

   B. Real-time

   C. Scheduled

   D. Signature-based

   ☑ **B.** A real-time scan is appropriate for continuous system protection. The antivirus will be able to inspect any application that the user attempts to execute (including the ones run from external media, like portable applications) and constantly monitor activity for malicious indicators.

   ☒ **A, C,** and **D** are incorrect. **A** is incorrect because an on-demand scan will only run if the user initiates it. However, that doesn't ensure protection against a malicious application that is installed or run at any moment in time. This feature is mostly useful if the user suspects malware is present on a system or a new device has been plugged in (i.e., external storage) and that needs to be scanned for malicious artifacts. **C** is incorrect because a scheduled scan would be preferred if the user would like to ensure a system is periodically scanned for malware. However, that won't have any effect on an application that the user is running before that scan is performed. **D** is incorrect because there's no scan type known as signature-based. This refers to the type of detection an antivirus is using. Signature-based means that the antivirus works by having a signature database, which contains signatures of known malware.

7. Your company is mainly using Windows and Apple devices and has recently implemented spam filtering and web proxy filtering and installed endpoint antivirus software on all devices. Which of the following presents the greatest risk to the company?

   A. AV with no update for the last month

   B. Unpatched RHEL 6.0 OS

   C. Fully patched Windows Vista OS

   D. Phishing e-mails

   ☑ **C.** Finding a machine running Windows Vista in a company actively using Windows presents a major risk, as that operating system's support ended in April 2017. That means that although it has been fully patched, no patches or security updates have been released from April 2017 onwards, leaving that host vulnerable to any exploits that have been released since then.

   ☒ **A, B,** and **D** are incorrect. **A** is incorrect because antivirus solutions were recently installed on all company endpoints, so even if they haven't been updated for a month, they pose a limited risk to the business. **B** is incorrect because an unpatched version of RHEL 6.0 wouldn't have any impact on a business not running Red Hat Linux. **D** is incorrect because even if company employees receive phishing e-mails on a regular basis, spam filtering and web proxy filtering have been implemented, which will provide a fairly good amount of protection against phishing e-mails.

8. You browse to a website and receive a pop-up message stating your computer is vulnerable and in immediate need of a missing patch. Which of the following might be present on that website?

A. PUA

B. Spyware

C. Virus

D. Scareware

☑ **D.** Scareware is a type of malware that prompts the user to install some type of security application, trying to entice an individual who visits a website where scareware is hosted by stating there's a missing update or patch or no antivirus present on the victim's machine. As soon as someone downloads and installs the application in question, various malicious tasks may start to take place, depending on what the goal of the scareware is (i.e., join the machine to a botnet or steal credentials).

☒ **A, B,** and **C** are incorrect. **A** is incorrect because a PUA (potentially unwanted application) would commonly not have a malicious goal but is mostly used to display annoying advertisements to the user or might perform some other trivial task like change the browser's default home page or search engine. **B** is incorrect because any software that is classified as spyware aims to obtain as much information about a user as possible by a variety of methods like logging keystrokes, obtaining usernames and passwords from browsers, or tracking user browsing behavior and purchasing habits. **C** is incorrect because a virus is a type of program that can cause a variety of symptoms on a target system like slowness and increased network or resource consumption, but in order for it to execute it first needs to be run by a user, and the question doesn't state anything about a file being downloaded and run. It just mentions a pop-up that was present when the user browsed to the website.

9. Which of these types of hardware would most commonly be virtualized to ensure the business reduces the related cost of physical equipment?

A. Server

B. Firewall

C. Router

D. VLAN

☑ **A.** Most companies have multiple servers within their environment in order to support a variety of tasks, like e-mail, DHCP, Active Directory, FTP, database, web, authentication, and licensing. Due to the cost of those devices and the effort required to maintain them, they tend to be virtualized quite often, as that significantly limits the associated cost and at the same time makes administration and troubleshooting easier. It also offers smaller downtimes because if a virtual server is damaged, it can be reconstituted from an image in a relatively short time. Whereas if a physical machine is experiencing issues, a technician would need to go to the data center to troubleshoot and possibly replace faulty hardware, which can take several hours at best.

☒ **B, C,** and **D** are incorrect. **B** is incorrect because although some vendors offer virtualized firewall versions, a firewall commonly requires substantial resources to be able to cope with network traffic and apply related rules from its ruleset (which might have thousands of rules that need to be evaluated in very short time). In addition, there are various concerns about virtual environment security and how easy it may be for an attacker that has compromised an ESXi server, for example, to gain access to VMs of security devices (i.e., firewalls) and alter related security settings to allow for access to the network. **C** is incorrect because networking devices mostly rely on specialized hardware to be able to perform decisions on how traffic should be routed in minimal time. Virtualizing such functions would take significant CPU power, not to mention it would also mean having virtual network interfaces, which would make the challenge even greater. **D** is incorrect because a VLAN (virtual local area network) is not a hardware device but a virtual component.

10. Which of these terms is unrelated to virtualization?

    A. Host

    B. VPN

    C. Hypervisor

    D. Guest

    ☑ **B.** A VPN (virtual private network) uses the word "virtual" in its title but has nothing to do with virtualization (i.e., using a virtual server). A VPN facilitates the creation of a secure connection over an insecure network (i.e., the Internet). It is called "virtual," as there's no actual physical tunnel between two remote ends, but because of the VPN's operation (providing enhanced security with encryption support), it's like building an isolated path between those devices for the duration of the session.

    ☒ **A, C,** and **D** are incorrect. **A** is incorrect because a host is the device where virtualization will be implemented, as the related virtualization software (i.e., Virtual Box or VMware) will be installed there. **C** is incorrect because a hypervisor is the actual software (i.e., Virtual Box or VMware) that offers virtualization. **D** is incorrect because any virtual machine that may be running on a host system is called a guest. Note that a physical host can support several guests, depending on its physical resource limitations.

11. Which of the following is not characteristic of a worm?

    A. Spreads over the network

    B. Consumes bandwidth

    C. Requires human intervention

    D. May bring a system to a halt

    ☑ **C.** A worm doesn't require any human intervention in order to execute and propagate. It has the ability to self-replicate to other machines and infect multiple hosts within a network. Note that a virus requires human intervention in order to be able to run.

☒ **A, B,** and **D** are incorrect. **A** is incorrect because worms tend to use networks to spread to as many hosts as possible. **B** is incorrect because worms consume a lot of network bandwidth when trying to locate possible hosts to infect. At the same time, they attempt to take advantage of any protocol that will allow them to replicate (like SMB or FTP), thus creating major spikes in bandwidth consumption. **D** is incorrect because a worm's execution is known to bring systems to a halt or even force them to restart frequently, as they are unable to cope with the amount of processing cycles and memory that a worm uses.

12. Which of these statements regarding virtualization is inaccurate?

   A. Improved elasticity

   B. Easier migration

   C. Better resource management

   D. Less robust system restoration

   ☑ **D.** Using a virtual machine offers more robust restoration (not less). That's because the process of restoring the virtual machine when something happens is very straightforward, since a previous snapshot can be used for restoration. Even if a machine goes down and needs to be rebuilt, that can be a matter of minutes or perhaps a few hours, while in the case of a physical server, it may even take days or at least several hours. That's especially true if a physical server malfunction requires a hardware replacement before restoration can start.

   ☒ **A, B,** and **C** are incorrect. **A** is incorrect because virtualization offers improved elasticity. If you have a virtualized file server and various clients start accessing files, you can always change the provisioning to account for the increased demand. If for some reason that stops, then the machine can be scaled down to address that, offering a high level of elasticity. **B** is incorrect because if migration to another machine is required, that can happen easily, as a set of files (which is what a virtual machine is composed of) will need to be copied to the new device so that restoration can take place there. **C** is incorrect because (as also mentioned earlier) a virtual machine can be provisioned according to the specific needs of an organization. If a robust web server is needed, it can be provisioned accordingly. Similarly, if an administrator notices that the machine stays idle too much, resources can be reduced to account for that. In addition, if more storage is required, that can be added with minimal interruption to the service being provided.

13. How can you best protect against VM escape?

   A. Patch the hypervisor software.

   B. Patch the guest OS.

   C. Use a next-generation firewall on the host.

   D. Use a host antivirus.

   ☑ **A.** VM escape is a type of exploit that can take place when an attacker manages to break out of the context of a virtual machine and interact directly with the host.

This is made possible due to a potential vulnerability within the hypervisor (the software that provisions the guest OS and controls how that interacts with the host). In order to ensure the risk is mitigated as much as possible, the hypervisor should always run the most up-to-date versions with the latest patches so that attackers can't use any known exploits to perform VM escape.

☒ **B, C,** and **D** are incorrect. **B** is incorrect because although patching the guest OS is quite important, it's the vulnerability within the hypervisor that ultimately allows an attacker to perform a VM escape. Please note that patching the guest OS will aid a lot in avoiding any risks from vulnerabilities that can lead to that machine being compromised. In a typical VM escape scenario, even if the hypervisor is vulnerable, the attacker will start by first compromising the guest OS, and after that is achieved, a hypervisor exploit will follow. However, if the hypervisor is sufficiently patched, then the only thing an attacker can achieve is to compromise the guest OS (assuming the attacker is not using a zero-day hypervisor exploit). **C** is incorrect because using a next-generation firewall on the host will most likely not achieve anything, as the attacker would perform this attack by compromising the guest OS and work through that to exploit the hypervisor. **D** is incorrect because using a host AV will not necessarily protect against this attack, as the attacker will initially compromise the guest OS and then exploit the hypervisor. It would be more beneficial to install an AV on the guest OS in the hope that the initial attack will be detected and stopped before the attacker manages to exploit the hypervisor.

14. Which of the following would be most crucial to investigate and address as soon as possible when attempting to harden a corporate e-mail server that also acts as a DNS server?

A. Open TCP port 53

B. OS license expiring soon

C. Open TCP port 80

D. Open UDP port 161

☑ **C.** Having TCP port 80 open indicates that there's possibly a web server running on the machine (assuming it's using the default port). However, this machine is classified as an e-mail and DNS server, not a web server, so there wouldn't be any reason for having TCP port 80 open. As such, this would need to be further investigated (possibly verify with the IT team if there's any reason for that port to be open) to ensure any risk is mitigated accordingly.

☒ **A, B,** and **D** are incorrect. **A** is incorrect because TCP port 53 is used by DNS for zone transfers and any requests over 512 bytes, so since the server is acting as a DNS server, this is required. **B** is incorrect because addressing a licensing issue wouldn't fall within the tasks performed during hardening, as it's not an immediate security concern. However, this would be something to report to the IT team so the issue is appropriately resolved. **D** is incorrect because UDP port 161 is used by default by SNMP (Simple Network Management Protocol), which would commonly be utilized to report the server's health status to a management console and alert the administrator of any issues.

15. One of the employees at your company is accessing social media websites. As the information security officer, you have been tasked with forming an appropriate document that prohibits that behavior. Which of the following would be best for that purpose?

   A. Security policy

   B. AUP

   C. Allowed application policy

   D. Related guideline

   ☑ **B.** An AUP (acceptable use policy) would be the most appropriate document to specify what actions are permitted or not allowed for corporate network users. An AUP document is something that all company employees have to adhere to. As such, including a statement about social media access not being allowed throughout the organization is something that all corporate employees will need to abide by.

   ☒ **A, C,** and **D** are incorrect. **A** is incorrect because a security policy is an overarching document containing corporate security goals and high-level objectives. It references specific documents (i.e., AUP, incident response policy, or physical security policy), which the organization will use to achieve its goals. **C** is incorrect because there's no type of policy known as "allowed application policy." This option is a distractor. **D** is incorrect because a guideline is a type of document used to provide related recommendations but is not obligatory. An AUP document, on the other hand, is authoritative and usually mentions possible sanctions in the event the related policy is not adhered to.

16. Which of the following provides hardware disk encryption and remote attestation?

   A. BYOD

   B. CYOD

   C. MDM

   D. TPM

   ☑ **D.** A TPM (Trusted Platform Module) is a hardware module that provides hardware encryption to devices supporting it. It works by storing the cryptographic keys that the OS uses for data encryption and decryption. It also provides remote attestation, meaning it provides an authorized party (like an OS vendor) the ability to verify if any tampering has taken place on the machine.

   ☒ **A, B,** and **C** are incorrect. **A** is incorrect because BYOD (bring your own device) is a policy regulating the use of personal devices (like laptops, phones, and tablets) on a corporate network and doesn't relate to encryption. **B** is incorrect because CYOD (choose your own device) is very similar to the concept of BYOD, but here the organization defines a list of preapproved devices from which the employee can select one that will be purchased and managed by the company. However, this doesn't relate to hardware encryption. **C** is incorrect because MDM (mobile device management) supports full disk encryption of enrolled devices but not remote attestation.

17. A friend of yours had her mobile phone stolen. Which of these actions would you recommend next?

A. Remote wipe

B. Remote lock

C. MDM

D. Encrypt the phone

☑ **A.** If a phone is stolen, you can report the theft to the police. However, if there's no immediate threat to human life, the odds of someone recovering that phone are very slim, unless the perpetrator is caught and the phone has not yet been sold to another party. When a device is stolen, it is more crucial to protect the data present on the owner's phone (e.g., stored credit cards) than hope to recover the device. Commonly, the best course of action would be to remotely wipe all data on the phone so that no third party can use it without the owner's knowledge.

☒ **B, C,** and **D** are incorrect. **B** is incorrect because using a remote lock would lock the phone and only allow someone who knows the related lock password to unlock it (note that the remote lock password is not the device's touch screen password but is placed when the owner activates the remote lock). However, that doesn't do anything to delete the phone data, and there's always a chance that a thief will be able to recover that. In addition, there's no point in locking the device and leaving the data intact if there's no real chance of recovering it. A lock would be a prudent step to take if you have left your phone in a coffee shop or a bus or a cinema, for example, and you are in the process of retrieving it. However, if that's not likely to happen (like in the case of theft), then the best course of action would be to remove all data from the device. **C** is incorrect because it is highly unlikely that your friend is using an MDM solution, as that's commonly used by companies since it comes with an associated cost. Even if she does, though, the solution would still be able to remotely wipe that phone, which is an option that most modern MDM solutions would offer. **D** is incorrect because encrypting the phone is a step that should have been performed prior to the theft in order not to allow a third party to be able to access the device's data.

18. Which of the following would provide an attacker with high-level system permissions and often appear as a legitimate process?

A. Logic bomb

B. Trojan horse

C. Rootkit

D. Macro virus

☑ **C.** The term rootkit is used to describe any application that acquires elevated operating system access and tries to hide its presence by a variety of methods (i.e., injecting itself into benign processes, appearing as a valid system application or process, intercepting OS API calls, or hiding in unallocated space).

⊠ **A, B,** and **D** are incorrect. **A** is incorrect because a logic bomb doesn't necessarily require elevated privileges to run, but even if it does, it won't usually try to hide its execution and usually won't have a rootkit's sophistication. Logic bombs are commonly used by developers or malicious insiders and are executed when specific conditions are met, that is, an employee removed from the HR database or a user account deletion. **B** is incorrect because a Trojan horse is a type of malware that performs a known function while executing malicious tasks without the user's knowledge. **D** is incorrect because a macro virus is a type of malware that is embedded in a file format that supports macro execution (i.e., in Word or Excel documents) and, once opened, runs a specific set of instructions. It is worth noting that in order for a macro virus to run, macros need to have been enabled on the target computer.

19. Which of these attacks allows an attacker access to forbidden file system locations and often targets a system's password file?

    A. XSS

    B. Directory traversal

    C. Buffer overflow

    D. CSRF

    ☑ **B.** A directory traversal attack is a type of web attack in which an attacker tries to access forbidden file system parts, that is, on a web server. The attacker would most commonly target the password file so user credentials can be harvested, but the term is used to describe access to any directory where access is not allowed.

    ⊠ **A, C,** and **D** are incorrect. **A** is incorrect because an XSS (cross-site scripting) attack would inject malicious code (i.e., JavaScript or HTML) to a web page, with the goal of bypassing existing access control and executing the malicious code. **C** is incorrect because a buffer overflow attack works by allowing the attacker to write into specific memory areas that shouldn't be normally available (i.e., an application using a buffer to hold data of a specific size, which is being overrun when more data is supplied and due to the application being vulnerable to a buffer overflow attack, it tries to store that information in the predefined buffer, thus resulting in writing to other memory areas). **D** is incorrect because a CSRF (cross-site request forgery) attack aims to utilize the user's browser to send a malicious request to a website without any indication to the user. Assume you are logged in to an online gaming website and want to transfer some of your credits to a friend. A CSRF exploit can be used while you are logged in to the website to have credits sent to the attacker's account instead.

20. A new company employee received an e-mail containing a Google Drive URL, which is supposedly used for exchanging data with the company's clients. When he tries to browse to it and log in, his browser presents him with a security warning stating that the connection to that site is not secure. Which term describes this attack more accurately?

A. Pharming

B. Phishing

C. Social network attack

D. Vishing

☑ **B.** This is a typical example of a phishing e-mail being used to obtain user credentials. The employee received what was supposedly a standard e-mail invitation to the company's Google Drive location to which he would probably log in using his corporate credentials, thus passing that to an attacker. There are two things that companies need to address to avoid this. One thing is to ensure employees get adequate training to distinguish illegitimate e-mails, and the second thing is to be cognizant of security warnings. If one is not certain what the reason for the displayed message is, it's best to reach out to the IT team than to just proceed with the activity.

☒ **A, C,** and **D** are incorrect. **A** is incorrect because pharming is a type of attack in which the victim tries to browse to a particular website but is instead getting redirected to a fake website because of DNS being exploited (i.e., a vulnerability in DNS itself or manual modification of the user's machine resolution ability, for example, by modifying the hosts file). **C** is incorrect because a social network attack would be performed using some social network invitation or e-mail supposedly originating from social media, that is, a LinkedIn connection invitation, to entice the user to click the URL contained in that e-mail and accept the new connection. **D** is incorrect because vishing is a type of social engineering attack that uses phone or VoIP and engages the victim in a discussion in order to extract useful personal information; for example, someone calling and posing as an electricity provider's employee and asking to confirm your full name, address, and date of birth to give you details about a new offer.

21. Which of the following tries to disable or attack the AV software?

A. Stealth virus

B. Multipartite virus

C. Polymorphic virus

D. Retrovirus

☑ **D.** A retrovirus is a type of virus that tries to attack a device's antivirus program. It may attempt to warn the victim that supposedly unsafe software has been found on the machine and then uninstall legitimate AV applications. Sometimes it has the ability to modify the virus signature database and corrupt or delete it altogether.

☒ **A, B,** and **C** are incorrect. **A** is incorrect because a stealth virus doesn't attack the AV application but actually tries to evade detection from it. Sometimes it does that by changing the offending file's name or size to make it seem like the infected file is the actual legitimate host file. **B** is incorrect, as a multipartite virus works by infecting various parts of a target system with the intent of making removal very difficult. **C** is incorrect because a polymorphic virus can change a malicious file in order to make signature detection more difficult; however, the replication and payload mechanisms remain unaltered.

22. Which of the following statements regarding Java applets is incorrect?

    A. Require JRE to be present so they can run.

    B. They're commonly used in web applications.

    C. They execute at the server.

    D. Work on various operating systems.

    ☑ **C.** Java applets are interactive components of a web page (i.e., buttons, text) that are executed on the client's web browser and use a VM (commonly known as JVM, or Java Virtual Machine) for execution. A typical example is capturing a user's mouse input so the program can manipulate it afterwards.

    ☒ **A, B,** and **D** are incorrect. **A** is incorrect because Java applets require JRE (Java Runtime Environment) to be installed in the client's browser so they can function properly. If that is not installed, a blank window is usually displayed stating that JRE is required in order for the applet to execute, which is something that attackers commonly try to exploit and redirect users to malicious websites, where they are supposedly downloading the latest JRE version while in fact malware is being delivered. **B** is incorrect because Java applets are used by many web applications, for example, to transfer the processing load to the client. **D** is incorrect because Java applets work on a variety of operating systems (i.e., Windows, Linux, UNIX, macOS), as they work on the client browser and are not dependent on the OS architecture.

23. What is the best method to protect against shoulder surfing?

    A. Clean desktop

    B. Privacy filter

    C. User education

    D. Screensaver

    ☑ **B.** A privacy filter (also known as a visual filter) can be quite effective against any shoulder surfing attack. When such a filter is used, the visible area of the screen is limited to only the person placed directly in front of the monitor. This can be extremely beneficial for people who travel a lot and tend to work in crowded places (i.e., train stations, buses, and airports).

    ☒ **A, C,** and **D** are incorrect. **A** is incorrect because a clean desktop entails clearing out the files and folders residing on a user's desktop, but that won't help in the case where individuals tend to work extensively with a variety of open documents (i.e., working all the time through presentations, spreadsheets, and various documents). **C** is incorrect because user education always goes a long way to limiting or preventing various types of social engineering attacks. However, the education aspect of this case would be to encourage individuals to use a privacy filter while working in public places so they can protect themselves from shoulder surfing attacks. **D** is incorrect because a screensaver won't help discourage shoulder surfing when a user is working on a computer. A screensaver is useful if the machine is left unattended for a short time. However, that will not have any effect if a password isn't set when the screen is locked, which is a common mistake.

24. Which of the following provides the least benefit against phishing e-mails?

   A. Install spam filters on all web servers.

   B. Users shouldn't open unsolicited e-mail attachments.

   C. Scan all e-mails for viruses.

   D. Maintain phishing campaign awareness.

   ☑ **A.** No e-mail accounts would be configured on a web server because that device should only be serving client web requests. Hence, there's no real benefit of having spam filters installed on it.

   ☒ **B, C,** and **D** are incorrect. **B** is incorrect because users shouldn't open e-mail attachments from people they don't know. This is, of course, a general rule of thumb, as sometimes it is very hard to do in reality, especially from people in HR, sales, and similar roles. **C** is incorrect because AV clients should be configured to scan all e-mail content for malicious URLs and all attachments for any suspicious files. **D** is incorrect because it is highly recommended for every individual to maintain vigilance about any large phishing campaign so appropriate attention can be demonstrated. For example, if you work at a fashion retailer, it would be great to know there's a large phishing campaign targeting fashion retailers these days so you maintain appropriate awareness.

25. Which of the following can't be provided by a TPM?

   A. Boot protection

   B. Encryption key storage

   C. Remote wiping

   D. Device identification

   ☑ **C.** A TPM (Trusted Platform Module) can't provide device remote wiping, which is a feature commonly supported by MDM (mobile device management) solutions.

   ☒ **A, B,** and **D** are incorrect. **A** is incorrect because TPMs offer boot protection by storing hash values of specific system files and other OS key metrics in order to allow the system to detect any alterations by unauthorized software. **B** is incorrect because the TPM is used to store any hard disk encryption keys. **D** is incorrect because device identification is achieved by a unique identification key, which is embedded in the TPM module by the manufacturer during its creation.

26. A cloud service can be accessed through a variety of operating systems. Which cloud characteristic does that relate to?

   A. Measured service

   B. Resource pooling

   C. Elasticity

   D. Broad network access

   ☑ **D.** Having the ability to access a cloud service from a variety of operating systems is known as broad network access. Usually, this feature uses two main methods. One is making an application available via a web browser, which is seamless to any operating system being used, as the application runs over the client's web browser. Another method is to allow a user to download the related software locally to a machine. But most cloud providers that use this feature make clients available for a variety of platforms, like UNIX, Linux, Windows, Android, and macOS.

   ☒ **A, B,** and **C** are incorrect. **A** is incorrect because a measured service refers to being able to get charged only for what is being specifically used. If a business has 50 cloud servers but is currently only using 20 of them while the rest are powered off, they have to be able to pay according to that. **B** is incorrect because resource pooling refers to being able to effectively manage resources so they are used as much as possible. If an eight-core server is only using two cores for client A, then use the remaining processing power to serve client B (if that is allowed). **C** is incorrect because elasticity refers to being able to scale up or down, according to the needs of the business, at any given moment in time. If you are an online travel agency and it's a school holiday period, you might find that you need much more resources than other periods of the year, so you should be able to increase your resources accordingly for that period and then scale down again with no service disruption.

27. Which of these cloud operation models would be better for easy storage and access, for a European company that needs to be in full control of sensitive data as well as conform with GDPR?

   A. Public cloud

   B. Private cloud

   C. Community cloud

   D. Hybrid cloud

   ☑ **B.** Since the company wants to maintain easy storage and access but also needs to conform with GDPR, the best option would be to use a private cloud. This will provide ease of storage (and associated administration) while the organization will have full control of all sensitive data, which will be residing in the company's private cloud instance. Of course, since GDPR conformity is a prerequisite, the instance can be located in any European company branch.

   ☒ **A, C,** and **D** are incorrect. **A** is incorrect because using a public cloud will not give the company full control over the data nor provide ease of access in case a public cloud instance is damaged, is under maintenance, or has its data stolen. **C** is incorrect because a community cloud is commonly implemented when different users want to share information over a common media; for example, two different universities with researchers participating in a common research project. However, the company is a sole organization, and the data in question would only be accessible by its employees and not anyone else. **D** is incorrect because a hybrid cloud combines two clouds (or more). As such, it wouldn't be suitable in this case because only a private cloud would provide full control over the data while maintaining easy storage and access.

28. Your company is thinking of migrating to a cloud model for a variety of services. However, security is of paramount importance, so all responsibility for OS and application security should reside with your company. Which of these cloud models would be more suitable?

   A. PaaS

   B. SaaS

   C. IaaS

   D. DaaS

   ☑ **C.** Since the company wants to remain responsible for its own security while using a cloud model of choice, the best option is to select a model in which the client has the greatest degree of control, which is IaaS (Infrastructure as a Service). In that model, the cloud provider is responsible for providing the hardware (i.e., servers, storage, networking) and the client is responsible for everything else (i.e., operating system and application installation and associated security).

   ☒ **A, B,** and **D** are incorrect. **A** is incorrect because in PaaS (Platform as a Service) the cloud provider is responsible for providing an operating system and associated applications (in addition to hardware) so the security of those resides with the cloud provider. **B** is incorrect because SaaS (Software as a Service) provides the least amount of control to a client since the cloud provider is responsible for everything and the client is just using a particular service (i.e., Dropbox). **D** is incorrect because there's no cloud model known as DaaS. This is a distractor.

29. Which of these types of attackers would most likely create and use a zero-day exploit?

   A. APT

   B. Insider threat

   C. Script kiddie

   D. Social engineering

   ☑ **A.** The term APT (advanced persistent threat) refers to individuals or, most commonly, groups of attackers who aim to compromise target networks or devices and stay undetected for long periods while persistency is maintained. They are usually politically motivated and often use very sophisticated attack mechanisms, including zero-day exploits, as they possess the manpower and technical skillset to create them.

⊠ **B, C,** and **D** are incorrect. **B** is incorrect because an insider threat would not have a need for a zero-day exploit to gain access to a system, but would instead usually take advantage of the already existing access due to being a company employee and possibly place some type of backdoor or try to perform privilege escalation. **C** is incorrect because a script kiddie wouldn't be technically skilled enough to create a zero-day exploit and would most commonly be restricted to using freely available tools or already prepared scripts. **D** is incorrect because social engineering is not a type of attacker but actually a type of attack. The individual using such an attack is called a social engineer.

30. Which of the following is the best option to ensure secure deletion of data stored on a public cloud?

   A. Use specialized software.

   B. Ask cloud provider to provide the hard disk.

   C. Use cloud provider's tool to securely delete data.

   D. Encrypt data prior to uploading and delete when no longer needed.

   ☑ **D.** Since the data is stored on a public cloud, it is very difficult to be certain it has been fully removed since the hard disk is owned by a public cloud provider. As such, the best option is to ensure data is encrypted before being uploaded, using a strong encryption algorithm. Even if your attempt to remove it from the public cloud results in some being left behind, it will still be encrypted and won't be easily usable by any third party managing to get a copy of it.

   ⊠ **A, B,** and **C** are incorrect. **A** is incorrect because it doesn't matter what software you use or how good it is—you can never be certain that data has been fully removed if you don't own the storage media being used to store it. **B** is incorrect because there's a slim chance of obtaining a hard disk from a public cloud provider, especially since it might hold other client data in addition to yours. Even if this was feasible, it's not a practical solution, as data may be spread across a variety of disks in different geographical locations. **C** is incorrect because using a tool provided by your cloud provider doesn't guarantee full deletion of the data, especially if you don't know how the tool exactly works or how credible it is, but also due to the fact that you have no way of verifying its operation.

31. Which of these attacks would most probably be used by a remote attacker who wants to steal sensitive files from a CEO's machine?

   A. XSS

   B. Trojan

   C. ARP spoofing

   D. SQL injection

   ☑ **B.** There are various categories of Trojans, like downloaders (created for downloading additional malicious files to a target machine), remote access Trojans (aiming to provide the attacker full control of a machine), backdoor Trojans (which will create a backdoor to a system so the attacker can gain remote access), and infostealer Trojans (which perform information theft from the machine they infect). An infostealer Trojan would be the best option for an attacker who wants to acquire sensitive data from a CEO's machine.

☒ **A, C,** and **D** are incorrect. **A** is incorrect because an XSS (cross-site scripting) attack would inject code (i.e., JavaScript or HTML) into a web page but wouldn't be suitable in the case of attacking the CEO's machine, as that's not running any web service. **C** is incorrect because ARP spoofing requires access to the local network in order to be able to launch a successful attack. That's because during an ARP spoofing attack, the attacker needs to be able to attach his or her machine to the local network so he or she can send ARP messages with the goal of impersonating a legitimate network host. However, as the question mentions a remote attacker, the attack wouldn't be useful in this scenario. **D** is incorrect because an SQL injection attack is an application attack commonly launched against web servers. As in the previous case of the XSS attack, this wouldn't be useful against a CEO's machine, which wouldn't be running any web service that can be exploited.

32. Which of the following exclusively refers to an illegal operation being present?

A. Botnet

B. Backdoor

C. Adware

D. None of the above

☑ **C.** Adware displays advertisements about a variety of products. The author either gains money by individuals viewing the ads or by enticing people to click a link, box, banner, or other advertisement element. As such, it is never considered something that a user would authorize as being installed, especially since some adware applications are known to have keylogging and spyware capabilities.

☒ **A, B,** and **D** are incorrect. **A** is incorrect because although a botnet may usually be referred to as something malicious, it doesn't necessarily make it the case. A botnet can be defined as a collection of machines working towards a common task. When that network of devices is used for nefarious purposes (i.e., to perform a DoS attack), then the botnet is definitely deemed malicious and illegal. But there are also legitimate purposes for such a network; for example, machines joined into the SETI (Search for Extraterrestrial Intelligence) program, which "borrow" computing cycles so that science is advanced by searching for extraterrestrial life. **B** is incorrect because backdoors (also known as programming hooks) are often implemented by developers so as to have emergency access in the event that the application or system experiences issues. However, if they aren't removed promptly, an attacker may discover them and gain system access, but that's more of an oversight or poor practice than something relating to an illegal operation or malware. However, if an attacker, disgruntled developer, or company employee was placing a backdoor to retain uninterrupted access to an application or system, this would be an illegal action. **D** is incorrect because this is a distractor.

33. A newly formed company wants to use cloud computing in order to save budget on hardware and administration. Which of the following responsibility models would be most appropriate for that purpose?

A. PaaS

B. Private cloud

C. Public cloud

D. IaaS

☑ **A.** The only two responsibility-related models that are mentioned as possible answers are PaaS and IaaS. The question mentions that the company is newly formed and needs to reserve hardware and administration budget, hence it would make sense to choose the model that would offload as many functions as possible to the cloud provider, which is PaaS (Platform as a Service). In PaaS, the cloud provider would be tasked with providing the necessary hardware, OS, and associated applications.

☒ **B, C,** and **D** are incorrect. **B** is incorrect because the term "private cloud" is used to refer to a cloud operation model, not a responsibility model. **C** is incorrect because the term public cloud is also used to refer to a cloud operation model and not a responsibility model. **D** is incorrect because IaaS (Infrastructure as a Service) entails a significant administration burden (as the customer is the one responsible for maintaining the OS and associated applications, including upgrading and patching), which is something that the company wants to avoid.

34. Which of these types of data residing in a cloud server would be protected by HIPAA?

A. Patient first name

B. Last four digits of patient credit card

C. Patient year of birth

D. Healthcare provider

☑ **D.** HIPAA (Health Insurance Portability and Accountability Act) relates to protection of PHI (protected health information), which is any information about an individual's health care, status, or related treatment provisioning. As such, an individual's healthcare provider is classified as PHI and should remain securely protected under HIPAA.

☒ **A, B,** and **C** are incorrect. **A** is incorrect because a patient's first name is not distinctive to the individual and doesn't require special handling. However, please note that the full name warrants protection under HIPAA. **B** is incorrect, as the last four digits of a credit card don't provide enough information to uniquely identify the card holder. In addition, even a full credit card number doesn't constitute PHI. That information falls under PII (personally identifiable information). **C** is incorrect, as a patient's year of birth is not classified as PHI since it doesn't provide enough information to uniquely identify an individual.

35. Your company requires data to be labeled appropriately so it can be placed in different cloud servers, depending on its importance. How would you classify data relating to company employees?

   A. Confidential

   B. Private

   C. Sensitive

   D. Public

   ☑ **B.** Any data relating to company staff would be classified as private since it's only intended to be used internally, and any intentional or unintentional release of the information would cause a very negative impact to the company.

   ☒ **A, C,** and **D** are incorrect. **A** is incorrect because a label of confidential would commonly refer to data that has grave importance to the company (like an acquisition of a new organization) and if leaked would have tremendous impact. **C** is incorrect because sensitive data refers to information that should be protected (i.e., salary ranges for different types of positions) but wouldn't have a detrimental effect if disclosed. **D** is incorrect because public data is available to the wider public, and employee data would never be freely available.

36. Which of these tasks would you avoid performing on a corporate host's virtual machine?

   A. Run another OS.

   B. Develop and test applications.

   C. Reverse-engineer malware.

   D. Host a file server.

   ☑ **C.** Virtual machines can be used to perform a variety of tasks, and several individuals do use them for reverse engineering. However, that is not recommended to be performed on the corporate network. If you intend to use a virtual machine to analyze malware, that should be done in an air-gap environment, with no possibility of communicating with the corporate network. Also, you need to consider the fact that some types of malware don't run on virtual environments, as they have the ability to detect them and stay dormant. Finally, another consideration would be to ensure your host system is adequately protected from common attacks and exploits (i.e., VM escape, insecure configuration of hypervisor and guest OS).

   ☒ **A, B,** and **D** are incorrect. **A** is incorrect because running another operating system is a common task for a VM. In fact, sometimes individuals (like developers or system administrators) tend to use them as an alternative to their primary operating system. **B** is incorrect because VMs can be used to develop and test applications. If a developer is creating a new application that is supposed to be running on four different operating systems, then there's no point in having four different physical machines. It would be much easier and cost-effective to just use four VMs. **D** is incorrect because hosting a file server can be easily achieved by a VM. Several companies have started to host various types of servers in virtualized environments in order to achieve more efficiency, less administration, and reduced cost.

37. Which of the following would prevent a zero-day exploit from running on your server?

   A. Signature-based AV

   B. Behavioral-based AV

   C. Network IPS

   D. None of the above

   ☑ **D.** The key takeaway from this question is that no security tool can guarantee prevention of a zero-day exploit. The challenge with those type of exploits is that they are, by definition, new to the security vendor and the vendor is vulnerable to the related exploit. As such, none of the options are guaranteed to prevent a zero-day exploit.

   ☒ **A, B,** and **C** are incorrect. **A** is incorrect because a signature-based AV works by using a signature database, which wouldn't include a zero-day exploit. **B** is incorrect because a behavioral-based AV wouldn't necessarily prevent a zero-day exploit. However, please note that any behavioral analysis is your best chance at identifying any suspicious activity, as it will analyze the activity patterns so there's a chance that an active exploit is detected. However, the question states what would prevent such an exploit, and this method is not guaranteed to prevent it. **C** is incorrect because a NIPS (network intrusion prevention system) would only be able to inspect and act on offending network traffic, but not at something taking place on your server.

38. Your company wants to develop a new application that will be distributed in a preconfigured VM (containing the application running on a Linux OS). Which of these terms best describes this?

   A. Host

   B. Guest

   C. Virtual appliance

   D. Hypervisor

   ☑ **C.** Your company aims to provide an easy way of delivering the application to its clients for use in a virtual environment. Hence, the application will be installed on a virtual machine running Linux, which will be ready for distribution to any client. That way, any client can obtain this preconfigured virtual machine, install it on their host operating system, and start using it. A virtual appliance is a VM with a preconfigured OS and one available application.

☒ **A, B,** and **D** are incorrect. **A** is incorrect because, as stated earlier, a host is the machine where virtualization will take place. It can be a server or a desktop or whatever other type of device the hypervisor will run on. **B** is incorrect because guest is a generic term used to describe any virtual machine running on a host. **D** is incorrect because a hypervisor is the software that offers virtualization (i.e., Virtual Box or VMware). Note that in the case of a virtual appliance, the goal is to create an image that can be deployed immediately from the client. But in order for that to happen, a specific hypervisor will need to be used. If the virtual appliance has been created to run on Virtual Box, then that's the hypervisor that needs to be used. If another hypervisor is used, the virtual appliance won't function.

Pre-assessment Test

Typically, people either love pre-assessment tests or they hate them. I used to belong to the second category. However, as I participated in many certification exams and had the privilege of teaching quite a large number of people over the years, I gradually realized that students don't actually hate pre-assessments but they do tend to be afraid of them (or assessments in general, for that matter).

The goal of this pre-assessment test is to allow you to adjust your studies according to the areas you're not familiar with at the level that the exam demands you to be. For example, most technical people know whether AES is a symmetric or asymmetric encryption algorithm. But do you know the possible key sizes it uses? Can you distinguish if a key of 56 bits can be an actual AES key?

That is the type of the thing the assessment can help you identify so your efforts are focused accordingly. However, if you don't know the answers to any of those AES questions, or you get a very low test score after taking this pre-assessment test, or you are not even in the mood to attempt the test, that really doesn't mean anything in terms of predicting your success. I have met people who didn't have any idea of what penetration testing is and as soon as they compromised their first machine they got hooked. They started putting in endless hours to master the techniques, eventually landed a junior ethical hacker role, and began winning their first capture the flag competitions within two to three years. The point is that if you are diligent and thorough in your approach, nothing will stop you from passing the exam and obtaining your SSCP certification.

Start reading the SSCP theory in order to get the hang of things, then create a study plan and stick to it. Even if you don't feel like taking the test to start with, you can always brush through the theory and take it at a later time. However, if you do decide to take it, you can greatly benefit from the fact that it might help you identify at the outset some areas that require improvement. This test contains a collection of 30 questions across all seven domains. The specific questions that relate to each domain are provided in the following table:

Domain	Exam Weight	Question numbers in Pre-assessment Test
1.0 Access Controls	16%	1–5
2.0 Security Operations and Administration	15%	6–10
3.0 Risk Identification, Monitoring, and Analysis	15%	11–14
4.0 Incident Response and Recovery	13%	15–18

Domain	Exam Weight	Question numbers in Pre-assessment Test
5.0 Cryptography	10%	19–22
6.0 Network and Communications Security	16%	23–26
7.0 Systems and Application Security	15%	27–30
Total	**100%**	

For example, if you take the test and find that you get the answers to the first four questions wrong, then it would be highly advisable to review the theory relating to domain 1.0 in detail. However, sometimes you might get a question wrong because you didn't understand it properly or because the answers related to items you are not familiar with.

On the other hand, a good score does not necessarily indicate that you are ready to take the exam. Don't forget that this pre-assessment test only comprises of 30 questions while the actual exam contains 125. Also, students tend to respond instinctively to questions they don't know by selecting random answers and sometimes those are correct. The time for random guessing is not when you take this pre-assessment test as that will not provide accurate results and will not help you study efficiently for your exam. If you put enough hours into preparing for the exam and testing your knowledge as you go along, you will very soon find out that you don't really need to guess on any answers.

Stick to the question facts. Read everything carefully. If you don't remember the theory behind the question, go back to supplement your knowledge and then give the question another go. Don't give up. Keep at it. Plan your studies. Assess yourself as you go along. Adjust your study plan accordingly (spend more time on those chapters that cover topics you are less familiar with). Don't rush. When you are studying, time is something you are working with, but when you are taking a real exam, it's what you are working against. Oh, and because I mentioned time, to make this a more realistic assessment, remember to only allocate about 43 minutes to complete this assessment. That is proportional to the three hours that is provided to complete the 125 questions of the actual exam.

Best of luck in your preparation journey, although I am sure you will do great!

Q

1. Bob wants to log on to a company system and is presented with a screen asking him to enter a username and password, followed by a second screen asking for an OTP. Which of these elements falls under identification?

   A. Password

   B. OTP

   C. Username

   D. Username and password combination

2. Captain Cramer is reviewing a biometric authentication system that will be used at a nuclear missile silo. Which of the following is the most likely reason that would prevent him from approving the usage of this device?

   A. Low CER

   B. Increased amount of type 1 errors

   C. Increased amount of type 2 errors

   D. High FRR

3. Felly Corp. wants to improve the level of current security policies. As such, employees won't be allowed to connect to critical infrastructure using corporate machines from the guest network. This is an example of:

   A. RBAC (Role-based Access Control)

   B. MAC

   C. ABAC

   D. DAC

4. A large law firm has a team (designated Alpha) representing a manufacturing client, while another team (designated Bravo) is working on a case relating to one of the manufacturing client's biggest competitors. Bravo team would greatly benefit from information that Alpha team has access to. Which of these models would be the most appropriate to ensure that a conflict of interest is avoided?

   A. Bell-LaPadula

   B. Biba

   C. Clark-Wilson

   D. Brewer-Nash

5. Which of the following is not an SSO technology?

   A. SAML

   B. SecureAuth IdP

   C. Kerberos

   D. OpenIDConnect

6. A network administrator is considering placing a new firewall at the network perimeter. Which type of control is this?

    A. Detective

    B. Corrective

    C. Preventive

    D. Recovery

7. A company backup policy primarily uses magnetic tapes for backups. They also regularly back up data to the company cloud. Which type of control does the company cloud represent?

    A. Detective

    B. Deterrent

    C. Recovery

    D. Compensating

8. Which of the following is not a security policy characteristic?

    A. Mission statement

    B. Enforcement section

    C. Sanctions statement

    D. Accountability statement

9. What process would take place if an (ISC)² member doesn't comply with the (ISC)² code of ethics?

    A. Any violators will be reported to the company the member is working for.

    B. (ISC)² will revoke their certifications.

    C. A review from a peer panel will take place.

    D. They will get a one-off warning.

10. In order for a merchant to comply with PCI-DSS, a network scan is required to be completed by which of the following?

    A. SAQ

    B. ASV

    C. QSA

    D. ISA

11. A company's single e-commerce server has gone down. The estimation of loss for each day it's not online is $500, and a technician charges $400 per day to repair it, with an initial estimation of repair time being one day. The monthly likelihood of such incidents is estimated at three. What is the ALE?

    A. $32,400

    B. $64,800

C. $15,600

D. $53,700

12. An IPS is placed in front of the DMZ segment housing an FTP and a web server. Suddenly, the network administrator receives a report of traffic from a specific external IP address not being received by the web server. However, a packet capture right before the IPS suggests that web traffic is passing properly. What is the most likely reason for this?

A. Malformed web request.

B. Packet capture has not been set to capture web traffic properly.

C. Physical link failure.

D. IPS dropping the traffic in question.

13. Which of the following is the most important consideration for a new SIEM implementation?

A. Configure time synchronization.

B. Adjust appropriate alert thresholds.

C. Ensure all available logs are ingested.

D. Provide security analyst access to individual log sources.

14. You are the head of security and your company is running a core finance application on a legacy Windows 2003 server. A recent vulnerability scan flagged the machine in question as being out of support (extended support for Windows 2003 ended in 2015). After contacting the application vendor, they alert you to the fact that the application is quite old and supported only on a Windows 2003 operating system. Which of these options do you choose?

A. Upgrade the server to the latest version.

B. Migrate the application to a new server.

C. Identify a new application that can be safely used.

D. Accept the risk.

15. A company's client database is stored on a server so that online purchases can take place. The database needs to be accessible constantly even if the server goes down. Which of the following would be more suitable for that purpose?

A. Failover cluster

B. Load balancing

C. Full backup

D. Differential backup

16. Using a proprietary forensic tool for investigation relates to which of these reliability factors?

    A. Clarity

    B. Error rate

    C. Credibility

    D. Testability

17. An organization performs a full weekly backup and is considering combining that with a differential or incremental one. Why would a full/differential backup be preferred over a full/incremental backup?

    A. A full/differential backup takes less time to complete during the week.

    B. When restoring a system, recovery time is reduced.

    C. A full/incremental backup takes less time to complete during the week.

    D. Differential backups are smaller in size.

18. A company's RPO is set at three days, while the MAO is four days. Which of these values indicates a realistic RTO?

    A. 3

    B. 5

    C. 7

    D. 9

19. Consider two text files: The first one contains the sentence "this is an SSCP example" and the second one contains the sentence "this is another SSCP example with different text". The MD5 hash of the first file is 063ba1995095c95c2e2184837fd47067, and the MD5 hash of the second file is 063ba1995095c95c2e2184837fd47067. What is this an example of?

    A. Work factor

    B. Collusion

    C. Rainbow tables

    D. Collision

20. A key escrow is used for storing:

    A. Public keys

    B. Digital certificates

    C. WOT certificates

    D. Private keys

21. Which of the following would be used for a new certificate registration request?

    A. WOT

    B. RA

    C. CRL

    D. OCSP

22. You want to ensure your company's e-mails are encrypted to maintain communication confidentiality. Which of these options would you choose for that purpose?

    A. DKIM

    B. SPF

    C. S/MIME

    D. DMARC

23. Which topology is the least resilient?

    A. Star

    B. Tree

    C. Mesh

    D. Bus

24. Which of the following would be performed by NAC?

    A. Authenticate a remote client.

    B. Create audit logs about the actions a machine performed while on the network.

    C. Check a client machine against an organizational health policy.

    D. Allow a client machine to issue specific commands.

25. You have a network composed of a hundred endpoints, ten firewalls, five routers, five IPS sensors, and three proxies across two geographical regions. Data from all of those devices is being forwarded to a SIEM platform. What would be the most crucial element for any type of security investigation you perform?

    A. Log integrity

    B. Verbose logging across all devices

    C. Appropriate alert thresholds

    D. Time synchronization

26. Which of these media types is most susceptible to electromagnetic interference?

    A. Shielded twisted pair

    B. UTP

    C. Optical fiber

    D. STP cat 6

27. How can you best protect against VM escape?

    A. Patch the hypervisor software.

    B. Patch the guest OS.

    C. Use a next-generation firewall on the host.

    D. Use a host antivirus.

28. Which of these attacks allows an attacker access to forbidden file system locations and often targets a system's password file?

    A. XSS

    B. Directory traversal

    C. Buffer overflow

    D. CSRF

29. Which of the following tries to disable or attack the AV software?

    A. Stealth virus

    B. Multipartite virus

    C. Polymorphic virus

    D. Retrovirus

30. Which of these types of data residing in a cloud server would be protected by HIPAA?

    A. Patient first name

    B. Last four digits of patient credit card

    C. Patient year of birth

    D. Healthcare provider

1. C	**11.** A	**21.** B
2. C	**12.** D	**22.** C
3. C	**13.** A	**23.** D
4. D	**14.** D	**24.** C
5. B	**15.** A	**25.** D
6. C	**16.** D	**26.** B
7. D	**17.** B	**27.** A
8. C	**18.** A	**28.** B
9. C	**19.** D	**29.** D
10. B	**20.** D	**30.** D

1. Bob wants to log on to a company system and is presented with a screen asking him to enter a username and password, followed by a second screen asking for an OTP. Which of these elements falls under identification?

   A. Password

   B. OTP

   C. Username

   D. Username and password combination

   ☑ **C.** Bob first enters a username to claim his identity. Please note that at this point he just claims to be Bob, without providing any further evidence to support that (like his password).

   ☒ **A, B,** and **D** are incorrect. **A** is incorrect because the password is used to authenticate the user and not identify him. **B** is incorrect because OTP (one-time password) is used as a second step of a two-step verification process. The user would typically encounter this screen only after entering a valid username and corresponding password (meaning he has claimed he is Bob and has provided Bob's correct password). **D** is a distractor, as a username and password pair can't be used in order to provide identification of a user. Passwords are used for authentication.

2. Captain Cramer is reviewing a biometric authentication system that will be used at a nuclear missile silo. Which of the following is the most likely reason that would prevent him from approving the usage of this device?

   A. Low CER

   B. Increased amount of type 1 errors

   C. Increased amount of type 2 errors

   D. High FRR

   ☑ **C.** A type 2 error (also known as FAR, False Acceptance Rate) can affect a system in a more negative way, as it means that it improperly allows access to illegitimate users, which would be detrimental in the case of a nuclear silo.

   ☒ **A, B,** and **D** are incorrect. **A** is incorrect because ideally a good biometric system needs to have a low CER (Crossover Error Rate), as that means it is performing better. **B** is incorrect because type 1 errors refer to FRR (False Rejection Rate), meaning the system doesn't allow access to a legitimate user. Although this is a nuisance, it doesn't even come close to how worse things can become by allowing illegitimate users to enter the secure premises (which is what answer C depicts). **D** is incorrect, as it has exactly the same meaning as B but instead of the term "type 1 error," FRR is used.

3. Felly Corp. wants to improve the level of current security policies. As such, employees won't be allowed to connect to critical infrastructure using corporate machines from the guest network. This is an example of:

   A. RBAC (Role-based Access Control)

   B. MAC

   C. ABAC

   D. DAC

   ☑ **C.** ABAC works by evaluating subject and object attributes (i.e., a user attempting to log in to a finance server from the guest network) and allows/rejects accordingly.

   ☒ **A, B,** and **D** are incorrect. **A** is incorrect because Role-based Access Control defines access by using roles or groups and isn't suitable for this scenario. **B** is incorrect because MAC uses labels for subject and object identification. **D** is incorrect because DAC models grant access to objects based on the identity of each subject (i.e., Alice has read and write permissions to a file).

4. A large law firm has a team (designated Alpha) representing a manufacturing client, while another team (designated Bravo) is working on a case relating to one of the manufacturing client's biggest competitors. Bravo team would greatly benefit from information that Alpha team has access to. Which of these models would be the most appropriate to ensure that a conflict of interest is avoided?

   A. Bell-LaPadula

   B. Biba

   C. Clark-Wilson

   D. Brewer-Nash

   ☑ **D.** The Brewer-Nash model (also known as the Chinese Wall model) is primarily used to avoid conflicts of interest. According to that, an ethical screen model is used to classify data to distinct conflict-of-interest classes. In this case, a simple way of classifying data would be to ensure that the manufacturing client is placed in one class while their competitor is in another one. Hence, if Bravo team has access to the competitor class, it can't access data from the conflicting class of the manufacturing client.

   ☒ **A, B,** and **C** are incorrect. **A** is incorrect because Bell-LaPadula is used for enforcing confidentiality. **B** is incorrect because Biba is used for enforcing integrity. **C** is incorrect because Clark-Wilson is also used to enforce integrity. Hence, the most appropriate choice is the Brewer-Nash model.

5. Which of the following is not an SSO technology?

   A. SAML

   B. SecureAuth IdP

C. Kerberos

D. OpenIDConnect

☑ **B.** SecureAuth IdP provides mobile device management and doesn't have anything to do with SSO.

☒ **A, C,** and **D** are incorrect. **A** is incorrect because SAML is used to provide SSO. **C** is incorrect because Windows domains and Linux/UNIX realms do use Kerberos for SSO. **D** is incorrect because OpenIDConnect is an SSO technology.

6. A network administrator is considering placing a new firewall at the network perimeter. Which type of control is this?

A. Detective

B. Corrective

C. Preventive

D. Recovery

☑ **C.** A firewall is classified as a preventive control, as it has the ability to prevent an attack by stopping offending traffic.

☒ **A, B,** and **D** are incorrect. **A** is incorrect because a detective control would only be able to identify an attack when it's taking place or after it has happened. **B** is incorrect because a corrective control would perform an activity to counter the attack. **D** is incorrect because a recovery control aims to restore a system after an incident has happened.

7. A company backup policy primarily uses magnetic tapes for backups. They also regularly back up data to the company cloud. Which type of control does the company cloud represent?

A. Detective

B. Deterrent

C. Recovery

D. Compensating

☑ **D.** The cloud provider is being used in case the backup tape (which is primarily used as a backup media) fails, thus making it a compensating control.

☒ **A, B,** and **C** are incorrect. **A** is incorrect because a detective control has the ability to provide event detection, which is not true in the case of a backup to the cloud. **B** is incorrect because a deterrent control aims to deter an attacker from performing a hostile action. **C** is incorrect because a recovery control aims to restore a system after an incident has happened. Please note that the question focuses on what type of control the company cloud is, making the correct answer a "compensating" one. However, if the question focused on what type of control a backup policy is, then the correct answer would be a recovery control.

8. Which of the following is not a security policy characteristic?

   A. Mission statement

   B. Enforcement section

   C. Sanctions statement

   D. Accountability statement

   ☑ **C.** A security policy doesn't have a "sanctions statement." Any related actions that can be pursued if the policy is not followed will be included in the "enforcement section."

   ☒ **A, B,** and **D** are incorrect. **A** is incorrect because a "mission statement" should be present and describe the overarching organizational vision. **B** is incorrect because an "enforcement section" would describe how a policy is going to be enforced and what steps might be taken in case personnel don't adhere to it. **D** is incorrect because an "accountability statement" would describe the specific role types (i.e., security staff) that have a responsibility to follow the policy.

9. What process would take place if an (ISC)² member doesn't comply with the (ISC)² code of ethics?

   A. Any violators will be reported to the company the member is working for.

   B. (ISC)² will revoke their certifications.

   C. A review from a peer panel will take place.

   D. They will get a one-off warning.

   ☑ **C.** In the event that a member violates the (ISC)² code of ethics, a peer review panel is formed so the case can be examined and a recommendation on how to proceed be made.

   ☒ **A, B,** and **D** are incorrect. **A** is incorrect because (ISC)² doesn't have the remit to reach out to the company a member might be working for. **B** is incorrect because certifications aren't revoked straight away. That might be a recommendation from an appropriate panel, but a ruling will come out after it convenes. **D** is incorrect because a code of ethics violation is a very serious matter, which doesn't warrant any warnings.

10. In order for a merchant to comply with PCI-DSS, a network scan is required to be completed by which of the following?

   A. SAQ

   B. ASV

   C. QSA

   D. ISA

   ☑ **B.** An ASV (Approved Scanning Vendor) is an external security entity that uses authorized scanners to perform a scan. Merchants of all levels are required to use such a provider for any scans that are performed.

☒ **A, C,** and **D** are incorrect. **A** is incorrect because an SAQ (Self-Assessment Questionnaire) can be used by an entity with a low number of credit card transactions to perform a compliance audit. **C** is incorrect because a QSA (Quality Security Assessor) is an external party that can perform an audit at a client site. **D** is incorrect because an ISA (Internal Security Assessor) is an internal company employee (who is ISA certified) able to perform specific client-site audits.

11. A company's single e-commerce server has gone down. The estimation of loss for each day it's not online is $500, and a technician charges $400 per day to repair it, with an initial estimation of repair time being one day. The monthly likelihood of such incidents is estimated at three. What is the ALE?

   A. $32,400

   B. $64,800

   C. $15,600

   D. $53,700

   ☑ **A.** In order to calculate the ALE, the following formula will be required: ALE = SLE × ARO. Furthermore, the SLE can be found by adding all related server costs, which are daily loss and repair cost. Based on that, the SLE will be $500 + ($400 × 1 day) = $500 + $400 = $900. The ARO is 3 monthly occurrences × 12 months = 36 occurrences per year. ALE = SLE × ARO = $900 × 36 = $32,400.

   ☒ **B, C,** and **D** are incorrect. All those figures are distractors, as none of them is correct.

12. An IPS is placed in front of the DMZ segment housing an FTP and a web server. Suddenly, the network administrator receives a report of traffic from a specific external IP address not being received by the web server. However, a packet capture right before the IPS suggests that web traffic is passing properly. What is the most likely reason for this?

   A. Malformed web request.

   B. Packet capture has not been set to capture web traffic properly.

   C. Physical link failure.

   D. IPS dropping the traffic in question.

   ☑ **D.** Since the packet capture shows web traffic being received by the web server without traffic from a specific source passing through the IPS, it seems that the traffic in question is being identified as malicious and thus is blocked from traversing the rest of the network.

   ☒ **A, B,** and **C** are incorrect. **A** is incorrect because although a malformed web request could have been sent, there's not enough information to suggest that this is the case and is the specific reason for dropping traffic from the IP in question. **B** is incorrect because there's no actual indication that web traffic is not being captured properly. In addition, the fact that only traffic from a specific IP is not seen by the web server suggests that packet capturing has been properly configured but some part of the traffic is just not passing through the IPS. **C** is incorrect because a physical link failure would result in no traffic reaching any of the servers in the DMZ, which is not the case here.

13. Which of the following is the most important consideration for a new SIEM implementation?

   A. Configure time synchronization.

   B. Adjust appropriate alert thresholds.

   C. Ensure all available logs are ingested.

   D. Provide security analyst access to individual log sources.

   ☑ A. In order for proper analysis to take place, a SIEM needs accurate data synchronization. If an analyst tries to track an attacker's actions through various device logs that are in different time zones, the analysis can become unmanageable. In addition, it becomes very difficult for cooperating third parties to track any reports that are produced when data from different time zones is referenced in various parts of the report.

   ☒ B, C, and D are incorrect. B is incorrect because although adjusting the alert thresholds is important to ensure that related teams are only engaged in the event of a valid security incident, this is something that can happen during the initial stages of the SIEM operation and usually happens gradually as more log sources are added and analyst teams become more familiar with its operation. It's difficult to ensure that thresholds are properly adjusted right at the beginning, as this takes substantial effort and time. C is incorrect because adding all available log sources to the SIEM (depending on their amount and volume) would result in overwhelming the tool as well as the analyst team supporting it. Organizations usually start by on-boarding the basic log sources that are required to achieve their goals and gradually adding more devices as they grow, while at the same time performing fine-tuning. D is incorrect because a SIEM works as a central logging and correlation platform. It allows analysts to view all the basic information to perform their tasks. Although having access to individual log sources can sometimes be beneficial (i.e., the analyst can review the raw logs that haven't been normalized within the SIEM, meaning all initial information is present), the whole point of the SIEM is to offer log storage and correlation without needing to access the end devices.

14. You are the head of security and your company is running a core finance application on a legacy Windows 2003 server. A recent vulnerability scan flagged the machine in question as being out of support (extended support for Windows 2003 ended in 2015). After contacting the application vendor, they alert you to the fact that the application is quite old and supported only on a Windows 2003 operating system. Which of these options do you choose?

   A. Upgrade the server to the latest version.

   B. Migrate the application to a new server.

   C. Identify a new application that can be safely used.

   D. Accept the risk.

☑ **D.** Accepting the risk may sometimes be the only way to move forward (that's why risk acceptance is a valid risk strategy, although it is not recommended to follow it unless all other avenues have been exhausted). As this is a core finance application, meaning its operation is crucial to the business, a way to continue using it must be identified. If upgrading the server (due to being out of support) or reverting to the application's vendor for a solution (i.e., if the application is only supported on a Windows 2003 system) are both nonviable options, accepting the risk seems the only viable solution.

☒ **A, B,** and **C** are incorrect. **A** is incorrect because upgrading the server to the latest version (which is several versions after the current one that the server is running) might disrupt the application's normal operation or even disrupt the functionality of the legacy application (only supported in Windows 2003). **B** is incorrect because migrating the application to a new server (judging by the fact that the application is old and not supported anymore) might again result in not being able to use it further. **C** is incorrect because although identifying a new application (given the age of the current one being used) might take some time, it seems like a viable way moving forward. However, this will possibly take several weeks or months, as the new application will need to be identified, then reviewed from the finance team to ensure that it fulfills all related needs, and then tested and accepted. However, that won't solve the challenge at hand (i.e., the machine being flagged as out of support and a core application being run on it), so this can only be a viable long-term approach.

15. A company's client database is stored on a server so that online purchases can take place. The database needs to be accessible constantly even if the server goes down. Which of the following would be more suitable for that purpose?

   A. Failover cluster

   B. Load balancing

   C. Full backup

   D. Differential backup

☑ **A.** A failover cluster is the most appropriate solution, as it can allow the database to be accessible if the server goes down. For that purpose, at least two servers are required, which can then be configured into a pair. One of them can be set to operate as the primary instance, while the other will be the secondary one. Once the secondary server detects any type of failure on the primary instance, it can assume its place as primary, thus guaranteeing minimal database downtime.

☒ **B, C,** and **D** are incorrect. **B** is incorrect because load balancing is primarily used for performance improvement, not for fault tolerance. **C** is incorrect because a full backup will not guarantee that the database will be accessible all the time. If a server goes down, an administrator would need to intervene and manually restore that backup in addition to containing only accurate information up until the moment the backup was taken. If a full backup was taken a week ago, then after a server failure, the backup that is restored will contain data that is a week old, so all other transactions would have been lost. **D** is incorrect because a differential backup won't be able to ensure constant access to the server database, as any type of restoration would need to be manually performed by an administrator, with substantial associated time if any failure occurs out of normal business hours, in addition to any transactions that are not contained in the backup that was lost.

16. Using a proprietary forensic tool for investigation relates to which of these reliability factors?

   A. Clarity

   B. Error rate

   C. Credibility

   D. Testability

   ☑ **D.** Testability relates to how much a tool or technique has been tested before being used in an investigation. Using a proprietary tool will not allow a variety of people from different industries to test the tool, hence its testability would be very low.

   ☒ **A, B,** and **C** are incorrect. **A** is incorrect because clarity refers to how easy it is to explain the tool or technique and its results to the court. **B** is incorrect because error rate refers to the tool's statistics regarding errors. **C** is incorrect because credibility refers to the individual handling a tool or using a method and how credible he or she is, as well as how reproducible the technique is by similar specialists.

17. An organization performs a full weekly backup and is considering combining that with a differential or incremental one. Why would a full/differential backup be preferred over a full/incremental backup?

   A. A full/differential backup takes less time to complete during the week.

   B. When restoring a system, recovery time is reduced.

   C. A full/incremental backup takes less time to complete during the week.

   D. Differential backups are smaller in size.

   ☑ **B.** Using a full/differential backup results in reduced recovery time, as the differential backup captures any changes from the last full backup. That means that at any given moment, a total of two backups will be required to perform system restoration: the most recent full weekly backup and the most recent differential one.

   ☒ **A, C,** and **D** are incorrect. **A** is incorrect because a full/differential backup takes more time to be completed during the week, as all changes from the moment the full weekly backup was taken need to be recorded. **C** is incorrect because a full/incremental backup does take less time to complete during the week (i.e., if taken daily, it records daily database transactions, which takes a relatively short time). However, that won't be a reason for choosing a full/differential backup solution over a full/incremental one. It's rather a statement regarding how the full/differential backup method works. **D** is incorrect because differential backups are larger in size (not smaller) because they include all changes since the last full weekly backup was taken, which may require substantial space.

18. A company's RPO is set at three days, while the MAO is four days. Which of these values indicates a realistic RTO?

A. 3

B. 5

C. 7

D. 9

☑ **A.** The time a crucial application or function can be unavailable without severe business impact refers to the MAO (maximum acceptable outage), which is stated as four days. The RTO is the time it takes (at most) for a system or service to be restored after an outage. Since the business can cope for up to four days (MAO set at four days), the RTO needs to be less than the MAO in order for the business to successfully recover and continue operations. From the provided options, only the first one (three days) allows for a viable RTO.

☒ **B, C,** and **D** are incorrect, as these are distractors.

19. Consider two text files: The first one contains the sentence "this is an SSCP example" and the second one contains the sentence "this is another SSCP example with different text". The MD5 hash of the first file is 063ba1995095c95c2e2184837fd47067, and the MD5 hash of the second file is 063ba1995095c95c2e2184837fd47067. What is this an example of?

A. Work factor

B. Collusion

C. Rainbow tables

D. Collision

☑ **D.** The two MD5 file hashes are identical; however, the content of the two files is different. This is known as a collision and relates to one of the basic principles of a hashing algorithm, which is to be collision free, meaning that two different files should never generate the same hash value. Even a slight change in a file that is used as input in a hashing algorithm should generate a different output.

☒ **A, B,** and **C** are incorrect. **A** is incorrect because the work factor relates to cryptography and expresses the time and effort that it would take to decrypt an encrypted message. **B** is incorrect, as it refers to the act of one or more individuals or companies conspiring to commit fraud. Although the syntax might be similar to the correct answer, this term has actually nothing to do with hashing algorithms. **C** is incorrect, as rainbow tables contain precomputed hash values intended to provide a reverse lookup resource for hash values.

20. A key escrow is used for storing:

   A. Public keys

   B. Digital certificates

   C. WOT certificates

   D. Private keys

   ☑ **D.** A key escrow is used for safely keeping private keys in order to be able to retrieve them in the event the company's private key is lost or damaged. Only specific people usually have permission to retrieve private keys from a key escrow facility due to the sensitivity of their nature.

   ☒ **A, B,** and **C** are incorrect. **A** is incorrect because public keys are publicly available and are contained in an individual's digital certificate. **B** is incorrect because any digital certificates would be issued and managed by the certificate authority. Please note that a CA (certificate authority) may be external (i.e., Symantec or VeriSign) or internal to the organization (i.e., when a certificate is needed for a system that is used only internally). **C** is incorrect because there's no such term as WOT certificate. WOT (web of trust) is a decentralized trust model with the goal of allowing a system to establish authenticity between a public key and its owner.

21. Which of the following would be used for a new certificate registration request?

   A. WOT

   B. RA

   C. CRL

   D. OCSP

   ☑ **B.** An RA (registration authority) can be used for an organization's certificate registration request. It is tasked with data verification, and after that is completed the request would be passed to the CA (certificate authority). Note that it is not mandatory to use an RA, but large companies do often use one. However, a request can also still just reach the CA directly.

   ☒ **A, C,** and **D** are incorrect. **A** is incorrect because a WOT (web of trust) is a decentralized trust model with the goal of allowing a system to establish authenticity between a public key and its owner. **C** is incorrect because a CRL (certificate revocation list) is a list of revoked certificates that the CA maintains and is used by clients to check a certificate's validity. **D** is incorrect because OCSP (Online Certificate Status Protocol) is another method of checking if a certificate has been revoked. The difference is that instead of a revocation list being provided (like in the case of CRL), the client would just send a request to the OCSP server asking if a certificate of interest is valid or not, and the server would return a verdict.

22. You want to ensure your company's e-mails are encrypted to maintain communication confidentiality. Which of these options would you choose for that purpose?

    A. DKIM

    B. SPF

    C. S/MIME

    D. DMARC

    ☑ **C.** S/MIME (Secure/Multipurpose Internet Mail Extensions) is a protocol that allows one to encrypt and digitally sign e-mails. This works by using the recipient's public key to encrypt an outgoing message. After that has been received, only the recipient can decrypt it (as that would require the recipient's private key), which ensures the security of that transaction. Furthermore, as S/MIME also supports digital signatures, a sender can sign the message that is sent so that the recipient knows it originated from a valid entity.

    ☒ **A, B,** and **D** are incorrect. **A** is incorrect because DKIM (Domain Keys Identified Mail) is a method of authenticating e-mail and identifying any attempt to spoof a valid sender. It doesn't support e-mail encryption; hence, it wouldn't be used to secure e-mail communications. **B** is incorrect because SPF (Sender Policy Framework) is used to authenticate e-mails and identify e-mail spoofing, not to encrypt them. Assume that you receive an e-mail originating from your bank (which is called amazing bank), sourced from e-mail account security@amazing-bank.com, asking you to change your password to a new value that is provided in the e-mail. If that e-mail is not actually sourced from "amazing bank" but is just an attempt by an attacker to spoof the source header so you are tempted to change your password to what is provided, that would be identified as forged e-mail. **D** is incorrect because DMARC (Domain-based Message Authentication, Reporting, and Conformance) is a protocol that allows organizations to specify if SPF or DKIM (or neither of them) is used and what action to take if validation fails (i.e., mark the message as spam) by publishing the relevant policy through DNS records. However, this protocol wouldn't be used for encrypting messages.

23. Which topology is the least resilient?

    A. Star

    B. Tree

    C. Mesh

    D. Bus

    ☑ **D.** When using a bus topology, any issue with one of the connected devices will bring the whole network to a halt. A bus topology uses T connectors for connectivity. That means that one end of a computer is connected to the bus and the other is connected to the next computer. If one of the computers or T connectors experiences an issue, the whole network stops working. In addition, if a lot of machines are connected to that network, identifying the issue may require vast amounts of time. This means the network will not be usable until the issue is resolved.

☒ **A, B,** and **C** are incorrect. **A** is incorrect because a star topology commonly uses a switch to allow the various machines to connect, which means that any issue with one machine doesn't affect the network's overall operation. **B** is incorrect because a tree topology uses a combination of a bus and a star, where multiple star networks connect over a common bus. If the bus experiences an issue, all the star networks are disconnected until the issue is resolved. **C** is incorrect because in a mesh topology, all machines are individually connected with each other, meaning that any issues with one connection don't affect the operation of the network.

24. Which of the following would be performed by NAC?

    A. Authenticate a remote client.

    B. Create audit logs about the actions a machine performed while on the network.

    C. Check a client machine against an organizational health policy.

    D. Allow a client machine to issue specific commands.

    ☑ **C.** A NAC (Network Access Control) device is primarily used to check if a client that is requesting to connect to the corporate network fulfills the minimum requirements to be allowed to join the network. If that is the case, a NAC device will allow the client to connect. If not, the client will usually be restricted to a quarantined network until it achieves the minimum company security requirements.

    ☒ **A, B,** and **D** are incorrect. **A** is incorrect because the authentication of a remote client would happen by an authentication server (i.e., RADIUS or TACACS+). **B** is incorrect because a NAC device wouldn't be able to perform auditing of a network client. That is a task that needs to be performed by the authentication server (i.e., a server supporting AAA, like RADIUS, TACACS+, or Diameter). **D** is incorrect because reviewing a client's permissions to issue specific commands takes place during the authorization process (which typically happens when a client logs on using an AAA server).

25. You have a network composed of a hundred endpoints, ten firewalls, five routers, five IPS sensors, and three proxies across two geographical regions. Data from all of those devices is being forwarded to a SIEM platform. What would be the most crucial element for any type of security investigation you perform?

    A. Log integrity

    B. Verbose logging across all devices

    C. Appropriate alert thresholds

    D. Time synchronization

    ☑ **D.** For any effective investigation to take place, appropriate time synchronization needs to be present for all the devices across the network. Even with a handful of devices, like five to six, analysis can become very complicated when those devices are not in a common time zone (i.e., UTC). Imagine you receive an alert from the SIEM with a time stamp of 14:00 UTC-8 (which might be the time zone of the tool or the location where it is installed) and you log in to individual devices to investigate further. Some of them are in UTC+4 and others in UTC-2. How are you going to be able to track a specific attacker's activities across all those time zones?

☒ **A, B,** and **C** are incorrect. **A** is incorrect because log integrity is crucial, but in this scenario the logs are being forwarded to a SIEM tool, which stores copies of them, so a good level of integrity is present. **B** is incorrect because verbose logging across various devices might be too intense (depending on the amount of traffic and device type) and cause issues with them, while it also consumes a lot of network bandwidth. SIEM platforms use EPS (events per second), and as that increases, the cost of the tool grows exponentially—not to mention that a more robust architecture will be required in order to cope with the excessive traffic being forwarded to the SIEM tool. However, if there's no time synchronization, even with an abundance of data, it will be very difficult to identify crucial artifacts of any attack. **C** is incorrect because for any SIEM to work effectively, appropriate alert thresholds need to be configured; however, those can be gradually defined as the tool is being used. Lack of time synchronization will pose a greater challenge when investigating malicious activities across logs of various devices in different regions (and various time zones).

26. Which of these media types is most susceptible to electromagnetic interference?

    A. Shielded twisted pair

    B. UTP

    C. Optical fiber

    D. STP cat 6

    ☑ **B.** UTP (unshielded twisted pair) is a cable type that is very commonly used in computer networks (especially for short to medium distances), CCTV circuits, and telephone systems, as it's very cost effective. However, its greatest disadvantage is that it is susceptible to both electromagnetic and radio frequency interference.

    ☒ **A, C,** and **D** are incorrect. **A** is incorrect because shielded twisted pair (STP) uses additional shielding to reduce the effect of electromagnetic interference. Although it is more expensive as a result, it is often used for outdoors implementations and signal transmissions over large distances. **C** is incorrect because optical fiber cabling uses light to transmit data and as such is not susceptible to electromagnetic interference. It's often used in high-speed networks and can allow high data transmission speeds over large distances, while also offering enhanced security in comparison to traditional media, like copper cables. **D** is incorrect because STP Cat 6 (also known as category 6) is a type of STP cable that is less prone to electromagnetic interference than common UTP cables.

27. How can you best protect against VM escape?

    A. Patch the hypervisor software.

    B. Patch the guest OS.

    C. Use a next-generation firewall on the host.

    D. Use a host antivirus.

    ☑ **A.** VM escape is a type of exploit that can take place when an attacker manages to break out of the context of a virtual machine and interact directly with the host. This is made possible due to a potential vulnerability within the hypervisor (the software that provisions the guest OS and controls how that interacts with the host). In order to ensure the risk is mitigated as much as possible, the hypervisor should always run the most up-to-date versions with the latest patches so that attackers can't use any known exploits to perform VM escape.

    ☒ **B, C,** and **D** are incorrect. **B** is incorrect because although patching the guest OS is quite important, it's the vulnerability within the hypervisor that ultimately allows an attacker to perform a VM escape. Please note that patching the guest OS will aid a lot in avoiding any risks from vulnerabilities that can lead to that machine being compromised. In a typical VM escape scenario, even if the hypervisor is vulnerable, the attacker will start by first compromising the guest OS, and after that is achieved, a hypervisor exploit will follow. However, if the hypervisor is sufficiently patched, then the only thing an attacker can achieve is to compromise the guest OS (assuming the attacker is not using a zero-day hypervisor exploit). **C** is incorrect because using a next-generation firewall on the host will most likely not achieve anything, as the attacker would perform this attack by compromising the guest OS and work through that to exploit the hypervisor. **D** is incorrect because using a host AV will not necessarily protect against this attack, as the attacker will initially compromise the guest OS and then exploit the hypervisor. It would be more beneficial to install an AV on the guest OS in the hope that the initial attack will be detected and stopped before the attacker manages to exploit the hypervisor.

28. Which of these attacks allows an attacker access to forbidden file system locations and often targets a system's password file?

    A. XSS

    B. Directory traversal

    C. Buffer overflow

    D. CSRF

    ☑ **B.** A directory traversal attack is a type of web attack in which an attacker tries to access forbidden file system parts, that is, on a web server. The attacker would most commonly target the password file so user credentials can be harvested, but the term is used to describe access to any directory where access is not allowed.

☒ **A, C,** and **D** are incorrect. **A** is incorrect because an XSS (cross-site scripting) attack would inject malicious code (i.e., JavaScript or HTML) to a web page, with the goal of bypassing existing access control and executing the malicious code. **C** is incorrect because a buffer overflow attack works by allowing the attacker to write into specific memory areas that shouldn't be normally available (i.e., an application using a buffer to hold data of a specific size, which is being overrun when more data is supplied and due to the application being vulnerable to a buffer overflow attack, it tries to store that information in the predefined buffer, thus resulting in writing to other memory areas). **D** is incorrect because a CSRF (cross-site request forgery) attack aims to utilize the user's browser to send a malicious request to a website without any indication to the user. Assume you are logged in to an online gaming website and want to transfer some of your credits to a friend. A CSRF exploit can be used while you are logged in to the website to have credits sent to the attacker's account instead.

29. Which of the following tries to disable or attack the AV software?

    A. Stealth virus

    B. Multipartite virus

    C. Polymorphic virus

    D. Retrovirus

    ☑ **D.** A retrovirus is a type of virus that tries to attack a device's antivirus program. It may attempt to warn the victim that supposedly unsafe software has been found on the machine and then uninstall legitimate AV applications. Sometimes it has the ability to modify the virus signature database and corrupt or delete it altogether.

    ☒ **A, B,** and **C** are incorrect. **A** is incorrect because a stealth virus doesn't attack the AV application but actually tries to evade detection from it. Sometimes it does that by changing the offending file's name or size to make it seem like the infected file is the actual legitimate host file. **B** is incorrect, as a multipartite virus works by infecting various parts of a target system with the intent of making removal very difficult. **C** is incorrect because a polymorphic virus can change a malicious file in order to make signature detection more difficult; however, the replication and payload mechanisms remain unaltered.

30. Which of these types of data residing in a cloud server would be protected by HIPAA?

    A. Patient first name

    B. Last four digits of patient credit card

    C. Patient year of birth

    D. Healthcare provider

    ☑ **D.** HIPAA (Health Insurance Portability and Accountability Act) relates to protection of PHI (protected health information), which is any information about an individual's health care, status, or related treatment provisioning. As such, an individual's healthcare provider is classified as PHI and should remain securely protected under HIPAA.

☒ **A, B,** and **C** are incorrect. **A** is incorrect because a patient's first name is not distinctive to the individual and doesn't require special handling. However, please note that the full name warrants protection under HIPAA. **B** is incorrect, as the last four digits of a credit card don't provide enough information to uniquely identify the card holder. In addition, even a full credit card number doesn't constitute PHI. That information falls under PII (personally identifiable information). **C** is incorrect, as a patient's year of birth is not classified as PHI since it doesn't provide enough information to uniquely identify an individual.

About the Online Content

This book comes complete with TotalTester Online customizable practice exam software with 250 practice exam questions.

System Requirements

The current and previous major versions of the following desktop browsers are recommended and supported: Chrome, Microsoft Edge, Firefox, and Safari. These browsers update frequently, and sometimes an update may cause compatibility issues with the TotalTester Online or other content hosted on the Training Hub. If you run into a problem using one of these browsers, please try using another until the problem is resolved.

Your Total Seminars Training Hub Account

To get access to the online content you will need to create an account on the Total Seminars Training Hub. Registration is free, and you will be able to track all your online content using your account. You may also opt in if you wish to receive marketing information from McGraw-Hill Education or Total Seminars, but this is not required for you to gain access to the online content.

Privacy Notice

McGraw-Hill Education values your privacy. Please be sure to read the Privacy Notice available during registration to see how the information you have provided will be used. You may view our Corporate Customer Privacy Policy by visiting the McGraw-Hill Education Privacy Center. Visit the **mheducation.com** site and click **Privacy** at the bottom of the page.

Single User License Terms and Conditions

Online access to the digital content included with this book is governed by the McGraw-Hill Education License Agreement outlined next. By using this digital content you agree to the terms of that license.

Access   To register and activate your Total Seminars Training Hub account, simply follow these easy steps.

1. Go to **hub.totalsem.com/mheclaim**.
2. To Register and create a new Training Hub account, enter your e-mail address, name, and password. No further personal information (such as credit card number) is required to create an account.

> **NOTE**   If you already have a Total Seminars Training Hub account, select **Log in** and enter your e-mail and password. Otherwise, follow the remaining steps.

3. Enter your Product Key: `67z2-n3ct-62w0`
4. Click to accept the user license terms.
5. Click **Register and Claim** to create your account. You will be taken to the Training Hub and have access to the content for this book.

Duration of License   Access to your online content through the Total Seminars Training Hub will expire one year from the date the publisher declares the book out of print.

Your purchase of this McGraw-Hill Education product, including its access code, through a retail store is subject to the refund policy of that store.

Neither McGraw-Hill Education nor its licensors shall be liable to any subscriber or to any user or anyone else for any inaccuracy, delay, interruption in service, error or omission, regardless of cause, or for any damage resulting therefrom.

In no event will McGraw-Hill Education or its licensors be liable for any indirect, special or consequential damages, including but not limited to lost time, lost money, lost profits or good will, whether in contract, tort, strict liability or otherwise, and whether or not such damages are foreseen or unforeseen with respect to any use of the McGraw-Hill Education Content.

TotalTester Online

TotalTester Online provides you with a simulation of the SSCP exam. Exams can be taken in Practice Mode or Exam Mode. Practice Mode provides an assistance window with hints, references to the book, explanations of the correct and incorrect answers, and the option to check your answer as you take the test. Exam Mode provides a simulation of the actual exam. The number of questions, the types of questions, and the time allowed are intended to be an accurate representation of the exam environment. The option to customize your quiz allows you to create custom exams from selected domains or chapters, and you can further customize the number of questions and time allowed.

To take a test, follow the instructions provided in the previous section to register and activate your Total Seminars Training Hub account. When you register you will be taken to the Total Seminars Training Hub. From the Training Hub Home page, select **SSCP Systems Security Certified Practitioner Practice Exams TotalTester** from the Study drop-down menu at the top of the page, or from the list of Your Topics on the Home page. You can then select the option to customize your quiz and begin testing yourself in Practice Mode or Exam Mode. All exams provide an overall grade and a grade broken down by domain.

Technical Support

For questions regarding the TotalTester or operation of the Training Hub, visit **www.totalsem.com** or e-mail **support@totalsem.com**.

For questions regarding book content, e-mail **hep_customer-service@mheducation.com**. For customers outside the United States, e-mail **international_cs@mheducation.com**.